FOOL'S GOLD?

SCOTT A. SHANE

FOOL'S GOLD?

The Truth Behind Angel Investing in America

OXFORD
UNIVERSITY PRESS

2009

OXFORD
UNIVERSITY PRESS

Oxford University Press, Inc., publishes works that further
Oxford University's objective of excellence
in research, scholarship, and education.

Oxford   New York
Auckland   Cape Town   Dar es Salaam   Hong Kong   Karachi
Kuala Lumpur   Madrid   Melbourne   Mexico City   Nairobi
New Delhi   Shanghai   Taipei   Toronto

With offices in
Argentina   Austria   Brazil   Chile   Czech Republic   France   Greece
Guatemala   Hungary   Italy   Japan   Poland   Portugal   Singapore
South Korea   Switzerland   Thailand   Turkey   Ukraine   Vietnam

Published by Oxford University Press, Inc.
198 Madison Avenue, New York, NY 10016

www.oup.com

Oxford is a registered trademark of Oxford University Press

Library of Congress Cataloging-in-Publication Data
Shane, Scott Andrew, 1964–
Fool's gold? : the truth behind angel investing in America
/ Scott A. Shane.
p.   cm.
Includes index.
ISBN 978-0-19-533108-0
1. Venture capital—United States.
2. Small business—United States—Finance.
3. Investments—United States.   I. Title.
HG4963.S52 2009
332.60973—dc22
2008012706

1 3 5 7 9 8 6 4 2
Printed in the United States of America
on acid-free paper

TO LYNNE, RYAN, AND HANNAH

Contents

Acknowledgments

I DECIDED TO write this book because I had trouble finding accurate data on angel investing. I had become interested in angel investing, having joined the North Coast Angel Fund, an angel group in Northeast Ohio, and having conducted a series of focus groups with leading angel investors in Atlanta, Cleveland, Denver, and Philadelphia on behalf of five of the Federal Reserve regional banks. As my interest in angel investing grew, I began to read everything I could about the topic and began a series of conversations with entrepreneurs, angels, and government officials. I attended the Angel Capital Association's annual and regional meetings and their Power of Angel Investing Seminars.

Unfortunately, the more people I talked to and the more things I read, the more confused I became, and the less I thought I understood angel investing. The problem was not that the sources of information were unclear—invariably I understood exactly what people were saying. Rather, the problem was that all the sources I consulted were long on opinion and short on data. While each opinion alone seemed to make sense, I had made the typical academic's mistake of examining a lot of sources and looking for patterns in the answers. As a result, I was left with a jumble of opinions that contradicted each other and little data to figure out which one was right.

Moreover, when a source provided data to back up its point of view, those data often had two troubling weaknesses. First, the data were not internally consistent. For instance, one source said that 50,000 U.S. businesses per year receive angel investments, but that 10 percent of

U.S. angel-backed companies go public every year. These two numbers cannot possibly be correct because they would indicate that 5,000 angel-backed companies go public every year in a country where there are fewer than 300 IPOs annually. I found that many books, articles, and presentations on angel investing suffered from this problem.

Second, it was very difficult to put the different numbers together. Everyone, it seemed, had a different definition of an angel investor. Like Justice Potter Stewart's view of pornography—I can't define it but I know it when I see it—many sources seemed to have implicit definitions of angel investors that they wouldn't or couldn't make explicit, and those definitions weren't the same. To some people, all informal investors were business angels. To others, only those who invested in businesses not run by their friends and family met the criteria. Some observers said angels had to be accredited investors,[1] while others explicitly acknowledged unaccredited investors as an important class of angels. Some writers said that angels were former entrepreneurs who helped give the founders of their portfolio companies the benefit of their experience through active involvement; others said many angels had no entrepreneurial experience and were passive investors. The list of definitional differences went on and on, filling the pages of my notebook and confusing me further.

Even when I could find different sources that used the same definition of business angels, the information about angel investors and the investments that they provided was so different that it made me wonder if they were really talking about the same thing. For instance, in one case, two authors defined angels as informal investors who invested in businesses not run by their friends and family and then offered estimates of the size of the angel capital market that differed by a factor of ten.

As a professor, I thrive on accurate facts. I find it difficult to understand something unless I can define and measure it, and I seek facts that are collected from an accurate and unbiased source in a careful and scientific way.

One day I decided that I wouldn't be able to understand angel investing unless I gathered the data on it, examined them, figured out which of the data could be believed, and looked for patterns in them. What I thought would be a few weeks effort to learn a little more about angel investing mushroomed. As I searched for the accurate facts and tried to map the accurate ones against each other, my files mushroomed. (Thankfully we now live in a digital age and I only needed a couple of new flash drives!)

As I started to write up some of the information that I found and began to show it to some of my academic colleagues, as well as to entrepreneurs, venture capitalists, and business angels that I know, several of them told me that I shouldn't keep this to myself. The patterns I had unearthed, they said, would be useful to many angels and would-be angels, entrepreneurs and would-be entrepreneurs, and public policy makers. So I ended up writing this book.

No book like this is ever really written by one author because the content comes from the data provided by others. This book would have been impossible without access to several data sources, including the Entrepreneurship in the United States Assessment, conducted by Paul Reynolds; the Survey of Business Owners conducted by the U.S. Census; the Survey of Consumer Finances and the Survey of Small Business Finances, conducted by the Federal Reserve Board of Governors; the Angel Capital Association Membership Survey, conducted by Marianne Hudson; and the Kauffman Firm Survey, conducted for the Ewing Marion Kauffman Foundation by Janice Ballou, Dave DesRoches, and Frank Potter of Mathematica-MPR. To Janice Ballou, Dave DesRoches, Marianne Hudson, Frank Potter, Paul Reynolds, and the anonymous researchers at the Census and the Fed, a thank you for your efforts to put these data together.

I would like to thank several people for their help in gaining access to these different data sources, in particular, Paul Reynolds of George Mason University for his help with the Entrepreneurship in the United States Assessment; Valerie Strang and Trey Cole for special tabulations of the Survey of Business Owners and the Business Information Tracking Series; Marianne Hudson of the Angel Capital Association for data from the membership survey of the Angel Capital Association; and Alyse Freilich and E. J. Reedy of the Kauffman Foundation for access to the Kauffman Firm Survey.

I also owe a debt of gratitude to Mark Sniderman of the Cleveland Fed; Kelly Edmiston of the Kansas City Fed; Will Jackson, formerly of the Atlanta Fed; and Christy Heavner of the Philadelphia Fed for their help in conducting focus groups with angel investors in Atlanta, Cleveland, Denver, and Philadelphia that were a source of information for this book.

The material from the focus groups discussed in this book was gathered under contract with the Federal Reserve Banks of Atlanta, Cleveland, Kansas City, Philadelphia, and Richmond, and was also provided in a working paper entitled, "Angel Investing: A Report Prepared for the Federal Reserve Banks of Atlanta, Cleveland, Kansas City,

Philadelphia and Richmond." Portions of this book were also provided in a working paper written under contract to the Office of Advocacy of the U.S. Small Business Administration and entitled "The Importance of Angel Investing in Financing the Growth of Entrepreneurial Ventures" (order number SBAHQ-07-Q-0016). Portions of Chapter 9 were also provided in a working paper entitled "Angel Groups: An Examination of the Angel Capital Association Survey."

I would also like to thank several entrepreneurs, business angels, academics, and policy makers who have given me generous amounts of their time to talk about angel investing over the past few years. Among those who stand out for special thanks are the anonymous participants in the angel focus groups; Dave Morgenthaler of Morgenthaler Ventures; Allan May of Life Science Angels; Steve Crawford of the National Governor's Association Center for Best Practices; John Huston of Ohio Tech Angels; Becca Braun, Kerri Breen, Lynn-Ann Gries, Ray Leach, and Kevin Mendelsohn of JumpStart; Clay Rankin and Todd Federman of the North Coast Angel Fund; and Emre Orgungor of the Cleveland Fed. Randy Bambrough, Simon Barnes, Jon Eckhardt, Tom Holmes, Allan May, Nicos Nicolaou, Barry Rosenbaum, and Gordon Schorr read the entire book and gave me very helpful feedback. This book would not have been possible without your help.

Last, I would like to thank my wife Lynne, daughter Hannah, and son Ryan. Each of them helped me in their own ways. Hannah and Ryan helped me by being excellent playmates when I needed breaks from writing. Lynne helped me by encouraging and supporting my efforts to create this book.

FOOL'S GOLD?

Introduction

THE TITLE OF this book is a pun. Some start-ups raise money from informal investors rather than institutional sources of funds, like venture capitalists and banks. Many observers refer to these informal investors as the three F's: friends, family, and fools, sometimes using the term "business angel" to refer to the third of these three categories. The phrase "fool's gold" refers to the money that angels make by investing in start-ups. But it also refers to iron pyrite, the shiny yellow rocks that miners sometimes mistake for real gold. So is angel investing a source of gold for informal investors or worthless, iron-pyrite? The answer to that question is the focus of this book.

Many investors and would-be investors believe that the *typical* investments people make in private businesses that have been founded by someone who is not a friend or family member—the definition of an angel investment—are "true gold." Similarly, many entrepreneurs and would-be entrepreneurs believe that the *typical* business angel is the most important and valuable source of capital for financing a new business. And many policy makers focus their attention on increasing the number of business angels, under the belief that they finance the creation of the high-growth technology companies that create new and high-paying jobs. But are these beliefs accurate?

If you read most books, articles, or Web sites about angel investing, you would think so. Most of the information you can find about angel investing tells the story of the best investments made by the most experienced, best-known, and most successful angels. Because good data are hard to get, numbers and statements are thrown around without consideration for whether they are accurate or consistent with each other. As a result, most people have gross misperceptions about what most business angels in America look like and what they do.

THE PROTOTYPICAL STORY

The typical story about angel investing goes something like this. After having invented a new piece of technology and founded a company in their garage, a pair of entrepreneurs—who by that point in time have maxed out their credit cards getting their business started—have worked their connections to wrangle an invitation to meet a business angel. This legendary figure is a former entrepreneur who started the most successful company in the previous generation of companies in the entrepreneurs' industry and who now occupies himself[1] sailing around San Francisco Bay, occasionally providing checks, with a sprinkling of sage advice, to young entrepreneurs who have started companies to develop the latest new, new thing.

At the time we join the story, the mythical angel has read the young entrepreneurs' business plan—which projects building the company to $100 million in sales in five years to be followed by an initial public offering (IPO) on NASDAQ—and is now meeting the two young entrepreneurs on the deck of his yacht, which is moored at a club in San Francisco Bay. The angel asks some questions, grilling the two entrepreneurs about their backgrounds and future plans, looking for holes in their patent, trying to gauge their strategy, seeking to determine whether the segment of the industry they are focused on is really growing as rapidly as the entrepreneurs say, getting a window on their personalities, and trying to figure out where the business stands.

The angel likes what he sees and agrees to conduct further due diligence on the entrepreneurs and their business. This mysterious process involves a variety of activities by the angel, including phone calls to Silicon Valley's leading venture capitalists (and sailing buddies of the angel), visits to the customers and suppliers of the company, conversations with the entrepreneurs' former employers and professors, visits to their place of business, examination of their financial records and their patents, and several other methods of kicking the tires and looking under the hood of the young company.

The due diligence shows that the company is likely to be a winner and, after a few days of intense negotiation, the angel agrees to write the entrepreneurs a check—$250,000 for 10 percent of their company—if they accept his terms. His term sheet is full of complicated clauses about anti-dilution protection (a contractual provision in an investment agreement that protects the investor from dilution of his or her portion of ownership that comes from later issues of stock at a lower price than the investor paid),[2] liquidation preferences, board seats, negative covenants, and convertible preferred stock. The entrepreneurs try to negotiate the terms of the deal, but short on cash, they know they need to take the terms and get the money. So they do.

Then it's off to the races. The angel works his magic Rolodex and helps the entrepreneurs assemble a top-notch management team, develop their new product, and get it launched. Through his sailing buddy at a leading venture capital firm, he finds them a vice president of marketing from a company that has just gone public. He gets the entrepreneurs introductions to C-list executives at the companies where they want to sell their product. Spending a couple of days each week helping the young entrepreneurs, the angel offers sage advice, based on his own start-up experience, which keeps the young entrepreneurs from stepping into a ruinous chasm on several occasions.

A year later, the angel introduces the entrepreneurs to another venture capitalist he knows—the one who financed his company originally—and the start-up secures follow-on financing. A couple of venture capital rounds and three-and-a-half years later, the company goes public. Launched on NASDAQ, the company is now worth $500 million. The angel, who was diluted down in a couple of the venture capital rounds, sells the 5 percent of the company he owns in the IPO and takes home a cool $25 million, a 100 times return of his initial investment in less than five years.

This latest American entrepreneurial dream catches the attention of the editors of a major financial magazine; they put a picture of the entrepreneurs and the mythical angel, who believed in them and their idea when their business was nothing more than a piece of paper, on the magazine cover. Inside, the angel and the entrepreneurs are interviewed for a story on the farsighted business angels whose prescience allows them to identify winning start-ups and drive the American economy forward. The cover picture, of course, shows the entrepreneurs and the business angels sitting on a 100-foot yacht in San Francisco Bay—but this time, it's the entrepreneurs' yacht.

Apocryphal? Yes. But if this exact story isn't the one told over and over again in books and magazine articles on entrepreneurship and angel investing, ones like it are. Everyone loves this kind of story. It's all about the American entrepreneurial dream and the wise private investors who make it all possible, enriching themselves and the entrepreneurs they back, and enhancing the American economy and society in the process.

So angels, academics, consultants, entrepreneurs, and reporters all write books and articles and Web blogs recounting stories like this, purporting to describe angel investing in America. Moreover, they tell us again and again about the successful and well-known companies that were financed by (and would not have been possible without the help of) business angels—companies such as Apple, Google, Ebay, Kinko's, Amazon.com, the Body Shop, Starbucks, and Yahoo.

They outline the extraordinary investments of these angels, recounting how Andrew Flipowski turned a $500,000 investment in Blue Rhino into a $24 million exit; how Sun Microsystems co-founder Andy Bechtolscheim made hundreds of millions of dollars from his $100,000 angel investment in Google; how an angel investor gave Steve Jobs and Steve Wozniak $91,000 to get that company started and ended up with an investment worth $154 million when Apple went public; how Thomas Alberg, the angel investor who backed Amazon.com, earned 260 times his $100,000 investment in that company; and how that investment was outdone by Iain McGlinn's 10,500 times return on the 4,000 British pounds he invested in return for half ownership of the Body Shop.[3]

There's only one problem with these fascinating, exciting, and uplifting stories about angel investing. They don't represent angel investing as it typically happens. They are the rarest of rare events. And because the stories of more typical angel investments in companies that did not become wildly successful and extremely well known aren't as interesting and uplifting, most authors don't tell those stories. The failures may be more typical than the successes, but they are harder to find and are less interesting to read about. So we are left with an inaccurate picture of angel investing in America, albeit one that would make a good Hollywood screenplay.

MY GOAL

I'm going to do something different. I'm not going to tell you the stories of the exciting and glamorous cream of the angel investing crop. Instead, I'm going to tell you about the typical investment made by the typical angel in the typical start-up that this investor finances. (I will tell you, though, what the most successful angels do differently from the typical ones.) While this means that I'm not going to be able to tell you stories about famous companies and glamorous investors—and I probably won't be able to sell the movie rights to this book—I am going to help you. The best information to provide the typical reader of a book about angel investing is information about the typical investment made by the typical angel because that's the kind of investment you're likely to encounter, whether you are an entrepreneur, angel, or policy maker.

I'm going to give you an accurate picture of the typical angel investment by taking a good, hard look at the data. And not just any data collected from an ad hoc group of really successful angels that some consultant or professor just happens to know. I'm going to use very accurate data, carefully collected from surveys of representative samples of angel investors by sources that know what they're doing—places like the Census Bureau and the Federal Reserve and leading academic institutions.[4]

(A representative sample is a sample that has the same characteristics as the overall population that you want to know about. For instance, if you want to know what kind of music American high school kids listen to, then a representative sample would be a set of teens randomly chosen from every high school in the country. A survey of the kids that go to Andover, Exeter, and Groton wouldn't be representative because high school kids that go to elite prep schools don't look like typical American kids. So asking them about their music preferences isn't very likely to give answers that resemble those of the overall population of high school kids in the country. Unfortunately, most surveys of angel investors are akin to asking the kids that go to Andover, Exeter, and Groton about their music tastes and trying to generalize from their answers; it won't work because the angels surveyed don't resemble the overall population of angels in the country.)

I'm going to use that data to tell the true story of angel investing in America and to challenge the myths, misperceptions, and inaccuracies that make up the received wisdom about angel investing today.

SO WHAT?

What difference does it make if we just read the stories about the most successful business angels? Why replace the interesting and uplifting Hollywood-like stories with accurate and precise information about typical angel activity? Isn't this just another example of academics counting angels on the head of a pin (pun intended)? No, it isn't. Having accurate information matters if you want to make the right decisions about angel investing. Whether you're an angel, entrepreneur, policy maker, or just a concerned citizen, you need to make good decisions about angel investing. Should you take some of your money and invest it in a stranger's start-up? Should you accept the terms that a business angel gave you to finance your business? Should you encourage angel groups to form in your city? Should you vote for a referendum to create an angel tax credit in your state? All of these things are examples of decisions that angels and would-be angels, entrepreneurs and would-be entrepreneurs, policy makers, and concerned citizens need to make about angel investing. Good information will help you make those decisions wisely. Bad information will lead you to make poor decisions that could end up hurting you.

Take the decision to invest in someone else's start-up. You need to have accurate information about how much money you will likely earn from making that investment and how much time you'll need to put into helping the entrepreneur get his business going. That way you can make an informed decision about whether you're better off putting your money into a stock index fund instead.

Now I'm not saying that you should make angel investments only if the financial returns to those investments are high. Even if you expect low returns from an investment, you might want to make it anyway to get involved with a start-up. But you don't want to make your decision thinking that you're likely to be an early investor in the next Google when that is very unlikely to happen.

While it might make you feel all warm and fuzzy inside to think that you'll be the next Thomas Alberg, turning your $100,000 investment in a start-up into $26 million, it's not going to help you make a smart decision. While it would be great if that happened, it is so unlikely that it wouldn't be prudent to make your decisions about angel investing thinking it will. No, to make smart decisions about angel investing, you need to know that the typical investor in an angel group—a select group of accredited angel investors worth an average of almost $11 million—earns less money on his investment (after the cost of his time is accounted for) than he would if he gave his cash to the average venture capitalist.[5] And the typical angel, who is not part of an angel group, does even worse. You need to make your decisions based on what is *likely* to happen, not what you dream will happen.

WHAT WILL YOU LEARN BY READING THIS BOOK?

Okay, so maybe you are willing to accept that we need to get the facts right about angel investing. But what do you need to know to be an angel, to raise money from one, to formulate public policy toward angel investing, or just to be an informed citizen? This book will tell you.

Of course, no book can answer every question a person might have about a topic. But I am going to answer the most commonly asked questions about angel investing. Things like this:

- What is angel investing and how is it different from other kinds of investing?
- Should you become a business angel?
- Should you try to raise money for your company from a business angel?
- How big is the angel capital market and how many companies do angels finance every year?
- How many people make angel investments and how often do they make them?
- Who is the typical angel investor and where can I find one?
- How do angels find deals and how do they evaluate them?
- What kinds of companies and entrepreneurs are angels looking for?
- What are the terms of the typical contract between an angel and an entrepreneur?
- How much money do angels make?
- What do the truly successful angels do that is different from the run of the mill investors?
- What makes some places better than others for angel investing?
- What public policies enhance angel investing in a region?

While these aren't the only questions the book will answer, they give you a flavor of where it's going.

WHO SHOULD READ THIS BOOK?

If you're a business angel or are thinking of becoming one; an entrepreneur who has received or is trying to get angel capital; a venture capitalist, banker or other business person who interacts with business angels; a friend or family member of an entrepreneur;

a public policy maker concerned with enhancing angel investing in your region; or just a person curious about angel finance, you should read this book.

- For entrepreneurs and would-be entrepreneurs, the book provides practical information about who angels really finance and how companies financed by angels actually get their money.
- For angels and would-be angels, the book provides useful information on the selection processes and financing terms that most angels *really* use, as well as their actual performance expectations and true investment returns.
- For venture capitalists, bankers, and friends and family members of entrepreneurs, this book provides insights into what angels look like and how they act, knowledge that will help you to identify the more valuable parts of the angel community and work more successfully with them.
- For policy makers, the book provides practical information on what policies actually enhance angel investing in a region and which do not—and may even do harm to the local economy.
- For those just curious about angel investing, the book provides an accurate picture of angel investing as it really is rather than as it is usually portrayed in the media.

Whichever category of reader you are, you will probably be surprised by what you read. The data overturn the conventional wisdom about angel investing and paint a much different picture. While this book might not make you feel as good about angel investing as many of the cheerleading books on the topic, it will be more helpful.

I want you to keep reading, so I am going to foreshadow some of the myths, inaccuracies, and misperceptions about angel investing that this book will correct:

- The size of the angel market is around $23 billion per year, about the same size as the venture capital market.
- Only 8 percent of informal investments—money from friends, family, or business angels—are angel investments.
- Angel investments are much smaller than most people believe; the typical investment is $10,000.
- Angel investment doesn't always involve equity; 15 percent of all angel deals are pure debt, and 40 percent of the funding that angels provide takes the form of debt.

- Angels don't finance only high-technology businesses; they invest in a wide swath of industries, focusing on the industries in which they have worked.
- Angels don't just invest in companies at the seed and start-up stage; in fact, more angels invest in companies that are cash flow positive than businesses that are little more than an idea.
- Angel investment deals are much more plain vanilla than received wisdom suggests; few angels have the kinds of term sheets that venture capitalists demand.
- Angel investors are not predominantly wealthy people; 79 percent of angel investments are made by individuals that don't meet Securities and Exchange Commission (SEC) requirements for accredited investors.
- Business angels aren't all that different from other sources of informal capital; on average, they have no more entrepreneurial experience, make no larger investments, have little more experience investing in start-ups, and make no more informal investments than friends and family.
- Only a tiny fraction of companies that receive angel investments get follow-on money from venture capitalists, and venture capitalists rarely co-invest with business angels.
- Angels don't get heavily involved with the companies they finance; the typical accredited angel investor who is part of an angel group—the most sophisticated of all angels—averages spending less than an hour per week per company in which he has invested.
- Angel investors don't do as well financially with their investments as received wisdom suggests, or as they expect; less than 2 percent of angel investments end in an IPO or acquisition.
- There is no shortage of angel capital in this country;[6] if anything, the data show a surplus of angel money, with more companies receiving angel money each year than meet the criteria for investment spelled out by many business angels.
- Very few of the factors associated with having a high level of angel investment activity in a region are things that policy makers can easily change; taxes explain little of the variation in angel investment activity across places.
- Angel groups are a small part of the angel capital market; accounting for only 1.8 percent of the companies receiving

angel investments, and 2 percent of the dollar value of angel investments made annually.

These are just a few of the things the data say about angel investing that most people are surprised to learn. If, as a would-be entrepreneur or investor, you're intrigued, read on; forewarned is forearmed.

ONE

What Is Angel Investing
and Why Do People Do It?

WHETHER YOU'RE INTERESTED in becoming a business angel yourself or you're trying to raise money from one, or you're a policy maker seeking to enhance angel activity in your region, or you're just someone interested in learning more about the topic, one of the first things that you're going to need to figure out is "what is angel investing?" You might think this is an easy question to answer. After all, how could people have possibly written all the books and articles and provided all the statistics out there about angel investing without defining the topic?

The answer is that they couldn't have, and the many authors who have written about angel investment have defined it. The problem is not the absence of a definition; it's that there are too many conflicting definitions. If you go on the Web and look up angel investing you'll find at least a dozen answers, all of them different. For instance, you might find these:

- " 'Angel' " is the term that is commonly used as a short form for the informal private investor. Angels invest their personal funds...in new or expanding small businesses started and operated by someone else."[1]
- "From a purely legal standpoint, an 'angel investor' (or 'business angel investor') is a 'high net worth individual,' usually an accredited investor (as the term is defined in Regulation D

under the Securities Act of 1933 or SEC Rule 501) who invests his or her own funds in private companies."[2]

- "The term angel refers to...individuals...who invest in and support start-up companies in the early stages of growth."[3]
- "Some angels are parents or relatives."[4]

If you think about these definitions for a while, you'll realize the problem. They are inconsistent. Is an angel someone who invests in all start-ups, including those founded and run by relatives, or is he somehow different from friends and family investors? Are all angels accredited investors or are there unaccredited investors who put money into other people's start-ups? Do all angels invest in the seed or start-up stage or do some invest in older, more developed companies? Do all angels provide support to the start-up companies in which they invest or are some of them passive investors? It's pretty clear that you can't understand angel investing unless you figure out which definition is right and then look at just the information that was gathered about investors and investments that fit that definition. Defining angel investing isn't going to be as easy as you might have thought from the recent article you read in *Inc.* magazine.

WHAT IS ANGEL INVESTING?

Before we go any further, I need to define angel investing. *An angel investor is a person who provides capital, in the form of debt or equity, from his own funds to a private business owned and operated by someone else, who is neither a friend nor a family member.*

Business angels are far from the only source of external capital that entrepreneurs can tap. The entrepreneurs' friends and family, venture capitalists, banks, trade creditors, credit card companies, and a host of other entities provide capital to private businesses.

To minimize the confusion about which capital sources are angel investors, I'm also going to define some other sources of funds for private companies:

- Institutional investor: A corporation, financial institution, or other organization (e.g., venture capital firm) that uses money raised from another party to provide capital to a private business owned and operated by someone else.

- Friends and family investor: An individual who uses his own money to provide capital to a private business owned and operated by a family member, work colleague, friend, or neighbor.
- Informal investor: An individual (not an institution) who uses his own money to provide capital to a private business owned and operated by someone else.

These definitions make it clear that the term "angel investor" is not synonymous with the term "informal investor". Rather, angel investors are a subset of all informal investors, which also include friends-and-family investors. That is, every angel is an informal investor, but not every informal investor is an angel; and individuals who make angel investments can, and do, make friends-and-family investments as well. Translated into more common parlance, informal investors encompass the three F's—friends, family, and fools (angels).

MANY KINDS OF ANGEL INVESTORS

While the definitions just provided indicate that the term "angel" is not synonymous with the term "informal investor" or "start-up investor," the angel category incorporates a wide range of different kinds of investors making a broad variety of investments. Unlike institutional investors, such as venture capitalists, who pretty much stick to making investments in high-technology companies that project generating $100 million or more in sales in five years, business angels invest in a broader array of industries, companies, and business opportunities. In one of the focus groups on angel investing that I conducted on behalf of several of the Federal Reserve regional banks, an investor explained that angels do not have to answer to anyone else for their investments and so invest in pretty much whatever they want.[5] As you will see in the chapters that follow, this variance in who angels are and what angels do has caused a lot of confusion for people trying to define what angel investing is.

Some angels are accredited investors; others aren't rich enough to meet SEC requirements for accreditation. Some angels are early stage capital providers; others put money into businesses that are cash flow positive at the time of investment. Some angels are passive investors, having scant involvement with the companies or founders after they invest; others get actively involved with the companies they finance. Some angels are quite knowledgeable about investing in private companies; others are quite naïve about entrepreneurship. Some angels take high risks to earn high returns; others seek lower risks and lower returns. Some angels invest alone; others invest as part of an organized group. These different dimensions affect the range of businesses in which angels will invest, the organizational arrangements they will employ, their investment criteria, their decision-making processes, and a host of other things—and these differences make describing business angels quite difficult.

To mitigate this difficulty, some observers have sought to define only some of these subgroups as angel investors. But this has only added to the confusion. Not only does that make it difficult to compare one observer's data to that of another, but also many of these definitions actually require another person's definition, and his or her data about angel investing, to be wrong. For instance, saying that angels must be accredited investors means that anything that anyone has found about unaccredited investors who put money into private companies run by people other than their friends and family members isn't relevant to angel investing, and that any information from studies that mix accredited and unaccredited angels isn't valid.

To mitigate some of this confusion, at least to the readers of this book, I'm going to identify and define several key categories of angel investors. I hope these definitions will help to show that different types of angel investors, such as accredited or unaccredited investors, or passive and active investors, are merely subsets of the broader group.

Unaccredited and Accredited Investors

- Unaccredited angel investor: An individual who does not meet the Securities and Exchange Commission's (SEC) accreditation requirements and who uses his own money to provide capital to a private business owned and operated by someone else, who is neither a friend nor a family member.
- Accredited angel investor: An individual who meets SEC accreditation requirements and who uses his own money to provide capital to a private business owned and operated by someone else, who is neither a friend nor a family member.

Active and Passive Investors

- Active angel investor: An individual who uses his own money to provide capital to a private business owned and operated by someone else, who is neither a friend nor a family member, and who invests his time as well as money in the development of the company.
- Passive angel investor: An individual who uses his own money to provide capital to a private business owned and operated by someone else, who is neither a friend nor a family member, but who does not invest his time in the development of the company.

Individual Angel, Angel Group, and Super Angel

- Individual angel: A person who acts on his own to provide some of his money to a private business owned and operated by someone else, who is neither a friend nor a family member.
- Angel group member: A person who acts as part of a group to provide some of his own money to a private business owned and operated by someone else, who is neither a friend nor a family member.
- Super angel: A person of very high net worth who provides some of his own money to a private business owned and operated by someone else, who is neither a friend nor a family member, through an office set up for that purpose.

CONFUSION ABOUT TYPES OF INVESTORS

Below, I highlight some of the most important sources of confusion about angels and other types of investors in private companies.

Informal Investing versus Angel Investing

Many observers define angel investors as informal investors. Take, for example, the following two definitions of angel investing culled from books, articles, and Web sites on angel investing.

- "A person, partnership, or corporation that uses his, her, or its own funds to invest in private companies, which are often early-stage companies but not exclusively."[6]

- "A private, non-related investor, investing their own money…alone or in syndication with other private investors."[7]

These definitions confuse "angel investing" which does not include investment in businesses run by family and friends with "informal investing" which incorporates *both* angel investing and friends-and-family investing. This confusion is a problem because many people believe that friends-and-family investing should be different from angel investing. The latter, the argument goes, will be influenced by the social relationship between the investor and the entrepreneur, which has earned it the nicknames "love money" and "believer capital."[8] As one author explains, "Angels are different from friends and family in that the investment is based on the financial risk/reward ratio as opposed to the affinity to the investment that is the predominant driver for friends and family."[9] In other words, the relationship between the investor and the entrepreneur that exists in friends-and-family investments makes these investments "emotional investments" as opposed to angel investments, which are "business investments."[10]

Passive versus Active Investors

Some observers limit angel investors to active investors—people who are willing to invest their time as well as their money in investing in private companies. Forgetting the fairly sizable number of passive angels, these observers argue that coaching and helping entrepreneurs to run their businesses is a part of angel investing.[11] In practice, however, many angels are passive investors who provide little more than money to the companies in which they invest. They do not sit on the boards of their portfolio companies and do not offer direct advice or assistance to their investees.[12] Passive investing is particularly common among members of angel groups organized as investment funds because the angels who participate in those groups can provide money but let other members make decisions on how to invest those funds.[13]

One participant in the Fed-sponsored focus groups explained that angels encompass both active investors who become heavily involved with start-ups as board members, assisting entrepreneurs with attracting customers, suppliers and additional investors, and even serving on the management team, and passive investors who provide money and nothing else.[14]

Knowledgeable versus Naïve Investors

Some observers distinguish business angels from other types of informal investors by saying that angels are "value-added" investors because of their knowledge of investing in private companies or because of their entrepreneurial experience. For instance, one observer writes, "Angel investors are typically cashed-out entrepreneurs or executives who provide early-stage funding to entrepreneurs in return for a portion of the equity in the venture,"[15] while another says that angels are "been there and done that" entrepreneurs.[16]

While it is certainly true that some angels are very knowledgeable about how to start and grow companies[17] and that some are former entrepreneurs,[18] defining angels as knowledgeable, value-added investors ignores those angels who have no start-up experience and are naïve about the entrepreneurial process.[19] In addition to including former entrepreneurs, angels also include executives and former executives in large companies, ex-bankers, people who have inherited their money, professional service providers who invest to build up their business relationships with entrepreneurs, and people who are investing money made in other professions.[20] One angel who participated in the Federal Reserve–sponsored focus groups explained that many angel investors are doctors, dentists, lawyers, and other professionals who have made a lot of money, but who have little entrepreneurial experience, and little experience investing in start-ups.[21]

Unaccredited versus Accredited Angel Investors

Perhaps the biggest source of confusion about angel investing is the tendency of many observers to limit angel investors to wealthy, accredited investors, forgetting about the large number of unaccredited investors who provide capital to private companies run by entrepreneurs who are neither their friends nor their family members. Take, for example, the following definitions:

- "Angels...are in many ways the same: wealthy individuals and families willing to invest in...deals offered by people they admire and with whom they seek to be associated."[22]
- "An angel investor [is] a high net worth individual (with investable funds of at least $1 million) who invests a portion of his/her assets in start-up ventures."[23]

However, as we will see in greater detail in Chapter 2, while some angels are accredited investors, many others are not. One angel who participated in the Fed-sponsored focus groups explained that much of the investing that many people would consider to be angel investing is not made by accredited investors.[24] Moreover, U.S. securities law clearly recognizes the existence of unaccredited angels. In fact, it imposes different rules for raising money from accredited and unaccredited angel investors. Under Regulation D of the Securities Act of 1933, the SEC allows companies to sell financial securities to an unlimited number of accredited investors but limits the number of unaccredited investors from whom money can be raised. In addition, if the effort to sell securities goes only to unaccredited investors, then a formal private placement memorandum, similar to that filed in a nonexempt filing, has to be provided to the investor, and the seller of the securities needs to show that the investors are "sophisticated."[25] By setting up separate rules for raising money from accredited and unaccredited angel investors, the SEC is clearly indicating that both categories of angel investors exist.

Size (of Investment) Doesn't Define an Angel

Some observers require investments to meet a certain minimum size to qualify as angel investments. For instance, one observer wrote, angels are people who "invest at least $20K in businesses not run by family."[26] However, there is nothing magical about a $20,000 investment. And, as we will see in Chapter 3, *the majority* of angel investors actually make investments that are smaller than $20,000 (the median, or typical, angel investment is $10,000). Moreover, some of the people who provide more than $20,000 in capital to private companies run by people who are neither their friends nor their family members also make investments of less than $20,000 in the same companies. Defining a single person's investments in the same company as both angel investments and non-angel investments just because one investment is $20,001, while the other is $19,999, doesn't make much sense.

Stage of Investment Doesn't Define Angel Investing

Investments in private companies are described as occurring at different stages of company development. Commonly referred to stages include seed, start-up, growth/expansion, and later stage. Seed stage investing occurs when a company has little more than a business plan or rough prototype of a product. Start-up stage investing occurs when a company has a new product and an initial organization but has not yet generated any revenues. Early stage investing occurs when a company has revenues but is not yet profitable. Later stage investing occurs when a company is already profitable.

Many observers define angel investing as primarily, or in some cases, as only that investing which occurs at the seed or start-up stage of a company's life. Take, for example, the following definition: "An 'angel investor' (or 'business angel investor')…invests his or her own funds in private companies, typically at the seed and early stages."[27] However, angel investing is not defined by the stage at which the investment is made. Some angels invest at the seed stage when the entrepreneur is the only other source of capital while others are late stage investors, providing bridge financing to companies that have already experienced substantial growth, or invest in management buyouts and leveraged buyouts of established companies.[28]

In fact, some observers believe that the stage at which angels invest is a strategic choice. For instance, some angels make later stage investments to obtain a better risk-return ratio and make seed stage investments only if there is no better option. In fact, one angel in the Fed sponsored focus groups explained that seed investments are done only when other investors have taken all of the later stage deals.[29]

Moreover, some angel investors focus on management buyouts and leveraged buyouts because that is where their expertise lies. In particular, retired executives of old economy, manufacturing companies often try to invest in turnaround opportunities where they can exploit proven management techniques, experience, and contacts to earn a financial return.[30]

Level of Risk Does Not Define Angel Investing

Some observers say that angel investments must be high-risk deals, excluding all deals that are not "high-risk."[31] However, defining only high-risk deals as angel investments doesn't make a lot of sense. For one thing, what's one person's high-risk investment is another person's moderate- or low-risk investment because the riskiness of an investment depends very much on the investor's knowledge. Therefore, a risk-based definition of angel investing is very subjective. Moreover, the preference of some angels for later stage companies and leveraged buyouts means that at least one group of angels doesn't make investments that involve technical risk (the risk that the entrepreneur may be unable to produce the product or service that he proposes offering) or market risk (the risk that the entrepreneur may not find a customer for his or her product or service).[32]

Making Equity Investments Does Not Define Angel Investing

Another odd way that angel investors have been defined has been to limit them to those people who make *equity* investments in start-up companies. For instance, one observer wrote, a business angel is "an individual who invests equity capital directly into a business, usually a small or medium-sized business."[33] This approach to defining angel investing doesn't make a whole lot of sense because angels use a wide range of financial instruments, from pure debt to pure equity. Because they have no fiduciary responsibility to others and are not regulated like banks, angels are not restricted in how they invest and can finance companies with whatever type of debt or equity they choose.

Moreover, in practice angels use debt fairly often. As will be shown in greater detail in Chapter 5, approximately 56 percent of all angel investments involve debt instruments. These instruments range from simple high-interest term loans to complex convertible debt that angel groups use to avoid placing a valuation on a portfolio company (for fear that it will cause conflict with the entrepreneur that will undo a deal or make it difficult to bring in later round investors).

Why the Long Treatise on the Definition of Angel Investing?

So why have I spent so much time clarifying the definition of angel investing used in this book and showing that many definitions used by other observers are contradictory and problematic? Because our ability to understand the basic facts about angel investing—the number of angels in the United States, the amount of money they invest, their attributes and the attributes of the companies and entrepreneurs in which they put money, the investment terms they use, and a host of other things—depends very much on having an *accurate* definition of angel investments and angel investors. If we define angels as active, knowledgeable, accredited, informal investors who make large, seed stage, high-risk equity investments in private companies instead of as individuals who use their own money to provide capital to private businesses founded by people who are neither friends nor family members, then we get wrong answers when we try to figure out who angels are, what companies they back, and how they make investments. (It's the same as saying let's figure out what horses are by using the definition of a zebra; you end up looking at the wrong animals at the zoo.) And inaccurate answers will make it difficult for would-be angels to understand whether they want to invest in private companies, for entrepreneurs to understand how to raise money from business angels, and for policy makers to set the laws and regulations that govern angel investing.

WHY DO PEOPLE BECOME ANGELS?

Another important question we need to answer about angel investing is why people become angels. Policy makers won't be able to design very good incentives to increase the number of angels in their communities if they don't know why people become angels, entrepreneurs won't do a very good job raising money from angels if they don't know why angels do what they do, and potential investors won't do a very good job of figuring out whether they should be business angels if they don't know why people make angel investments. Unfortunately, it turns out that explaining why people become business angels isn't so easy.

Unlike the motivations of institutional investors, whose goal is to make money for their own investors from the deals that they strike with entrepreneurs, the motivations of business angels aren't so clear-cut. Sure, making money is a motivation for some angels, but it isn't the only motivation, or even the defining motivation, for many. In fact, two thirds of angel investors report that making money isn't their primary motivation for investing in private companies.[34] And some angels value the nonfinancial benefits of investing in private companies so much that it might be better to view their activity as consumption rather than as investment, much as we look at the purchase of art or expensive homes.[35] The fact that making money isn't the primary, let alone sole, motivation for many angel investors means that we need to figure out the answer to the question: Why do people become business angels?

To Make Money

Let's start by dispensing with the money issue. Some angels invest in start-ups to make money.[36] For instance, one study of 230 business angels in Germany found that the desire to earn money was one of the top four reasons that people invest their own money in other people's companies.[37]

The financial motivation for investing in start-ups is pretty straightforward. People become business angels because they believe they can obtain financial returns from investing in private companies that exceed the returns they can obtain from other kinds of investments.

These types of angels tend to say that they won't invest in other people's companies unless the investment is likely to provide the chance to earn a high return. Take, for example, one angel who participated in the Federal Reserve–sponsored focus groups. He explained that he would not invest in a company that promised to stay in state no matter what because the company would not be doing everything possible to keep costs down and, thus, enhance investors' returns.[38]

It is important to note that the financial motivation is valid regardless of whether angels actually earn higher returns on their investments in private companies than in their other investment alternatives. As long as they believe that they will make more money investing in other people's businesses than investing in other things, then the financial motivation can explain why they become angels.

To Get Involved with Private Companies

But angels tend to express a lot of other motivations for investing in other people's companies. Some people say they become angels because they find the process of building new companies to be enjoyable but don't want to start another company.[39] Being an angel allows them to work with entrepreneurs and participate in this building process without having to put in the tremendous amount of effort that is necessary to make a new company successful.[40] As one angel put it quite succinctly, "They want to stay in the game, but not stay up to 2 A.M. anymore."[41]

One study found that having the opportunity to contribute to the development of new companies is one of the major reasons people become business angels.[42] Of course, this is probably a greater motivation for people who have had entrepreneurial experience themselves and who have had a good time building start-up companies in the past.

Some angels enjoy becoming involved with start-ups and working with entrepreneurs because of the satisfaction they get from building something new. In the focus groups on angel investing that I conducted, several angels explained that they make these investments because they like to grow something from nothing by helping an entrepreneur transform a technology into a new product or service or convert an idea into an organization.[43]

This motivation is particularly true of angels who were successful entrepreneurs. Once these angels exit their own companies, some of them look for ways to help other entrepreneurs create and grow successful companies because they enjoy being part of efforts of building companies from nothing.[44]

Angel investors also enjoy getting involved with other people's companies because it allows them to make use of expertise they have developed in an industry, with a particular technology, or in building companies. Investing in private companies provides a way for the angels to give others the benefit of their expertise, whether that expertise involves commercializing new technologies, selecting managers to run companies, or something else.[45] For instance, one angel who participated in the Federal Reserve–sponsored focus groups explained that he is primarily interested in investment opportunities that leverage his skills.[46]

In particular, many angels say they want to pass on the skills they have developed to the next generation of entrepreneurs[47] and to help young entrepreneurs develop as businesspeople.[48] As one angel explained, "I…have been involved in building companies…myself. I enjoy helping other people who are doing the same thing."[49]

Many angels have strong beliefs about what actions help and hinder the growth of companies. By investing as angels, these individuals believe that they can increase the upside potential of business opportunities.[50] One angel said, "I've had both success and failure as an entrepreneur and…I was driven to take that experience and help people, so…they wouldn't make…the same mistakes I made."[51]

Several angels explained that they invest to get entrepreneurs to compensate them for their expertise. Many private companies cannot pay cash for assistance, so an expert in marketing, product development, or whatever the angel believes is the source of the value that he provides to start-ups needs to take his payment in the form of equity. If the company he is helping also needs capital, the expert often ends up making an angel investment.[52]

Ironically, some angels say they invest in other people's companies for precisely the opposite reason. Rather than getting compensation for their expertise, these angels say that they invest money in new companies because entrepreneurs will not listen to their advice if they don't have to pay for it. In fact, at least one angel group was established because retired executives who wanted to share their knowledge and experience with entrepreneurs found that the entrepreneurs wouldn't listen to them unless they also invested in the entrepreneurs' ventures.[53]

To Learn New Things

Another reason people make angel investments is to learn something new. Some angels want to learn about how companies develop. Because investing in private companies allows people to become involved with more than one company at a time, some people find it to be a particularly effective way to do this.[54]

Other angels recount that they like to invest in private companies because they like to challenge themselves and their ideas in an open forum and debate different views.[55] Still other angels say that they like to learn about new technology before it reaches the marketplace, or even before many other people have heard about it.[56]

As a Hobby Job

Some people make angel investments as a hobby,[57] in some cases because they have found retirement to be boring.[58] Some angels even describe their investment activity as a "hobby" and explain that it is more fun than reading books or playing golf, in part because they are better at building companies than at doing these other things. Other angels explain that investing in private companies is more fun than other hobbies because it is more intellectually stimulating and exciting than trying to put a ball in a hole 350 yards away or because it involves the rush of winning a game that depends both on luck and on skill.[59]

One angel described the personal enjoyment that she gets from angel investing with an analogy that sums up the hobby perspective. She said, "I liken it to fly-fishing. [If] a venture capitalist...doesn't come home with fish then he loses his job, like a commercial fisherman. A fly fisherman...really wants to catch a fish, but enjoys the experience. If he doesn't bring home a fish, it's not the end....His livelihood doesn't depend on it."[60]

Ironically, angel investing may be a cheaper hobby than many others. While investing $10,000 in one new company every other year might not be cheap, it is still a lot less expensive than traveling, sailing, or art appreciation. As one angel said, "It's cheaper and more fun than buying a yacht."[61]

To Find a Job

Some people become angel investors to find a job. This subset of angels usually makes investments in just one company at a time because they make those investments as entrée into companies where they want to have their next gig as CEO or other type of executive. One angel who participated in the Fed-sponsored focus groups explained that these investors often put a lot of their time and effort into the companies in which they invest, along with their money.[62]

To Help the Community

Some people become angels to support the community in which they live and work.[63] A part of this motivation is a desire to give something back to a place that has supported them in some way. In focus groups conducted with business angels, several of them explained that angel investing gave them a psychological return from community building.[64]

Another part of this motivation is a desire to encourage economic development, something that some angels call "writing economic development checks."[65] By spurring economic development through investments in private companies, the angels believe that they can keep jobs, technology, and talented people in the community in which they live. In places that have declined from their economic peak, this motivation is often expressed as a desire to get the community "back on its feet again" or to make it the community a place where young people will choose to live after they finish their education. One participant in the Federal Reserve–sponsored focus groups explained that some angels invest because they like the psychic return that comes from helping to build businesses in the community.[66]

A related motivation comes from a belief in the value to society of the products and services that entrepreneurs provide. Sometimes angels invest because they believe the world needs something. For instance, some angels invest in life science companies because those companies have a treatment for a medical condition that the angel wants treated. As one angel explained, "To the motivations I would also add curing a disease or condition that has affected one's family or loved ones. This is a relatively common theme in life science angel investing."[67]

Because a Friend of a Friend Has a Business

Some people become angels because a friend of a friend has a business and needs capital. Some part of this motivation is a belief in the idea that everyone should have a chance to run his or her own company. Another part of the motivation is the desire not to disappoint a person who is a friend of a friend, no matter how distant the connection is. This motivation for angel investing is just another way people "pay it forward," as in the 2000 movie with Kevin Spacey.

IN CONCLUSION

So what's the message of this chapter? It's pretty straightforward, even if points out the complexity of understanding angel investing. First, an angel investor is a person who provides some of his own money, in the form of debt or equity, to a private business that he doesn't run and that isn't run by a friend or family member. Thus, angel investing is a subset of all informal investing, which also includes investments made by friends and family. Moreover, it is just one of many sources of capital for private companies, which also include venture capitalists, banks, trade creditors, asset-based lenders, and the entrepreneurs themselves, among a host of others.

While angels are a distinct source of entrepreneurial finance, they aren't homogenous. Some angels are accredited investors; others are unaccredited. Some angels are early stage capital providers; others are late stage investors. Some angels are passive investors; others are actively involved in the companies in which they invest. Some angels are quite knowledgeable about entrepreneurship; others are quite naïve about it. Some angels take high risks to earn high returns; others seek lower risks and accept lower returns. Some angels invest alone; others put their money in start-ups as part of a group. While people falling along all of these different dimensions are angels, the differences between them affect the range of businesses in which they will invest; the types of organizational arrangements that they will use;

their investment criteria; their decision-making processes; and a host of other things, which make describing business angels quite difficult.

Second, unlike institutional investors, who are in the business of investing in start-ups to make money, the motivations of business angels aren't clear-cut. Some angels invest to make money, but that isn't the only motivation, or even the defining motivation, for many. Some people become angels to be involved with private companies without starting companies themselves; others do it to learn something new. Some people become angels to find a new job; others do it because they need a hobby. Still others become angels to give back to the community in which they live and work or to pay it forward. The diversity of reasons people become angels makes understanding the patterns in what they do more difficult but also more interesting.

But before we talk about who these people are and what they do, let's take a look at the market for angel capital and how it fits into the broader market of capital for new businesses, the subject of the next chapter.

TWO

How Big Is the Angel
Capital Market?

HOW MANY ANGELS are there? How much do they invest? How many companies get angel capital? These are important questions to entrepreneurs seeking capital, the angels providing it, and the policy makers hoping to marry the two. The good news is that we have answers to these questions. The bad news is that there's no shortage of answers to them, and the answers don't come close to agreeing. For example, estimates of numbers of companies receiving angel investments every year are as low as 15,000 and as high 700,000; estimates of the number of people who make angel investments are as low as 100,000 and as high as 3 million; and estimates of the amount of money that angels invest every year are as low as $20 billion and as high as $150 billion. Therefore, many of the reported statistics on angel investing—whether they are on the number of firms receiving angel investments, the number of angel investors, or the amount that angels invest—are incorrect by a very large order of magnitude. The question is: which ones are correct?

To figure this out we need to look at studies of samples of people and firms that are representative of the population of the people and companies in the United States. Estimates that extrapolate from surveys of wealthy individuals who are known to have invested in start-up companies provide inaccurate numbers because the angel investment activity by these individuals is very different from that of the general population.

Let me give you an analogy to show you what I mean. Suppose you want to know how many home runs the typical major leaguer will hit in a season. You're going to run into problems if you look at Mark McGwire, Sammy Sosa, and Barry Bonds to figure that out. Their home run hitting patterns are different from those of the typical major league player. And the bigger the thing you try to extrapolate to—say, home runs in a career instead of home runs in a week—the more off course your estimates get.

Now add to this problem the fact that many estimates confuse angel investing with other types of informal investing and are actually measuring the amount of angel investing *plus* friends-and-family investing, and you get estimates that aren't very good and aren't very useful.

HOW ARE NEW BUSINESSES FINANCED?

Before we start talking about angel investing, we have to put external financing of new businesses in context. Getting money from *any* source other than the founders of the business is a rare activity for a new company. For instance, the Census Bureau's most recent Survey of Business Owners—our government's effort to look at all businesses in this country—showed that 63.6 percent of firms used the entrepreneurs' own money to finance the start of their businesses, while only 2.7 percent raised money from an outside investor—a venture capital firm, a strategic investor, a friend or a family member.[1]

Even among very rapidly growing businesses—the kinds of firms that many people say business angels are targeting—most capital comes from the founders, followed by their friends and family. In 2005, *Inc.* magazine looked at the 2004 Inc. 500 companies—the 500 fastest growing private companies in the United States—and reported where they got their start-up capital. The majority—70 percent—got it from the founders' personal assets, and 10 percent got it from the founders' friends and family. Only 4 percent got their start-up capital from any kind of private equity source, a proportion *half* as large as the proportion that received money from a commercial bank or other financial institution, and equal to the percentage that got it from a supplier, customer, or other business entity.[2] In short, getting money from an outside investor, any kind of outside investor, is a pretty rare thing for a start-up.

In 2004, in the United States, approximately $310 billion was invested in young companies. As Figure 2.1 shows, this capital came primarily from four sources. Approximately $124 billion came from the entrepreneurs themselves;[3] another $20 billion came from venture capitalists; and $4 billion came from Small Business Investment Companies (SBICs). However, the bulk of the money—$162 billion—came from informal investors.[4] (As explained in the previous chapter, an informal investor is an individual who uses his own money to provide capital to a private business run by someone else.)

The amount of informal investment undertaken in the United States every year is substantial, equaling 1.3 percent of the U.S. gross domestic product (GDP).[5] Moreover, the Global Entrepreneurship Monitor, a massive effort by academic researchers around the world to sample a group of adults who represent the adult-age population of each country, found that 3.4 percent of adults had invested in a business start-up founded by another person between 1997 and 2001.[6] In the United States, the proportion of the adult-age population that made at least one informal investment over the previous three years

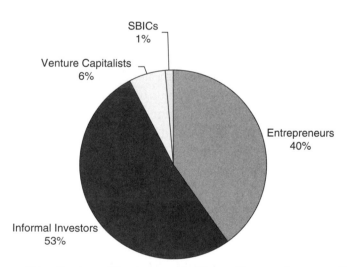

FIGURE 2.1. Distribution of Investment in Young Companies across Venture Capitalists, SBICs, Informal Investors, and Entrepreneurs. *Source*: Created from data contained in Reynolds, P. 2007. *New Firm Creation in the U.S.: A PSED I Overview*. Berlin: Springer-Verlag and from data downloaded from www.altassets.com/knowledgebank/surveys/2006/nz8218.php.

ranged from 7 percent in 2000 to 3.5 percent in 2004.[7] Because there were 212 million adult Americans in 2004, this means that an estimated 7.4 million U.S. adults made an informal investment between 2001 and 2003.

We can also estimate the average number of informal investments made by American investors over the 2001 to 2003 period. Because those people who made informal investments over the three-year period made an average of 1.91 of them, American adults made 14.1 million informal investments from 2001 through 2003.[8]

Many observers have looked at numbers like these and concluded that the angel capital market is quite large. However, drawing that conclusion is a mistake. As we will see in a short while, almost all informal investment comes from friends and family, *not* from business angels.

It is also a mistake to look at the numbers for informal investment and conclude that accredited investors are responsible for a lot of informal financing (let alone a lot of angel financing). Most informal investments are *not* made by accredited investors. Accredited investors are a small portion of the population, and they do not make informal investments at a high enough rate to account for the majority of informal investments. George Haynes of Montana State University and Charles Ou of the Office of Advocacy of the U.S. Small Business Administration examined data from the Federal Reserve Survey of Consumer Finances and found that in 1998, only 12.7 percent of households that met the minimum net worth requirements for being accredited investors held an informal equity investment.[9] And the numbers for the more recent Entrepreneurship in the United States Assessment, conducted in 2004, revealed that only 10.5 percent of accredited investors had made an informal investment during the previous three-year period.[10]

INFORMAL EQUITY MARKET

The informal capital market that we've been talking about isn't just providing equity to companies; it's also providing debt. In fact, *more than half* (56 percent) of all informal investment provided to new companies takes the form of debt. That shouldn't be surprising to those of you who've seen the Web site Prosper.com, which matches individuals who want to borrow money to individuals who want to lend it. Debt instruments are a lot easier to use, especially when the companies receiving the capital are sole proprietorships or partnerships, which make up the majority of U.S. businesses.

The numbers might not be surprising, but they do point out an important caution: if what we want to understand is *equity* investments made in young companies, we have to adjust the estimates that we just made for the informal capital market.[11] If we do that, we find that the informal equity capital market in the United States is approximately $71.3 billion per year.

And that money goes to a small number of companies. The 2003 Federal Reserve Survey of Small Business Finances indicates that only 2.5 percent of companies that are less than five years old receive an informal equity investment annually. Even older businesses are not much more likely to get informal equity investments. The Fed data show that only 2.6 percent of all small businesses received an informal equity investment in the previous twelve months.

What about the number of informal equity investors? Approximately 4.6 million American adults made an informal *equity* investment during the three-year period from 2001 through 2003.[12]

The stock of informal equity investments held by U.S. households isn't that different from the annual flow. George Haynes of Montana State University and Charles Ou of the Office of Advocacy of the U.S. Small Business Administration used data from the 1989 through 1998 Surveys of Consumer Finances (SCF) to measure the informal *equity* holdings of U.S. households. They found that in 1998, 1.4 percent of American households held an informal equity investment.[13] Based on these numbers, in 1998, approximately 1.4 million U.S. households held an informal *equity* investment.

However, the numbers are much smaller if we are interested in informal equity investments made by *accredited* investors. Data from the 1998 Federal Survey of Consumer Finances shows that only 0.3 percent of U.S. households met both the net worth requirement for being accredited investors ($1 million)—and held an informal investment.[14] That is, the vast majority of the informal investments in this country are held by households that do not meet accreditation requirements, at least on the net worth side.

TYPES OF INFORMAL INVESTORS

Most informal investments are not angel investments, but are actually friends and family investments (see Figure 2.2).[15] The data from the Entrepreneurship in the United States Assessment, conducted in 2004, indicate that 54 percent of all informal investments in the United

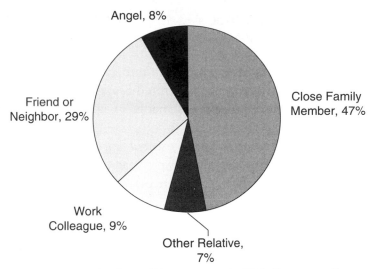

Angel, 8%

Friend or
Neighbor, 29%

Close Family
Member, 47%

Work
Colleague, 9%

Other Relative,
7%

FIGURE 2.2. Sources of Informal Investments in U.S. Start-ups. *Source*:
Created from data contained in Reynolds, P. 2004. *Entrepreneurship in the
United States Assessment*. Miami, FL: Florida International University.

States are made in businesses run by the investor's relatives, and another
38 percent are made in businesses run by his friends, work colleagues,
and neighbors, making 8 percent of investments angel investments.
Similarly, the 2003 Federal Reserve Survey of Small Business Finances
data show that 7.4 percent of businesses that received an informal equity
investment that year got that investment from a business angel.

Friends and Family

The vast majority of informal investments—92 percent—are friends
and family investments, so it is useful to take a look at the characteristics of that market. Estimates using data from the Entrepreneurship
in the United States Assessment indicate that the friends and family
capital market is about $139 billion annually.

Angel Investors

These statistics suggest that the angel capital market is much more
modest than what received wisdom tells us. Although some observers
claim that business angels have between $100 billion and $300 billion
in money invested in new companies[16] and that the annual flows of
angel funds are approximately "$56 billion a year,"[17] the data from the
Entrepreneurship in the United States Assessment indicate that annual

flows of angel funds are about $23 billion per year. Over the 2001 through 2003 period, approximately 331,100 people made an angel investment.

This funding is provided to a limited number of companies. According to the Entrepreneurship in the United States Assessment data, in 2003, Americans made angel investments in approximately 57,300 companies.

This estimate is higher than the estimate of the number of companies receiving angel investments every year from the 2003 Federal Reserve Survey of Small Business Finances, which found that 0.19 percent of U.S. businesses with fewer than 500 employees—a number that extrapolates to 44,100 companies—had "received an equity investment from a business angel in the previous 12 months."[18] Based on information from other sources on the proportion of angel investments that do not involve equity, the Fed data give us an estimate of 50,700 companies that receive an investment from a business angel each year.

As we will see in greater detail in Chapter 6, regardless of which estimate we use, very few of these companies are seed or start-up stage businesses. Most are companies with existing cash flow. Therefore, the number of seed and start-up stage companies receiving equity investments made by angel investors is considerably smaller than 44,000 companies per year.

Even the most successful high-growth companies aren't likely to ever receive angel funding. For instance, one study found that 88 percent of the Inc. 500 companies never received money from business angels, whereas one third of them raised money from friends and family.[19]

Unaccredited and Accredited Angel Investors

As the previous chapter pointed out, only some angel investors meet the SEC income or net worth requirements to be accredited investors. But what portion of the angel capital market is made up of accredited investors? The data contained in the Entrepreneurship in the United States Assessment suggest that 79 percent of the angel investments made by American adults over the three year period from 2001 through 2003 were made by unaccredited investors.[20]

We can estimate the number of companies that receive accredited angel investments every year from venture capitalist co-investment rates gathered by Andrew Wong of the University of Chicago. Wong identified companies that had received angel capital during the 1994 to 2001 period by looking at media mentions of investments (which almost certainly restricted him to the identification of companies that received money from accredited investors). He found that venture capitalists co-invested in 21 percent of the investment rounds.[21] By applying this co-investment rate to the number of venture capital investments reported annually by PricewaterhouseCoopers' Venture Capital Money Tree during this time period, we get an estimate of 13,000 companies that receive angel investments from accredited investors every year.[22] In short, only a small number of companies get money from *accredited* angel investors every year.

This may be because a very small percentage of the accredited investor population makes angel investments. An analysis of the Wisconsin angel tax credit system shows that in 2005, one quarter of 1 percent of tax filers with adjusted gross incomes higher than $200,000 (the income level for a single person to be considered an accredited investor) received an angel tax credit in that state.[23] While the Wisconsin tax credit data might not capture investors who invest in companies in other states, most angel investors limit their investments to companies that are geographically near by. Therefore, even if we were to adjust this estimate for people living in places like Milwaukee and investing in companies in places like Chicago, the proportion of people making more than $200,000 per year and investing in private companies that are owned and operated by someone else is still very small. Therefore, at least in Wisconsin, a minuscule portion of accredited investors makes angel investments.[24]

Accredited angel investors account for a larger portion of the dollar value of the angel capital market than their share of angel investments made. Because their investments tend to be much larger than those of unaccredited angels, data from the Entrepreneurship in the United States Assessment suggest that accredited angels provide about 54 percent of the angel dollars invested annually. That is, in 2004, unaccredited angels invested approximately $10.6 billion in private companies, while accredited angels invested around $12.4 billion.

"Been-There-Done-That" Entrepreneurs

Some observers don't consider all accredited investors who invest in private companies to be business angels, arguing instead that the true angels have entrepreneurial experience. Taking that perspective, how many business angels are there? Business angel Bill Payne says that there are "more than 400,000 active angels" with angels being defined as "accredited investors" who put money into businesses founded by people other than friends and family and who are "been-there-and-done-that" entrepreneurs.[25] However, the true number is much lower.

Estimates from the Entrepreneurship in the United States Assessment suggest that 61,200 accredited investors who have made an angel investment also have started and run their own businesses.[26] But just because you have started a business doesn't make you a "been-there-done-that" entrepreneur. You also need to accomplish something with that business. If the criterion for "been-there-done-that" entrepreneur status is to have a business worth at least $1 million, then 16,500 people that made at least one angel investment in the 2001 through 2003 time period meet the criterion. But if the standard is to have a business worth at least $10 million, the number of households that have made at least one angel investment in that time period and meet the criterion drops to 9,400.[27]

And there's one other thing to consider. A number of these people inherited or purchased their businesses. If an angel is an accredited investor who started a company that is worth at least $10 million and who has made at least one angel investment in the past three years, then there are probably no more than 9,000 households in the country with an angel in them.

EXTERNAL EQUITY INVESTMENT

It is often difficult to distinguish angel investments from investments made by friends because angels sometimes know the people whose companies they choose to invest in. Therefore, it's useful to consider the size of the market for equity finance that comes from both friends and angels, to ensure that the failure to differentiate investments by friends and angels doesn't cause us to misunderstand the patterns in angel investment activity.

When we include equity investments by friends with equity investments by business angels to measure the external equity market, we find that this market ($66.7 billion per year) is almost five times as large as the $13.8 billion per year angel equity market. However, by the standards of most financial markets, this is tiny. By comparison, the average *daily* trading volume on the New York Stock Exchange is $25 billion.

Several sources, including the Panel Study of Entrepreneurial Dynamics, the Federal Reserve Survey of Small Business Finances, and the Census Bureau's Survey of Business Owners (SBO), indicate that very few companies receive equity investments from anyone other than the founders of the business. Estimates from the SBO data put the portion of businesses less than six years old receiving an external equity (friends and angels) investment at only 1.3 percent.

COMPARISON WITH OTHER TYPES OF INVESTMENT

So how important a source of capital are business angels? The received wisdom is that they are *the dominant source* of capital for new companies. For instance, one observer writes, "Simply put, private investors, or business angel investors, are a primary if not *the* primary source of capital for early-stage and growing companies."[28]

However, as you probably figured out from the data provided earlier in this chapter, this statement can't be true. Although some observers claim that business angels invest in "thirty to forty times more ventures each year than venture capitalists,"[29] that would have angel investors financing between 74,000 and 167,000 companies per year, depending on which source for the annual number venture capital-backed start-ups is to be believed. Estimates based on the data from the Federal Reserve Survey of Small Business Finances and the Entrepreneurship in the United States Assessment put this number between 50,700 and 57,300 annually.

Moreover, surveys of companies about the financing that they receive do not suggest ratios this high. For instance, data from 2003 Federal Reserve Survey of Small Business Finances show that the same proportion of businesses less than five years old received an angel investment as received a venture capital investment in the previous year. For businesses of all ages, 11.5 times as many businesses had received an angel investment in the previous year as had received a venture capital investment in that same period. The Kauffman Firm Survey (which combines investments by friends and angel investments) indicates that 3.5 times as many new firms received equity from an individual other than the spouse, parents, in-laws, or children of the owners in their first year of operation as received money from venture capitalists.[30] Because the Kauffman Foundation data include friends as angel investors, the ratio of the number of angel-backed companies to venture capital-backed companies must be less than 3.5.

The story is no different for high-growth businesses. In 2005, *Inc.* magazine reported where the 2004 Inc. 500 companies got their start-up capital. "Private equity," of which angel investors are a subset, provided the start-up capital for only twice the number of Inc. 500 firms as venture capitalists. Moreover, the magazine reported that in the time since the businesses were founded, 17 percent of them had raised money from business angels while 12 percent of them had raised venture capital, a ratio of less than 1.5 to 1. Therefore, it appears that business angels do not finance as many more new companies than venture capitalists as previous research suggests.

The data indicate that it is not business angels who finance many more businesses than venture capitalists; rather, it is the *other* types of informal investors who do. To understand what I mean, take a look at the following information from the Federal Reserve's Survey of Small Business Finances. The surveyors asked entrepreneurs if they had received an equity investment from individual investors (which included friends, family, and angels) or venture capitalists in the previous twelve months, as well as whether these individual investors were "business angels" or something else. The data reveal that *more than 13 times* as many businesses less than five years old received an equity investment from some kind of individual investor as received an investment from an angel investor! The very large difference in the number of companies that received investments from individual investors and angel investors indicates that it is not "angels" who provide capital to so many more new companies than venture capitalists but rather it is friends and family.

The number of businesses financed by business angels is also small in comparison to the number financed by many other sources. While studies show that few companies ever receive an angel investment, almost every start-up gets money from its founders. Moreover, the founders of 65 percent of all new businesses use personal debt to obtain money for their companies, with 28.3 percent using their credit cards and 23 percent getting bank loans.[31]

But what about the amount of money that young companies receive? After all, many observers say that business angels account for a large portion of the capital provided to new businesses. For instance, the experts write:

- "Nearly two thirds of funding for new enterprises is obtained from angels."[32]
- "Angels account for 90 percent of the early stage financing in the United States that is not provided by friends or family."[33]
- "BAs [business angels] fund an annual amount of two to five times more money to entrepreneurial firms than the VC [venture capital] industry."[34]

Unfortunately, these estimates are a greater reflection of the authors' fervent belief in the importance of business angels than they are a representation of the actual proportion of financing that angels provide. The actual numbers break down as follows: In 2004, approximately $310 billion was invested in young companies in the United States. Of this total, $124 billion came from the entrepreneurs themselves; $139 billion came from friends and family; $20 billion came from venture capitalists;[35] $4 billion came from small business investment companies,[36] and $23 billion was invested by business angels. Thus, business angels accounted for just over 7 percent of the total amount of money invested in young companies in the United States in 2004.

Moreover, the angel capital market is only one sixth the size of the friends-and-family market and is no larger than the venture capital market.[37] It's also very small in comparison to other financial markets that you might be familiar with. It is half the size of the initial public offering market ($43 billion in 2004),[38] and is dwarfed by the mergers and acquisitions market ($749 billion in 2004),[39] which itself is tiny in comparison to the $12 trillion public equity market.

The dollar values are not that different when looked at from the point of view of the financing received by companies. One study that looked at data from the Federal Reserve's Survey of Small Business Finances found that 3.6 percent of the capital that the companies had received had come from business angels as compared to 1.9 percent from venture capitalists.[40]

This study also showed that the proportion of the capital that young companies receive from business angels is also very small in comparison to the proportion that comes from banks, which are the *leading source* of external debt financing for new businesses. The Federal Reserve's Survey of Small Business Finances data indicate that commercial bank lending accounts for 16 percent of the total financing of businesses

KEY FACTS TO REMEMBER

Amount invested by informal investors in a typical year	$162 billion
Amount invested by friends and family investors in a typical year	$139 billion
Amount invested by business angels in a typical year	$23 billion
Amount invested by accredited business angels in a typical year	$12.4 billion
Number of companies financed by business angels in a typical year	50,700–57,300

that are two years old or less, 3 percent more than the next highest source, trade credit.[41]

IN CONCLUSION

Our collective belief in the size and importance of the angel capital market appears to be misplaced. Contrary to the statements of many observers, the data show that the angel capital market is not very large in comparison to other sources of start-up financing and downright minuscule in comparison to the public equities or mergers and acquisitions markets.

The received wisdom on the role of angels within the informal capital market also appears to be incorrect. The data indicate that friends-and-family investors are a much more important source of capital than business angels. The numbers show that angel investors only account for about $23 billion of the $162 billion in informal investment made in 2004; and around only 8 percent of all informal investments are angel investments. Moreover, only a tiny fraction of companies in existence receive an angel investment in any given year.

Although many observers argue that angel investors are much more important than venture capitalists to the financing of start-ups, this belief appears to be more a wish than a reality. The data show that angels provide the same amount of money to start-ups as venture capitalists.

The angel capital market also differs from the way it is generally described by observers in two important ways. First, it is not primarily an equity market. A substantial portion of angel transactions involve some form of debt. Second, it is not composed solely or even primarily of accredited investors. Unaccredited investors account for the vast majority of angel investors and a substantial portion of the funds that angels put into private companies every year.

Having set the record straight on the size and importance of the angel capital market, I turn now to who business angels are and what they look like.

THREE

Who Are Angel Investors?

W HO ARE THESE angel investors that you hear about all the time? Considered by many to be a central feature of the American entrepreneurial system, business angels are thought to be wealthy, Silicon Valley former entrepreneurs, sipping chardonnay on the decks of their 100-foot yachts while writing checks to twenty-something geeks who have invented the latest widget. After all, this is how they are described time and time again in books and articles, Web sites and blogs.

If you read the popular press and think you know the answer, you will be in for a surprise. Actual business angels look very different from the way that they are described in the media. The typical business angel is less wealthy, less well-educated, younger, and less likely to be retired than suggested by the stereotypical description of angels. And he doesn't have significantly more experience starting companies or investing in them than other kinds of informal investors. So let's take a look at what business angels really look like.

ANGEL INVESTORS AREN'T ALL WEALTHY

The received wisdom is that angels are wealthy people.[1] A quick trip to the bookstore or around the Worldwide Web pretty much shows that. The Web sites, books, and articles on angel investing consistently refer to angels as "wealthy individuals" or "high net worth investors." For example, one observer writes, "Angels today...are in many ways the same: wealthy individuals and families willing to invest in high risk deals.... Angels are also financially sophisticated private investors willing to provide seed and start-up capital for higher-risk ventures."[2]

The only problem with the *obvious* point that most business angels are wealthy people is that it isn't true. Wealthy people may be more likely than poor people to become business angels, but that doesn't mean that people have to be wealthy to make angel investments (more on this point in Chapter 11). The data from the Entrepreneurship in the United States Assessment shows that the *majority* of people who made an angel investment from 2001 through 2003 do not have the income or net worth to be accredited investors. As Table 3.1 shows, 66.7 percent of all angels *fail to meet* the $1 million minimum net worth for SEC accreditation. Moreover, 16.7 percent of business angels in the United States actually have a *negative* net worth, roughly the same proportion—16.7 percent—that have a net worth of more than $2 million!

The numbers on household income are similar; the *vast majority* of angels don't even come close to meeting SEC accreditation requirements. Only 13.6 percent of angel investors are married and have a household income of more than $300,000 per year (the minimum for a married couple to be accredited), while only 22.7 percent of angel investors have a household income of more than $200,000 per year (the minimum for a single person to be an accredited investor). In fact, many more angel investors have low incomes than have high incomes. The data show that 31.8 percent of business angels have a household

TABLE 3.1. Income and Net Worth of Angel Investors

Income or Wealth Category	Share of Angel Investors
Less than $1 Million Net Worth	66.7%
Negative Net Worth	16.7%
Married with More than $300,000 in Household Income	13.6%
More than $200,000 in Household Income	22.7%
Less than $40,000 in Household Income	31.8%
Less than $25,000 in Household Income	22.7%

Source: Created from data contained in the Entrepreneurship in the United States Assessment and Reynolds, P. 2004. *Entrepreneurship in the United States Assessment.* Miami, FL: Florida International University.

income of *less than* $40,000 per year. Similarly, 22.7 percent of angel investors have a household income of *less than* $25,000 per year.[3]

This pattern is not just present in the data from the Entrepreneurship in the United States Assessment. The data from the Global Entrepreneurship Monitor provides similar, if less precise, support for the view that the typical angel investor is not wealthy. This survey, conducted on a representative sample of adult-aged Americans annually from 1999 through 2004, shows that 8.3 percent of the business angels in the United States were in the lowest third of income for Americans, and 21.7 percent were in the next third, leaving only 70 percent of angel investors in the top third of income in the United States (the cutoff to enter the top third of U.S. income earners is $75,000 per year).[4]

We find similar evidence from data from the state of Wisconsin's Revenue Division on taxpayers who took advantage of that state's angel tax credit in 2005. The data show that *more than half* (52 percent) of the tax filers who received an angel tax credit and 54 percent of the tax filers who received a seed angel investment credit had an adjusted gross income of less than $200,000 per year.[5]

FEW ANGELS ARE RETIRED

Another common misperception about angel investors is that they are predominantly retired, successful entrepreneurs who want to remain involved with start-up companies. It turns out that only a small portion of angel investors are retired—23.1 percent, according to the data from the Entrepreneurship in the United States Assessment.

Moreover, angels are no more likely to be retired or out of the labor force than other types of informal investors; the proportion of angel investors who are in different labor force categories is not statistically different from that of friends-and-family investors or even the rest of the adult population. According to data from the Entrepreneurship in the United States Assessment, 63.7 percent of friends and family investors are working full- or part-time compared to 65.4 percent of angel investors.[6] Approximately 25.3 percent of friends-and-family investors are retired compared to 23.1 percent of angel investors, while 11.1 percent of friends and family investors are not in the labor force compared with 11.5 percent of angel investors.[7]

And these patterns are not unique to the Entrepreneurship in the United States Assessment. Other surveys of representative samples of the adult population show similar patterns. For instance, data from the

Global Entrepreneurship Monitor indicate that in the United States, 75 percent of friends and family investors and 71.4 percent of angels are employed full- or part-time.

GENDER DOESN'T AFFECT THE ODDS OF BEING A BUSINESS ANGEL

Many observers have noted that more than 80 percent of angels are male,[8] a point made to argue that gender affects the odds that a person will become a business angel.

While most angels are, in fact, male, this does not mean that being male increases the odds that a person will become a business angel—for two reasons. First, gender might affect the odds that a person makes an informal investment but not the odds that the informal investment is an angel investment rather than an investment in a business run by a friend or family member. Second, gender might not account for the differences in the odds of making an angel investment. Rather, it might simply reflect the fact that men score higher than women on some characteristic, such as the number of entrepreneurs that they know, which increases the odds of making an angel investment. Once this characteristic is taken into consideration, gender has no additional effect on the odds that a person will make an angel investment.

It turns out, in fact, that both of these things are true. Gender, itself, has no effect on the odds that a person will make an angel investment. Analysis of the Entrepreneurship in the United States data shows that once the effect of other factors are taken into account, men are no more likely than women to be business angels and that being female has no effect on the odds that a person is a business angel rather than another type of informal investor.[9]

BLACKS AREN'T UNDERREPRESENTED IN THE ANGEL COMMUNITY

Many observers have inferred that Blacks are underrepresented in the angel community because almost all angel investors are White.[10] However, the fact that few angel investors in the United States are Black says nothing about whether Blacks are underrepresented among angel investors any more than the fact that few angel investors in West Africa are White says anything about whether Whites are underrepresented

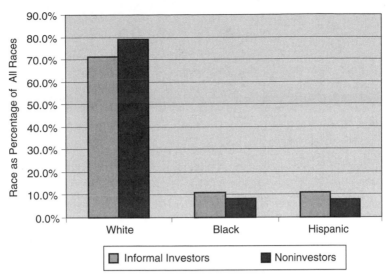

FIGURE 3.1. Black, White, and Hispanic Shares of Informal Investors and Noninvestors. *Source:* Created from data contained in Reynolds, P. 2007. *Entrepreneurship in the United States: The Future Is Now.* New York: Springer.

among angel investors in that region. To have a large portion of angel investors in the United States be Black would require Blacks to be highly *overrepresented* among angel investors since they account for only 12.8 percent of the U.S. population. Moreover, even if surveys showed that just 3 percent of *accredited* angel investors were Black, this actually would be an indication that Blacks are *overrepresented* among accredited *angel* investors since only 2.5 percent of accredited investors are Black.[11]

The data from the Entrepreneurship in the United States Assessment suggest that Blacks are actually *overrepresented* among informal investors. As Figure 3.1 shows, Blacks and Hispanics are *more likely* than Whites to be informal investors.[12] Data from the Entrepreneurship in the United States Assessment show that to the extent that Blacks are underrepresented in any informal investor group, they are underrepresented among friends-and-family investors.[13]

AGE HAS NO CLEAR EFFECT ON ANGEL INVESTING

The general perception is that business angels tend to be older and that the likelihood that a person is a business angel increases with age.[14] However, this perception is not accurate. Angel investors can

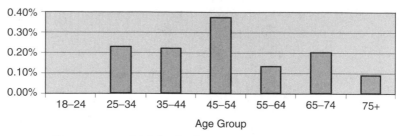

FIGURE 3.2. Percentage of Adults Making Angel Investments for Different Age Groups. *Source:* Created from data contained in the Entrepreneurship in the United States Assessment and Reynolds, P. 2004. *Entrepreneurship in the United States Assessment.* Miami, FL: Florida International University.

be of any age, with the Entrepreneurship in the United States Assessment showing that they range in age from 26 to 76, and the Global Entrepreneurship Monitor showing angels aged 18 to 76. Second, the likelihood that a person will be an angel investor doesn't increase with age over his lifetime. Rather, as Figure 3.2 shows, the likelihood peaks in the 45- to 54-year-old age group,[15] a younger age than that at which net worth peaks (between the ages of 55 and 64).[16]

BUSINESS ANGELS ARE LESS EDUCATED THAN YOU THINK

The prevailing wisdom is that business angels are highly educated people,[17] with one observer saying "most business angels are well educated"[18] and another describing the typical business angel as having a "postgraduate degree, often technical."[19]

However, it turns out that the average business angel is less educated than most observers think. The data from the Entrepreneurship in the United States Assessment reveal that only 28 percent of angels have an advanced degree and 24 percent did not graduate from college. Only a minority are MBAs, lawyers, doctors, and other people with a professional degree.

Moreover, it is not clear that education has much effect on the likelihood that someone will become an angel investor. Analysis on the data from the Entrepreneurship in the United States Assessment indicates that once the effect of education is isolated from the effect of other things,[20] it has no effect on the likelihood that a person will be a business angel rather than just a member of the adult population, and it has no effect on the likelihood that a person will be a business angel rather than another type of informal investor.

HOUSEHOLD STATUS

Our image of angels as married men with nonworking spouses and grown children—which probably results from the general sense that they are older and retired—is also inaccurate. According to data from the Entrepreneurship in the United States Assessment, the majority— 54 percent—of business angels live in two-earner households.[21] And many angels have small kids. Approximately 30 percent have children aged 5 and under, 15 percent have children between 6 and 11, and 37 percent have children aged 12 to 17.

ANGELS AREN'T PARTICULARLY EXPERIENCED ENTREPRENEURS

One of the justifications that many observers make for getting an angel investment is that angel money is "smart money." As one expert on angel investing explained, angels are "smart money" because the typical angel has "started up, operates, or sold a successful business."[22] This entrepreneurial experience, the argument goes, allows angels to provide advice and assistance as well as money.

Friends-and-family investors are believed to lack similar experience and so are thought to be less valuable investors. For instance, one observer writes, "Many entrepreneurs are still limited to family-and-friends capital.... [T]hese sources...do not really fill the needs of most early-stage ventures, which need: capital, experience, contacts. The true angels can provide all of these."[23]

Although angels have a great deal of entrepreneurial experience— 88 percent have experience starting a company—and 89 percent believe that they have the experience and skills necessary to start a business (according to data from the Entrepreneurship in the United States Assessment)—the framing of this information in most publications gives the impression that business angels have much more entrepreneurial experience than other sources of informal capital. However, this turns out not to be the case. According to data from the Global Entrepreneurship Monitor, the percentage of angels who currently own and manage their own businesses is not that much higher than the proportion of friends-and-family investors who do. Moreover, roughly the same percentage of friends-and-family investors as angel investors believe that they have the skills to start their own businesses.

Statistical analysis that isolates the effect of entrepreneurial experience shows that having more business start-up experience, being an owner-manager of a business, and perceiving that one has the skills to start a business have no effect on the odds that a person will be an angel investor rather than another type of informal investor.[24] Moreover, experience as an entrepreneur isn't related to being an effective business angel. Studies show that an angel's amount of entrepreneurial experience *is not correlated* with his financial returns from angel investing.[25]

A lot of authors say that entrepreneurs are an important source of angel capital. They give the impression that many, if not most, successful entrepreneurs become business angels. For instance, one author writes, "Financial angels have earned their wings through prior business success, accumulating wealth and wisdom that they re-deploy in ventures founded by the next generation of entrepreneurs."[26]

However, in point of fact, very few entrepreneurs become business angels. Studies have shown that the proportion of entrepreneurs who make informal investments may be as low as 10.8 percent,[27] and almost certainly is no more than one fifth of all entrepreneurs.[28] Because business angels are a subset of all informal investors, the proportion of entrepreneurs that become business angels cannot be higher than these percentages.

And this proportion may be declining. In his examination of the Federal Reserve's Survey of Consumer Finances, Bart Hamilton of Washington University in St. Louis found that the percentage of current business owners who make informal investments declined from 1992 to 1998.[29]

Moreover, some very carefully conducted research suggests that entrepreneurs are actually *less* likely to make informal equity investments than non-entrepreneurs. While people who run their own businesses are more likely than others to be informal investors, this pattern appears to exist because people who are running their own businesses tend to have higher net worth than those who are not. Once the effect of household wealth is accounted for, business-owning households are actually *less* likely to make informal equity investments than non-owner households.[30] In other words, wealthy people are more likely than poor people to be informal equity investors, but entrepreneurs are no more likely than non-entrepreneurs to be such investors.

ANGEL INVESTORS TEND TO BE INEXPERIENCED INVESTORS

Much of the literature on angel investing gives the impression that the typical angel investor is quite experienced at financing private companies.[31] This framing of angels as experienced investors helps to justify the position that angels are "smart money" and can provide a lot of help to the companies in which they invest. If, as the argument goes, angels make a lot of investments in private companies, then they can take what they have learned from one investment and apply it to another. Because angels are thought to make more investments than other kinds of informal investors, they are again argued to be "smarter money" than friends and family.

However, it turns out that business angels are much less experienced than many people think. Data from the Entrepreneurship in the United States Assessment puts the typical number of informal investments made by angel investors at less than one per year.[32] The Federal Reserve's Survey of Consumer Finances shows that informal equity investors hold an average of only 1.6 informal investments (the median, or typical number, is one). And the Entrepreneurship in the United States Assessment shows that the average number of informal investments that angels have made in their careers is 5.1 (typically they have made four).

Moreover, the variance across angels in their amount of investing means that only some angels make investments at the average pace. One study showed that 35 percent of business angels in the United Kingdom had made only a single investment in their lifetimes.[33]

Similar patterns can be seen in informal *equity* investments. The Federal Reserve's Survey of Consumer Finances shows that approximately 80.4 percent of informal investors have made only one informal *equity* investment in their lifetimes, only 8.2 percent have made two, and only 2.5 percent have made more than four.

Angels don't even make more informal investments than friends-and-family investors. Statistical analysis that accounts for a variety of other factors shows that there is no (statistically significant) difference in the number of informal investments made over the individual's career, between business angels and other types of informal investors.[34]

ANGELS THINK LIKE THE REST OF US

Do angels think differently from other types of start-up company investors about the role of start-ups or the bearing of risk or any of the myriad of other things related to investing in private companies? If you have read a lot of books or articles on angel investing, you probably think so because much has been made of the notion that angels think differently from other people.[35] However, it turns out that there is *no* systematic scientific evidence that business angels think differently from the rest of the population or from other types of informal investors.

Examination of the data from the Entrepreneurship in the United States Assessment shows that angels don't think differently about entrepreneurship from the rest of the population or other types of informal investors on several dimensions.[36] They are no more likely than the rest of the population or other types of informal investors to say any of the following:

- Fear of failure would stop them from starting a business.
- Most people would prefer all Americans to have the same standard of living.
- Starting a business is a good career choice.
- There are a lot of stories about successful entrepreneurs in the media.[37]

That's not to say that carefully designed studies of representative samples will not find differences in the attitudes of business angels and the rest of the population, or between business angels and other types of informal investors. But no one has done these studies yet, so no one has evidence of these differences. Moreover, the odds are against finding many differences in the attitudes of business angels and friends and

KEY FACTS TO REMEMBER	
Portion of angels with less than $200,000 in annual income	77.3 percent
Portion of angels with less than $1 million in net worth	66.7 percent
Portion of angels who are retired	23.1 percent
Age with highest odds of making angel investments	45 to 54
Portion of angels who didn't graduate from college	24 percent
Portion of angels who live in two-earner household	54 percent

family investors because many people make both types of investments. Because a large portion of angels also makes other types of informal investments, the same attitudes are held by most angels and friends and family investors. All of this, of course, makes it startling to see angels described as thinking differently from the rest of the population.

Maybe business angels will prove to have different attitudes from the rest of the population or other kinds of informal investors. But until someone shows that they do, we should probably assume that they think the same way as the rest of us. Otherwise, we risk creating myths about angel investors that aren't true.

IN CONCLUSION

Most people have a preconceived notion of what angel investors look like—and it's wrong. Angels aren't all wealthy, high-income, well-educated, older, retired, White, male, former entrepreneurs with a great deal of experience investing in start-up companies. The majority live in dual income households, and relatively few angels are retired. In fact, they aren't even that old, with an average age of less than 50. Most of them still have kids living at home.

We have no evidence that Blacks are underrepresented among angel investors and no evidence that gender affects the odds of being an angel. And business angels are much less educated than most people think, with close to one quarter failing to graduate from college.

The assumption that angels are "smarter money" than friends-and-family investors isn't supported by any real data. Angels aren't particularly experienced entrepreneurs, having no more entrepreneurial experience than other kinds of informal investors. They also tend to be inexperienced investors in private companies, making less than one angel investment every two years, on average. Finally, angels tend to have similar attitudes about start-ups and investing in them as the rest of the adult-aged population. In short, angels look a lot more like everyone else than they look like the stereotypical creatures portrayed in the media. And, as we will see in the next chapter, relatively few companies need them.

FOUR

How Many Companies
Need Angels?

A COMMON STORY about angel investing goes something like this. Angels are a special breed of investor who provides the risk capital that start-up companies use to transition between founder and friends-and-family money, and venture capital funds. The role of angels in filling this capital gap is crucial to economic growth because no other source of capital is available to companies making this transition, and the companies making this transition are vital contributors to the economic development of our country. Because many more companies need angel capital than can get it, the shortfall of angel capital holds back economic growth and hurts society.[1]

This story is often trotted out to justify government intervention in the angel capital market. Because angels play a unique role in the venture finance system and the market fails to provide angel capital to an adequate number of companies, the argument goes, the government needs to step in and subsidize angel investing. By increasing the number of angels and the pool of available capital, this subsidy helps to overcome the failure of the market to provide sufficient angel money to the start-up companies that need it—and benefits us all.[2]

But just because companies don't obtain angel financing when they seek it doesn't mean that the angel capital market is failing and that government intervention is necessary. It could be that the companies didn't obtain the capital because they *shouldn't* get it. The opportunities that they are pursuing could be insufficiently valuable to justify external investment or the talent of the entrepreneurs pursuing the opportunities could be too low to justify any party's making an investment. In fact, it's possible that there is actually a surplus of angel capital. That is, there aren't enough good opportunities to absorb all of the angel capital available.[3] Therefore, crucial questions to answer are these: "How much demand is there for angel capital?" and "How does that demand compare to the supply of angel money?" This chapter seeks to answer these questions.

THE GAP-FILLING ROLE OF ANGELS

Much of the writing on angel investing argues that business angels fill the financing gap between the $100,000 maximum seed stage investment that friends and family are said to be willing to provide and the $5 million expansion stage investment that venture capitalists are thought to be willing to offer.[4] Because friends and family don't have enough money to invest much beyond $100,000 and the cost of making venture capital investments leads venture capitalists to avoid investments less than several million,[5] companies needing between $100,000 and $5 million have to go to business angels.

This argument is pervasive in books and articles on angel investing. Take, for example, the following:

- "Business angels fill the classical 'equity gap,' where the firm is too risky and asset-free to warrant bank lending, and the size of funds demanded are too small for the traditional formal venture capitalist."[6]
- "Angel investors perform the important role of plugging the gap between what the entrepreneur can raise to get the firm off the ground and the level at which institutional investors and creditors will invest."[7]
- "Angel funding today generally represents the second round of financing or the first outside round in the early days of a company. It's where you turn after you've tapped out your credit card and devoured friends-and-family money but don't have enough progress to merit the attentions of venture capitalists. It fills the financial gap between $100,000 and what a company might expect to receive from a venture capital firm, which begins somewhere around $5 million."[8]

Although this view presents a nice perspective on angels—it says they are special and unique—it is inaccurate and misleading in a number of ways. First, it implies that in the absence of business angels many companies would fail to obtain the capital they need to grow. While some companies no doubt obtain capital from business angels after getting money from friends and family and before raising money from venture capitalists, it is not at all clear that those companies would *fail to get* money from venture capitalists if they did not first get money from business angels. In fact, we have no good evidence that getting money from business angels *increases* the probability that a firm will receive venture capital (see Chapter 5 for more on this point). Therefore, business angels may not play any unique role in the system of financing start-ups in this country. It could be that in the absence of business angels, banks, trade creditors, or someone else would step in and fill the same role.

Second, the "gap-filling" perspective on angel investing gives the impression that most of the firms that receive friends and family financing *will also* need venture capital. This is far from true. In fact, a very tiny portion of companies that receive friends-and-family money ever get venture capital financing. Therefore, this "gap-filling" role cannot be important for very many companies that have received financing from friends and family. The *maximum* number of firms that are founded each year for whom the receipt of angel capital could have filled a gap between friends-and-family money and venture capital cannot be larger than the total number of companies that receive non–seed stage venture capital, which, in 2004, was 2,465 businesses, out of the estimated 2 million new employer and non-employer businesses created that year.

Third, the gap-filling argument gives the impression that business angels actually provide capital to a significant number of companies that need between $100,000 and $5 million in financing. However, most observers have found that angels will rarely put more than $500,000 into any new business. And this is not just the case with individual angels. Data from the Angel Capital Association's annual survey of angel groups shows that a very small percentage of those groups make investments of between $500,000 and $2 million in a company, let alone invest between $2 million and $5 million. Therefore, it is unclear how angels can be responsible for plugging the financing gap that might exist between the $100,000 in seed money that entrepreneurs get from friends and family and the $5 million in expansion capital that venture capitalists are said to be willing to provide.[9]

Fourth, the argument that angels are special investors because they fill a financing gap between friends and family and venture capitalists is predicated on the assumption that most companies need equity capital to grow. Banks, credit card companies, and trade creditors are not substitutes for angel investors because young companies cannot borrow money. However, if new companies are able to borrow money from creditors at a young age, then this gap-filling argument for the unique role of business angels is weakened considerably.

Contrary to the received wisdom,[10] *most* new companies are able to obtain debt financing at the same age and stage of development at which they tend to obtain angel money. The data from the Federal Reserve's Survey of Small Business Finances show that new companies are financed by equity and debt to approximately the same degree;[11] 47.9 percent of the funding for businesses less than two years old is equity, while 52.1 percent is debt.[12]

The numbers are even more extreme when we focus on *external* investment in new companies because most of the equity financing of new companies comes from the founders, while debt is much more likely to come from an external source. For instance, one study showed that half of all new firms borrow money from someone other than the founder, but less than 10 percent receive an equity investment from a nonfounder.[13]

In short, business angels seem to be less a *unique source* of financing for new companies that fills a gap between friends and family and venture capitalists than a *choice* of capital provider, along with credit card companies, banks, factors, asset-based lenders, and venture capitalists. Some entrepreneurs choose to finance their businesses by going to business angels, but others prefer to go directly to venture capitalists for seed stage financing or obtain debt from credit card companies, trade creditors, or banks (rather than give up some equity and control to a private investor). Still others prefer to bootstrap their businesses through retained earnings, going to neither debt nor equity providers.

HOW MANY NEW COMPANIES ARE APPROPRIATE FOR ANGEL FINANCE?

One of the problems with the argument that there is excess demand for angel capital is that it doesn't jibe with the evidence that angel capital is appropriate for very few new companies. As one pair of authors explains, "Although many ventures look for capital, only a very small percentage deserve capital investment."[14] The authors of this statement are consultants who assist companies in obtaining angel capital. They explain that of the 5,000 business plans sent to their company every year, only 100 meet the criteria for angel investment.[15] Because angels don't fund people who are self-employed independent contractors but rather fund new companies, the pool of businesses from which the 2 percent of young companies that the authors consider appropriate for angel investing is drawn, is the roughly 600,000 new employer firms founded in the United States every year. Stated another way, these authors believe that every year approximately 12,000 new employer firms are created that are appropriate for angel financing. That's a rate of formation of angel-appropriate companies that is much smaller than the number of companies that receive angel money every year.

Other researchers have come up with similar estimates of the number of companies appropriate for angel investment. One source estimated that 95 percent of new businesses are too small and have too limited growth potential to get outside equity financing,[16] meaning that around 30,000 new employer businesses founded in the United States every year are appropriate for this activity. Another study estimated that of the 5.3 million employer firms in the United States with fewer than 500 employees, no more than 200,000 of them have the growth potential to allow them to receive an external equity investment. Because only about 12.7 percent of employer firms are less than four years old, this study suggests that only about 25,500 young businesses in the United States existing at any point in time have the growth potential to receive an angel investment.[17] These estimates are all lower than the number of companies that get angel money every year.

ALIGNMENT OF SUPPLY AND DEMAND

There isn't any evidence that the supply and demand for angel deals is mismatched. If there were excess demand for angel capital (or a shortage of supply), we should see something happening to the angel capital market that we don't see. The excess demand for angel capital would drive up the price of angel capital. Because the price of angel capital is the amount of equity that entrepreneurs pay for the money they receive, excess demand would mean that entrepreneurs would have to give up very large amounts of equity, and valuations of companies would be very low. Thus, if there were excess demand for angel capital, we should expect to see a lot of entrepreneurs reporting that angel investing doesn't make sense and that the angels aren't "fairly" valuing their companies, stating that they are worth too little and asking for too much equity.

However, we don't see widespread reports that angels are "undervaluing" companies, nor do we see evidence that angels are demanding too much equity. Moreover, we don't see much evidence of entrepreneurs walking away from term sheets (the nonbinding letters of intent that outline the financial, legal, and other terms of a possible investment[18]) and seeking alternative forms of financing. In fact, the one study that examined this issue found that few angel deals were lost because the entrepreneur walked away from the terms of the deal and went elsewhere for money.[19]

GROWTH EXPECTATIONS OF START-UPS

The distribution of founders' expectations for business growth also suggests that there is no excess demand for angel capital. Many angels report that they look for high-growth companies. If this is true, then a shortage of angel capital could exist only if there are more entrepreneurs that say they want high-growth companies than companies that angels say they finance. For instance, if all the founders of companies started in the United States create companies that they don't intend to grow, then there will be zero companies that would meet angels' growth projections and there couldn't be a shortage of angel money.

So what do the data say? One study, conducted on behalf of the U.S. Small Business Administration found that *half* of a representative sample of new business founders in the United States expects their firms to have sales of *less than $100,000* in their fifth year of operation.[20] Another study, this one conducted by Paul Reynolds and his colleague Samis White, showed that *half* the founders of a representative sample of start-ups in the United States expected to have only three employees in their third year of operation.[21] Clearly, half of all founders expect to have businesses that are way too small to justify seeking angel money. So we shouldn't think of those businesses as somehow "failing" to get angel capital that they need.

We also can look at estimates of the number of companies whose founders project rates of sales growth that make their businesses appropriate for business angels to see how many companies that represents. Although there is some disagreement about what level of sales growth makes companies appropriate (see Chapter 6 for more on this issue), with different investors indicating that they are looking for companies that project making $10 million, $50 million, or $100 million in sales in five years after founding, we can look at the numbers of companies that *project* these sales levels to see how many of them would interest business angels. The Panel Study of Entrepreneurial Dynamics asked the founders of a representative sample of new businesses founded in United States what their expectations for their businesses' sales in five years would be. Approximately 4 percent of the founders reported that they expected to have businesses that would generate $10 million or more in revenue in the fifth year. This means that about 80,000 (of an estimated 2 million new businesses) are created annually in which the founders expect to meet the minimum size that *some* angels believe makes companies appropriate for angel financing. As you no doubt realize, this is not much more than the number of companies that receive angel investments every year, estimated from a representative sample of the adult-age population. Therefore, even if *every entrepreneur* who has a company that he wants to grow large enough to justify angel financing also *wants* to get angel financing (instead of relying on his own investment, retained earnings, banks, asset-based lenders, trade creditors, or friends and family to provide the needed capital), the number of companies whose founders *intend* to grow large enough to justify angel investment is not much higher than the number of companies in which angels invest every year.

And of course, that's if the right target for an angel-financeable company need only achieve $10 million in sales in five years. If the right target is closer to the $50 million or $100 million reported by some angels, then the number of companies that receive angel financing every year greatly exceeds the number of companies that intend to grow large enough to justify it.[22] In short, the sales growth projections of start-up company founders provide little evidence of a shortage of supply of (or excess of demand for) angel capital.

NEW FIRMS' CAPITAL NEEDS

Another way to look at the question of demand for angel financing is to examine new firms' capital needs. The number of firms that require the amount of money that angels are said to provide gives information about how many businesses are appropriate for angel investing.

Some experts say that companies seeking angel financing typically need between $25,000 and $500,000 dollars.[23] Approximately 15.1 percent of new business founders surveyed in the Entrepreneurship in the United States Assessment say that they need between $25,000 and $500,000 from an external source.

But not all new businesses are appropriate for angel financing. Angels tend to invest only in corporations, rather than sole proprietorships or partnerships, because they want to make investments in entities from which they can exit with reasonable ease, and they generally want some mechanism to protect themselves against malfeasance and opportunistic behavior by entrepreneurs. In fact, the data from the Federal Reserve Survey of Small Business Finances indicates that *only* businesses taking a corporate legal form receive angel financing.

If we look at the number of new businesses founded every year that take a corporate form,[24] the number of companies needing an angel-appropriate amount of money is not very large. As Figure 4.1 shows, only an estimated 71,382 new businesses are founded every year that take the appropriate legal form for angel investing and need between $25,000 and $500,000 in financing from someone other than the founder.

However, there might be an excess *supply* of angel capital. That's because some observers believe that companies don't seek angel financing until their capital needs are significantly greater than $25,000.

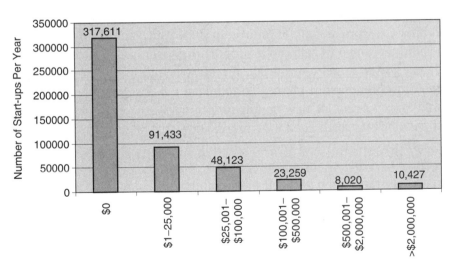

FIGURE 4.1. Number of New Businesses Founded Annually that Take the Appropriate Legal Form for Angel Financing and Need Different Amounts of Funding. *Source:* Created from data contained in the Entrepreneurship in the United States Assessment and Reynolds, P. 2004. *Entrepreneurship in the United States Assessment.* Miami, FL: Florida International University.

According to business angels John May and Cal Simmons, for instance, entrepreneurs don't tend to look for money from business angels until their funding needs exceed $100,000.[25] At the same time, they say that companies generally need to go to venture capitalists when they need $2 million or more. If angels fund companies that need between $100,000 and $2 million, then only an estimated 31,279 new companies founded each year need the amount of money that angels can provide and take the appropriate legal form for angel financing. And that's assuming that every company that needs this amount of money wants it from angels, as opposed to banks, asset-based lenders, friends and family, credit card companies, and so on.

Even this number might be too large because angels generally finance only employer firms rather than businesses that employ no one other than the founder. Only an estimated 3,597 new *employer* corporations that need between $100,000 and $2,000,000 in financing are founded in the United States every year.[26] Even if we include all new employer corporations that need between $25,000 and $2,000,000, only an estimated 9,131 companies are started annually. In fact, only an estimated 20,800 new employer corporations that need *any* capital beyond that provided by the entrepreneurs are founded in the United States each year.

In practice, for businesses to be right for angel investors, they need to offer a reasonable rate of return. So these estimates should probably be adjusted down to reflect the proportion of companies that offer the chance for an angel-appropriate investment multiple. The data from the Entrepreneurship in the United States Assessment indicate that only 39.5 percent of new company founders expect a rate of return of 20 times invested capital or more, only 57.6 percent expect a rate of return of 10 times or more, and only 73.7 percent expect a rate of return of 5 times or more. In fact, 11.8 percent of the founders expect to do little more than get their initial capital back. And, of course, these estimates are provided by the founders themselves, who are probably overly optimistic about these numbers.[27]

HOW MANY COMPANIES ACTUALLY LOOK FOR ANGEL MONEY?

Another source of information on the demand for angel capital is data on the number of companies that are actually seeking angel money at any point in time. Because companies cannot get angel money if they don't look for it, their willingness to look for angel money is an indirect indicator of their need for angel capital.

Many observers have offered estimates of the number of companies that are looking for angel money at any point in time. For instance, one observer writes, "Upward of 400,000 to 500,000 companies are attempting aggressively to raise capital at any given time."[28] However, a brief look at the data demonstrates how implausible this estimate is.

One study that examined data from the Federal Reserve Survey of Small Business Finances shows that only 4 percent of corporations *sought* an equity investment from a non-founder during the previous three years.[29] If we take the number of small businesses in operation and weight it by the proportion that take a corporate form, are employer firms, and are less than four years old, we find that there are 238,000 employer corporations less than four years old in operation in the United States. If 4 percent of these businesses sought an informal equity investment in the past three years, then 9,500 small, young corporations are looking for equity from informal investors.

Other studies provide similar evidence. A study in Canada found that in 2004, only 1.2 percent of all employer businesses with fewer than 20 employees *sought* an informal equity investment.[30] Because the Canadian data are not restricted to corporations—the only legal form of business that gets angel investment in the United States—it makes sense that the proportion is lower than that shown in the Fed data. Nevertheless, the order of magnitude in both studies suggests that, at any time, only a few new businesses are looking for informal equity, let alone seeking angel money.

ACTUAL SALES ACHIEVED

As you might expect, fewer companies *reach* a level of sales appropriate for angel investors than *project* reaching these sales levels. So the actual number of companies for which angel investing turns out to have been appropriate is even smaller than the numbers identified earlier in the chapter. We can figure out the actual sales achieved by start-up companies by looking at data from the Business Information Tracking Series. This survey is the U.S. Census's effort to gather information from every business in the United States. Because the survey asks the company representatives who fill out the survey to indicate the year in which the company began, we can see what level of sales the companies have achieved by the time they are six years old. And by matching first year and sixth year sales data, we can see the rate of sales growth.

According to the Business Information Tracking Series, only 9.2 percent of employer firms founded in 1996 had reached $1 million in sales by 2002.[31] That works out to 47,140 businesses that are started every year that hit the $1 million in sales mark at the end of six years. But reaching $1 million in sales in this time period isn't very fast growth and may not meet the targets of business angels (see Chapter 6 for more on business angels' growth targets). Obviously, a smaller percentage of new businesses grow to $10 million, $50 million, or $100 million in sales over this time period. But how much smaller?

To get a picture of this distribution, I commissioned a special tabulation of the Business Information Tracking Series from the U.S. Census to look at the cohort of companies founded in 1996 over the 1997 through 2002 period.[32] Table 4.1 shows the number of firms achieving different levels of sales over that time period. According to the Census Bureau, approximately 511,000 new single establishment businesses were founded in 1996. By 2002,

- 8,154 firms had achieved sales of $5 million or more.
- 3,608 firms had achieved sales of $10 million or more.
- 474 firms had achieved sales of $50 million or more.
- 175 firms had achieved sales of $100 million or more.

Angels often say that they try to invest in situations in which one out of ten of their investments works out.[33] If this is true, then for the 1996 cohort, the following numbers of companies were appropriate for angel investors to investigate, depending on the angels' targeted sales for portfolio companies after six years of operation (more about which target is correct in Chapter 6):

- 81,540 firms, if the target is sales of $5 million or more.
- 36,080 firms, if the target is sales of $10 million or more.
- 4,740 firms, if the target is sales of $50 million or more.
- 1,750 firms, if the target is sales of $100 million or more.

If the observed number of companies that receive angel investments in the United States every year is correct, then the typical angel must target companies with sales of $5 million after six years of operation.

As Chapter 8 explains in greater detail, almost all angel investments exit through acquisition. Data from Pratt's Stats—a service provider that collects information on the mergers and acquisitions of private companies—shows that the median, or typical, value of an acquisition

TABLE 4.1. Number of New Firms Founded in 1996 Achieving Different Levels of Sales in 2002

Sector	Number of Start-ups	Number Failed	Number <$100,000	Number $100,000– $499,000	Number $500,000– $999,000	Number $1,000,000– $4,999,999	Number 5,000,000– $9,999,000	Number $10,000,000– $49,999,999	Number $50,000,000– $99,999,999	Number $100,000,000+
All Sectors	510,654	260,970	50,598	113,451	38,495	38,986	4,546	3,134	299	175
Agricultural Services, Forestry, Fishing	11,412	5,538	1,497	3,121	798	433	18	7	0	0
Mining	1,554	825	119	312	123	137	17	19	2	0
Construction	67,384	34,786	4,970	15,365	5,471	5,853	548	346	32	13
Manufacturing	23,545	12,180	1,745	4,210	1,855	2,682	429	393	27	24
Transportation, Communication, Utilities	24,160	13,829	2,451	4,641	1,403	1,519	193	95	17	12
Wholesale	34,209	17,603	1,702	5,026	2,837	5,101	1,033	797	68	42
Retail	102,706	56,228	6,963	22,009	8,379	8,032	577	450	56	12
Finance, Insurance, Real Estate	43,975	20,773	5,272	10,652	3,239	3,191	458	319	38	33
Services	198,524	96,414	25,729	47,945	14,355	12,005	1,272	706	59	39

Source: Created from data contained in a special tabulation of the Business Information Tracking Series of the U.S. Census.

of a private company is 0.68 times one-year sales. Therefore, the typical company of angel-targeted size is worth $3,400,000 at the time of probable exit. As we will see in later chapters, these numbers indicate that either the perceived rates of return that angels typically earn, or the valuations of angel investments that are typically reported, must be incorrect. The typical angel portfolio company simply cannot have both the valuation that is reported *and* the rate of return that is reported, given the *actual* valuation of the typical company, and the *actual* distribution of sales growth among start-ups.

INDUSTRY DISTRIBUTION OF HIGH-GROWTH COMPANIES

Of course, high-growth companies are not evenly distributed across all sectors of the economy. They are much more likely to be found in certain industries than in others. That much is clear by looking at the different industry sectors shown in Table 4.1. Because angels often say they focus on certain industries, it is important to understand the industry distribution of high-growth companies to understand demand for angel investment.

We can do this by looking at the percentage of businesses that achieve different levels of sales across industries. I am going to focus on the proportion that achieves $50 million in sales. (For reasons that will become clearer in Chapter 6, this seems to be the level of sales that many observers say angels look for companies in which they seek to invest.)

Industry is measured by the Standard Industrial Code (SIC). This is a system that the U.S. government used to use to classify businesses activity by industry. (It has since been replaced by another system called the North American Industry Classification System, which is harmonized with the system used in Canada, but that isn't important here.) The purpose of SIC codes is to categorize companies in different industries based on what they are doing. For instance, companies that engage in forestry are in a different SIC code from companies that engage in coal mining because the two businesses are different in terms of what the companies do and the customers they serve.

SIC codes are also nested, which means that four-digit codes are more precise classifications than three-digit codes, which are more precise than two-digit codes, which are more precise than one-digit codes. For instance, the three-digit code "drugs" is composed of both "pharmaceutical preparations" and "medicinal chemicals and botanical products," which have different four-digit SIC codes. The three-digit code "drugs" is part of the two-digit code "chemicals and allied products" along with other industries, such as "industrial inorganic chemicals." And "chemicals and allied products" is part of the one-digit code "manufacturing" along with several other manufacturing industries, such as "textile mill products" and "fabricated metal products."

Table 4.2 shows the proportion of firms in different two-digit industries that achieve different levels of sales after six years of operation. In some industries, there are almost no high growth start-ups. For instance, *no* new petroleum and coal products companies that were founded in 1996 achieved $50 million in sales by 2002, and this includes all businesses in petroleum refining; asphalt paving and roofing materials; asphalt felts and coatings; miscellaneous petroleum and coal products, lubricating oils and greases; and petroleum and coal products not elsewhere classified.

Strangely, the industries that angels are reported to focus on the most don't seem to be the industries with the largest proportion of high growth firms, at least not over the period for which the data were available. The data show that only four two-digit SIC codes—electronic equipment, chemicals and allied products, paper and allied products, and insurance carriers—have more than *1 percent* of start-ups that reach the $50 million level of sales in this time period. Two of these industries—paper and allied products and insurance carriers—are not industries in which most experts say that angels tend to invest.

Perhaps more important is the actual number of companies that achieve the level of sales that angels are reported to target. It's tiny. While just over 500,000 new single establishment businesses are started every year, most of those, paradoxically, are started in industries in which much less than 1 percent of start-ups reach $50 million in sales after 6 years of operation. In the two (two-digit) industries in which more than 1 percent of companies reach $50 million in sales, and angels are reported to invest regularly, only a handful of companies reach the targeted level of sales: there are only six chemicals and allied products companies and ten electronics and electrical equipment companies that reached $50 million in sales in six years.

If angels really are targeting situations in which one-in-ten companies turn out to achieve $50 million or more in sales, this means that out of the 1996 cohort of new single establishment businesses in the United States, there were sixty chemicals and allied products companies and 100 electronics and electrical equipment companies that angels should

TABLE 4.2.   Percentage of New Firms Founded in 1996 Achieving Different Levels

SIC Code	Industry	Number Started in 1996	Number with 2002 Sales of $50 Million +	Sales in 2002 <$100,000	Sales in 2002 $100,000– $499,000
0700	Agricultural Services	10,835	0	13.03%	27.71%
0800	Forestry	266	0	15.41%	16.54%
0900	Fishing, Hunting, and Trapping	311	0	14.15%	24.12%
1000	Metal Mining	74	0	1.35%	10.81%
1200	Coal Mining	121	0	0.83%	5.79%
1300	Oil and Gas Extraction	1,114	2	9.34%	22.71%
1400	Nonmetallic Minerals, Except Fuels	245	0	5.31%	17.96%
1500	General Building Contractors	22,599	29	6.20%	18.71%
1600	Heavy Construction, Except Building	2,478	6	5.17%	20.74%
1700	Special Trade Contractors	42,307	10	8.13%	25.11%
2000	Food and Kindred Products	1,236	5	4.05%	15.21%
2100	Tobacco Products	18	0	11.11%	5.56%
2200	Textile Mill Products	391	1	5.12%	16.88%
2300	Apparel and Other Textile Products	2,553	0	8.50%	12.93%
2400	Lumber and Wood Products	2,735	1	5.96%	19.89%
2500	Furniture and Fixtures	934	0	7.17%	18.52%
2600	Paper and Allied Products	190	3	3.16%	9.47%
2700	Printing and Publishing	3,712	0	10.34%	19.94%
2800	Chemicals and Allied Products	512	6	3.32%	11.91%
2900	Petroleum and Coal Products	51	0	1.96%	1.96%
3000	Rubber and Miscellaneous Plastics Products	832	4	4.33%	12.50%
3100	Leather and Leather Products	112	1	8.04%	14.29%

Sales in 2002 $500,000–$999,000	Sales in 2002 $1,000,000–$4,999,000	Sales in 2002 $5,000,000–$9,999,000	Sales in 2002 $10,000,000–$49,999,000	Sales in 2002 $50,000,000–$99,999,000	Sales in 2002 $100,000,000+
7.05%	3.77%	0.15%	0.06%	0.00%	0.00%
5.64%	2.63%	0.38%	0.00%	0.00%	0.00%
6.11%	5.47%	0.32%	0.00%	0.00%	0.00%
2.70%	6.76%	0.00%	1.35%	0.00%	0.00%
4.13%	7.44%	2.48%	2.48%	0.00%	0.00%
8.35%	8.53%	1.08%	0.99%	0.18%	0.00%
9.39%	11.43%	0.82%	1.63%	0.00%	0.00%
8.07%	10.39%	1.03%	0.75%	0.09%	0.04%
8.84%	12.51%	2.14%	1.69%	0.20%	0.04%
8.11%	7.55%	0.62%	0.32%	0.01%	0.01%
8.17%	13.03%	2.27%	2.75%	0.08%	0.32%
5.56%	0.00%	0.00%	5.56%	0.00%	0.00%
8.44%	14.32%	2.05%	2.05%	0.26%	0.00%
5.09%	5.17%	0.51%	0.63%	0.00%	0.00%
8.78%	10.05%	0.84%	0.91%	0.04%	0.00%
8.57%	11.78%	2.14%	1.50%	0.00%	0.00%
7.37%	27.89%	5.26%	4.74%	1.58%	0.00%
7.68%	8.30%	1.16%	0.65%	0.00%	0.00%
8.40%	18.95%	3.32%	5.47%	0.98%	0.20%
5.88%	15.69%	1.96%	9.80%	0.00%	0.00%
7.69%	17.91%	4.93%	3.85%	0.24%	0.24%
10.71%	10.71%	3.57%	0.00%	0.00%	0.89%

(*continued*)

TABLE 4.2. (*continued*)

SIC Code	Industry	Number Started in 1996	Number with 2002 Sales of $50 Million +	Sales in 2002 <$100,000	Sales in 2002 $100,000–$499,000
3200	Stone, Clay, and Glass Products	760	0	8.55%	19.21%
3300	Primary Metal Industries	245	2	2.04%	17.14%
3400	Fabricated Metal Products	1,860	4	6.88%	18.55%
3500	Industrial Machinery and Equipment	3,483	7	9.88%	20.87%
3600	Electronic and Other Electric Equipment	977	10	5.12%	13.10%
3700	Transportation Equipment	868	3	3.92%	19.82%
3800	Instruments and Related Products	620	3	6.29%	17.26%
3900	Miscellaneous Manufacturing Industries	1,456	1	7.42%	20.67%
4100	Local and Interurban Passenger Transit	1,805	0	12.35%	18.39%
4200	Trucking and Warehousing	13,893	5	9.64%	20.13%
4400	Water Transportation	610	0	8.85%	22.95%
4500	Transportation by Air	761	1	7.10%	17.08%
4600	Pipelines, Except Natural Gas	3	0	0.00%	33.33%
4700	Transportation Services	3,755	1	13.64%	19.49%
4800	Communications	2,465	14	6.17%	13.47%
4900	Electric, Gas, and Sanitary Services	868	8	13.48%	20.39%
5000	Wholesale Trade-Durable Goods	21,312	55	5.11%	15.07%
5100	Wholesale Trade-Nondurable Goods	12,897	55	4.75%	14.07%
5200	Building Materials and Garden Supplies	3,413	0	5.24%	19.92%
5300	General Merchandise Stores	1,080	0	5.37%	19.54%
5400	Food Stores	12,263	0	5.09%	20.71%
5500	Automotive Dealers and Service Stations	9,747	61	2.82%	12.51%

Sales in 2002 $500,000–$999,000	Sales in 2002 $1,000,000–$4,999,000	Sales in 2002 $5,000,000–$9,999,000	Sales in 2002 $10,000,000–$49,999,000	Sales in 2002 $50,000,000–$99,999,000	Sales in 2002 $100,000,000+
6.84%	13.68%	2.24%	2.24%	0.00%	0.00%
11.43%	14.69%	4.90%	4.90%	0.82%	0.00%
10.11%	15.22%	2.74%	1.77%	0.05%	0.16%
8.38%	11.71%	1.44%	1.23%	0.09%	0.11%
7.47%	18.22%	2.05%	3.58%	0.20%	0.82%
7.14%	11.75%	3.80%	3.57%	0.23%	0.12%
8.55%	15.65%	3.23%	1.94%	0.48%	0.00%
6.94%	7.76%	1.24%	0.96%	0.07%	0.00%
6.70%	7.81%	0.50%	0.28%	0.00%	0.00%
5.55%	5.66%	0.66%	0.20%	0.04%	0.00%
8.52%	8.69%	1.64%	1.15%	0.00%	0.00%
6.18%	9.99%	1.45%	0.79%	0.13%	0.00%
0.00%	0.00%	33.33%	0.00%	0.00%	0.00%
5.62%	5.94%	0.61%	0.32%	0.00%	0.03%
5.03%	7.06%	1.30%	1.18%	0.32%	0.24%
8.87%	7.49%	1.84%	0.92%	0.35%	0.58%
8.59%	15.54%	2.98%	2.08%	0.16%	0.10%
7.81%	13.88%	3.08%	2.74%	0.26%	0.16%
10.67%	13.65%	0.97%	0.26%	0.00%	0.00%
6.67%	6.02%	0.46%	0.19%	0.00%	0.00%
9.33%	9.44%	0.72%	0.38%	0.00%	0.00%
8.38%	19.16%	2.35%	3.15%	0.52%	0.10%

(*continued*)

TABLE 4.2.   (*continued*)

SIC Code	Industry	Number Started in 1996	Number with 2002 Sales of $50 Million +	Sales in 2002 <$100,000	Sales in 2002 $100,000– $499,000
5600	Apparel and Accessory Stores	4,690	0	6.14%	22.47%
5700	Furniture and Homefurnishings Stores	7,775	1	6.32%	20.41%
5800	Eating and Drinking Places	39,051	0	7.84%	23.28%
5900	Miscellaneous Retail	24,687	6	8.05%	22.79%
6000	Depository Institutions	638	1	8.46%	22.41%
6200	Security and Commodity Brokers	4,058	12	10.99%	22.01%
6300	Insurance Carriers	708	13	6.50%	14.27%
6400	Insurance Agents, Brokers, and Service	9,421	3	13.02%	32.60%
6500	Real Estate	21,262	9	12.45%	23.93%
6700	Holding and Other Investment Offices	4,514	27	14.13%	17.72%
7000	Hotels and Other Lodging Places	4,165	9	10.20%	26.58%
7200	Personal Services	16,420	0	19.01%	24.07%
7300	Business Services	47,367	35	10.99%	19.07%
7500	Auto Repair, Services, and Parking	15,255	0	8.66%	29.46%
7600	Miscellaneous Repair Services	5,791	0	12.31%	26.42%
7800	Motion Pictures	3,465	1	10.74%	21.01%
7900	Amusement and Recreation Services	9,237	16	12.45%	23.46%
8000	Health Services	26,021	14	7.11%	26.83%
8100	Legal Services	12,204	2	10.82%	33.14%
8200	Educational Services	3,871	1	14.96%	21.96%
8700	Engineering and Management Services	30,106	16	13.73%	22.25%
8900	Services, Not Elsewhere Classified	2,060	0	15.49%	22.91%

Source: Created from data contained in a special tabulation of the Business Information

Sales in 2002 $500,000–$999,000	Sales in 2002 $1,000,000–$4,999,000	Sales in 2002 $5,000,000–$9,999,000	Sales in 2002 $10,000,000–$49,999,000	Sales in 2002 $50,000,000–$99,999,000	Sales in 2002 $100,000,000+
7.87%	4.84%	0.28%	0.11%	0.00%	0.00%
9.70%	8.82%	0.45%	0.17%	0.00%	0.01%
7.43%	4.74%	0.14%	0.04%	0.00%	0.00%
7.93%	6.93%	0.49%	0.21%	0.02%	0.00%
6.58%	12.07%	5.02%	2.82%	0.00%	0.16%
7.12%	7.42%	1.28%	1.18%	0.15%	0.15%
5.79%	8.33%	1.55%	1.13%	0.71%	1.13%
5.84%	3.87%	0.36%	0.21%	0.02%	0.01%
7.77%	6.83%	0.68%	0.31%	0.02%	0.02%
8.51%	12.63%	2.97%	3.06%	0.38%	0.22%
12.15%	9.05%	0.70%	0.53%	0.12%	0.10%
3.19%	1.47%	0.06%	0.04%	0.00%	0.00%
5.66%	6.19%	0.86%	0.50%	0.04%	0.03%
7.76%	3.63%	0.14%	0.07%	0.00%	0.00%
5.96%	3.87%	0.21%	0.17%	0.00%	0.00%
5.86%	6.00%	0.78%	0.35%	0.03%	0.00%
6.29%	5.29%	0.70%	0.45%	0.10%	0.08%
14.10%	10.81%	1.03%	0.49%	0.02%	0.03%
8.76%	7.12%	0.48%	0.16%	0.00%	0.02%
7.34%	8.01%	0.88%	0.39%	0.03%	0.00%
6.56%	6.49%	0.89%	0.51%	0.05%	0.01%
7.04%	7.18%	0.34%	0.29%	0.00%	0.00%

Tracking Series of the U.S. Census. (The industries are measured at the two-digit SIC Code level.)

have thought were appropriate in terms of expected levels of sales. Moreover, there were only forty-two (two-digit) industries in which there were *any* companies that angels should have thought would meet their expectations for sales level achieved after six years of operation, and many of those industries are ones in which angels are not thought to invest very often.

HOW MANY COMPANIES ACHIEVE ANGEL-TARGETED GROWTH RATES?

Estimates based on sales growth *rates* yield similar results. Very few companies achieve the rate of growth reported to be targeted by business angels. We can look at the data from the Business Information Tracking Series to see this distribution. But before we do that we need to define what "high growth" means. Some observers have called high-growth companies "gazelles" and defined them as businesses that grow their sales at a rate of 20 percent per year.[34]

So how many new businesses started every year are gazelles? Figure 4.2 shows the distribution of firm growth rates from 1997 to 2002 for the 1996 cohort of start-ups. A 20 percent per year rate of growth leads to an increase in revenues by 2.5 times over this time period. Thus, of the approximately 511,000 new single establishment businesses created in 1996, 30,168, or 5.9 percent, are "gazelles."

There's just one problem with this line of reasoning. Contrary to popular opinion, most gazelles don't increase their sales fast enough to meet business angels' sales growth rate expectations. This somewhat surprising fact is borne out by a look at the sales growth rates that experts say are necessary for companies to be angel-appropriate.

According to several experts on angel investing, even a ten times increase in sales over six years, which only 1.2 percent of new businesses (6,128 companies) achieves every year, isn't enough for companies to hit the common angel targets for sales in their sixth year of operations. The typical start-up that seeks angel funding, at least from the North-coast Angel Fund (an angel group in Northeast Ohio of which I am a member), has projected sales of $654,000 in its first year. This means that at a tenfold rate of growth, the typical start-up would *project* reaching only $6,540,000 in sales at the end of its sixth year. While that's a large increase, and higher than 98.8 percent of all U.S. companies, it's not high enough to be attractive to angel investors interested in earning a financial return on their angel investments, at least not the

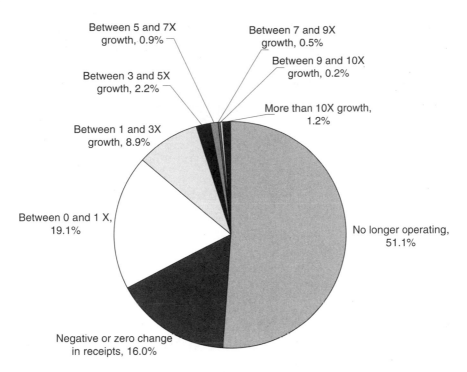

Between 5 and 7X growth, 0.9%

Between 7 and 9X growth, 0.5%

Between 9 and 10X growth, 0.2%

Between 3 and 5X growth, 2.2%

More than 10X growth, 1.2%

Between 1 and 3X growth, 8.9%

Between 0 and 1 X, 19.1%

No longer operating, 51.1%

Negative or zero change in receipts, 16.0%

FIGURE 4.2. Distribution of Five-Year Revenue Growth Rates of New Businesses Founded in 1996, between 1997 and 2002. *Source:* Created from data contained in a special tabulation of the Business Information Tracking Series of the U.S. Census.

angels referenced in most books on angel investing. That level of sales would not compensate the angel for the risk of failure, cost of capital, or opportunity cost of not investing in alternative opportunities.

So what is the level of sales growth over the first six years of a business's operations that would make it attractive to angel investors? Perhaps, a more than *sixty-fivefold* increase. The businesses that sought funds from the North Coast Angel Fund actually projected an average increase in revenues of 66.7 times.[35] And it turns out that this is roughly the same rate of revenue growth as that shown in the Gunner Circuit Systems Inc. case study that is used in the Angel Capital Association's Power of Angel Investing seminar to teach novice angels how to evaluate investment opportunities.[36] So perhaps a more than sixty-fivefold rate of increase in sales over six years is what makes a business interesting to business angels, at least the ones sophisticated enough to join angel groups or to attend the Power of Angel Investing seminar.

But this is just the companies that *sought* funds from the North Coast Angel Fund. The companies that get funds probably have a higher projected rate of sales growth. In fact, the managing director of the Northcoast Angel fund indicated that a projected increase of revenues of 81 times what is generated in the company's first year over the next five years is the rate of growth necessary for companies to be selected by that group's angel investors.[37] And how many new companies actually meet this growth target every year, you might ask? The answer is less than 400 companies.

So either business angels invest in fewer companies than many people say they do, or they don't really have the sales growth targets that many observers say they do, or they don't really have as high a proportion of their investments meet those targets as many observers say they do. Given the actual rate of new business sales growth reported by the Census Bureau, at least one of these three things can't be true.

IN CONCLUSION

Most books and articles about angel investing tell a very nice story about angels. They explain that these investors play a special role in the system of financing start-ups by filling a capital gap that exists between

KEY FACTS TO REMEMBER	
Number of new businesses founded every year that project $10 million in sales in 5 years	80,000
Number of new employer corporations founded every year that need between $25,000 and $2,000,000 in external capital	9,131
Number of companies founded each year that achieve $5 million or more in sales in 6 years	8,154
Number of companies founded each year that achieve $10 million or more in sales in 6 years	3,608
Number of companies founded each year that achieve $50 million or more in sales in 6 years	474
Number of companies founded each year that achieve $100 million or more in sales in 6 years	175

friends and family and venture capitalists. Because there is a shortage of angel capital, the story goes, angels cannot fill this role completely and government intervention is necessary to increase the amount of angel capital provided to new businesses. While this story provides a nice, neat explanation for the role of angel investors in entrepreneurial finance, and provides a nice, neat justification for government subsidies for angel finance, there's one problem with it. It's just a story.

Angels don't play a special role in filling the so-called financing gap. We have no studies that show a *causal* relationship between getting angel money and receiving venture capital. And even if we did, that causal relationship would apply to only a minuscule number of firms. Added to that, few angels invest money in the amounts necessary to fill this gap, and most young companies get debt rather than equity financing. In short, there is little evidence for the financing gap story of angel investing.

Moreover, there is no evidence that there is a shortage of angel capital. A variety of different ways of calculating how much angel capital is needed by start-ups yields estimates of *more* companies receiving angel money every year than companies in need of that capital. The actual sales of start-up companies, and the industry distribution of those companies, also fails to suggest a shortage of angel money; nor is there any evidence of the effects of an angel capital shortage, such as upward pressure on the price of angel capital.

In short, even though Chapter 2 pointed out that the angel capital market is smaller than many observers believe, there is no shortage of angel capital in the United States. The market for angel capital is relatively small because only a small number of companies need money from business angels. While it is possible that some people choose not to start companies because they don't think they will be able to get the funds they need (from angels or other sources) skewing the statistics reported in this chapter, we don't appear to have a shortage of angel money, given the demand for angel capital in this country.

FIVE

What Do Angel Investments Look Like?

Most of the books and articles that have been written about angel investing spend a lot of time talking about what angel investments look like. In fact, you might say that this is their core. The basic premise of the authors of these books and articles is that angel investments differ from other kinds of informal investments. Angels, the story goes, invest more money, and put it in different types of businesses, using a different set of financial instruments, than other informal investors, taking an approach more akin to venture capitalists (VCs) than friends and family. As a result, those interested in angel investing, as entrepreneurs, policy makers, or would-be angels, need to think about angel investments differently.

While this approach might sell a lot of books—if what angels do is unique, then there is good reason to buy a book to learn the angels' way of doing things—it's not accurate. In practice, angel investors tend to make the same types of investments, in similar sizes, using similar investment instruments, and structuring deals in similar ways as other kinds of informal investors.

ANGEL INVESTMENTS ARE NOT
AS BIG AS YOU THINK

How big are the investments that angels make in start-ups? If you believe the conventional wisdom—big. And definitely bigger than the investments made by other types of informal investors. The conventional wisdom is that angels invest no less than $25,000 and as much as $1.5 million.[1] The typical (median) level of investment is reported to be as high as $91,000.[2]

However, it turns out that the typical angel investment is much smaller than most people say it is. The data from the Entrepreneurship in the United States Assessment, which was conducted in 2004, indicate that the size of the *typical* angel investment is only $10,000. Even angel investments by sophisticated angels that involve equity are not that large. One study showed that even equity investments by business angels in California who made "Series A" investments in private companies (primarily in information technology) for whom the legal work was done by the now defunct law firm, Brobeck, Phleger & Harrison, had a median value of only $27,100.[3] (A "Series A" investment is the first round of sale of equity to investors by the founders of a company.[4])

The argument that angels make larger investments than other types of informal investors is also belied by the data. The average angel investment is not (statistically) different in size from the average friends-and-family investment, according to data from the Entrepreneurship in the United States Assessment.[5]

ANGEL INVESTMENTS ARE MORE VARIED
THAN MANY PEOPLE IMPLY

Most books and articles report the size of the average angel investment (mean) rather than the size of the typical investment (median) when discussing these investments. This approach leads to inaccurate estimates because the average size investment is very much influenced by a small number of super large investments. Take, for example, estimates from the 2003 Federal Reserve Survey of Small Business Finances, which measures the amount of informal equity investment made in small businesses. The median level of investment made by the most recent investors in businesses less than five years old was $50,000, but the investments ranged from $3,000 to $13.5 million!

Not only does the focus on the average size angel investment cause people to think the typical angel investment is larger than it really is, but also the lack of discussion of the variation in the size of angel investments masks the importance of considering *why* some angel investments are so much larger than the average or typical ones. It turns out that a variety of factors affect the size of an angel investment. For instance:

- The average and typical size of first-round investments are smaller than the corresponding numbers for later rounds.[6]
- The average investment is larger when there is venture capital co-investment.[7]
- The average investment is smaller for angels who invest alone, as opposed to those who invest with others.[8]
- The average investment is larger for ventures that have a management team in place.[9]
- The average investment is larger for ventures in higher growth industries (industries with higher market-to-book ratios).[10]

These patterns indicate that an accurate understanding of the size of angel investments requires estimates to be made from a sample of investments that are representative of the population of all investments. If the sample from which the information is gathered is one of later round investors who are part of angel groups that invest largely in conjunction with venture capitalists, and only in companies founded in high-growth industries that already have revenues and a management team in place, then the estimates of the size of investments will be much larger than most other angel investments—and not in any way applicable to the typical one.

ANGELS ALSO LEND MONEY

Many people view business angels as providers of only equity capital.[11] For instance, one observer writes, "No right-minded investor will put forth money without getting equity...in return."[12] However, it turns out that the focus on angels as a source solely of equity capital is not very accurate. Because angels don't have a fiduciary responsibility to other investors, as is the case for venture capitalists, and they are not regulated, as is the case for banks, they can and do invest using a very wide range of financial instruments, from pure debt to pure equity.

Not only can angel investments involve loans, but also a lot do. Debt accounts for 40.2 percent of the money that angels provide to start-ups, according to the Entrepreneurship in the United States

Assessment.[13] And, according to this same source, 14.8 percent of all angel deals are pure debt. Even among deals in which angels invest in return for some equity, debt is also used approximately 29.8 percent of the time.

MANY ANGELS JUST USE COMMON STOCK

Much has also been made of the tendency of angel investors to use convertible preferred stock—stock with a liquidation preference that can be converted into common stock at the investor's option[14]—as their investment instrument.[15] So strong is this belief that many angels indicate that they won't invest in common stock (a type of security that provides an interest in the ownership of a company[16]). For instance:

- One angel says, "I will never do another common stock financing."[17]
- Another angel says, "I have a rule, I will not invest in common stock, I will only invest in something that will be a preferred instrument."[18]
- A third angel says, "I've done common. It tends to be a mistake. It screws up the option plan. You don't offer the investors the type of protection that the investors really should have, like liquidation preferences. And I've made that mistake before and I don't intend to make it again."[19]

Why the strong feelings about preferred stock, a topic that the lay reader might think should not inspire the passions of, say, the Yankees–Red Sox rivalry? The answer is that convertible preferred stock offers the following advantages over common stock:

1. Liquidation preference—the ability to get your money back before other investors in the event that the business does poorly and its assets need to be liquidated.
2. The option for dividends (payments made to a company's shareholders, often in the form of cash[20]).
3. The ability to strengthen the balance sheet of the recipient company (because it is a purchase of stock rather than a loan, making it equity rather than debt).
4. The chance to avoid the negative tax consequences that occur when investors pay more than founders for the company's common stock, thereby creating a "bargain" for tax purposes.[21]

While convertible preferred stock offers many advantages to investors, the frequent discussion of its use in angel investing probably overstates its importance. Fixing an exact rate at which angels use convertible preferred stock is difficult because the only studies of its use are convenience samples of companies known to receive angel financing that might be different from other samples.

(A convenience sample is a group of people who are easy for a surveyor to find but who don't represent the larger group of people that he wants to understand. For instance, a convenience sample of investors in the stock market might be hedge fund managers who live in Greenwich, Connecticut, whom a *Business Week* columnist knows. While these fund managers certainly invest in public equities, their approach to investing is likely to be different from those of the general stock buying public, making their average answers to the survey unrepresentative, and not predictive, of the average American's approach.)

Nevertheless, the relatively high rate at which common stock is used among samples of known business angels is instructive. One study of sophisticated business angels investing in high potential companies—the very situation in which convertible preferred stock would be most likely to be used—found that common stock was used in 40 percent of investment rounds that involved only angels.[22] While we don't have direct evidence of this, it seems plausible that if 40 percent of sophisticated business angels use common stock in angel only investment rounds, then the *typical* angel who makes an equity investment purchases common stock.

Why would so many business angels use common stock rather than convertible preferred stock if several angels have gone on record saying that they will never use it? Because the transaction costs of more complex securities may not be worth incurring for the small investments that most angels make.[23]

CONVERTIBLE DEBT ISN'T USED VERY OFTEN

Another investment instrument often discussed in angel investing is convertible debt, which is a loan that carries the right to be converted to equity at the option of the investor at some time in the future. Many people say that convertible debt is a very useful investment instrument because it provides the opportunity for angels to earn high financial returns (because it can be converted to equity) while offering the liquidation preferences of debt in the event the venture fails. Perhaps more important, the argument goes, convertible debt allows an investor to put off the valuation of a company until a later round of investment—typically the first venture capital round—thus facilitating the initial financing of new ventures. Many observers believe that the ability to skirt the dicey issue of valuation helps entrepreneurs and angel investors reach an agreement on the financing of new companies[24] and helps angel investors avoid making an error in the valuation that will make the business unattractive to venture capitalists in a later round.[25]

While it's true that convertible debt offers a liquidation preference and the potential to earn high returns, and allows initial investors to pass off valuation to a later investor, it actually isn't used very often. In an investigation of the terms of angel investment agreements for high potential deals, Andrew Wong of the University of Chicago found that convertible debt was used in only 6.7 percent of investment rounds in which angels invested.[26] Because more typical angels would be even less likely than those in Wong's study to use convertible debt, the use of this financial instrument among business angels is probably rare.

ANGELS RARELY STAGE THEIR INVESTMENTS (EVEN IF THEY SHOULD)

One of the most powerful tools available to start-up company investors is the ability to stage investments. Staging—the investment of money in a company over time conditional on the achievement of milestones—helps to protect the investor against uncertainty by preserving the right to abandon an investment if it doesn't develop in a way favorable to the investor. If, for example, an entrepreneur is developing a new piece of electronic equipment, the investor can provide the entrepreneur with a small sum of money to figure out how to make the equipment work. If it does, he can then provide more money to see whether potential customers are interested in it. If that milestone is met, the investor can provide even more money to see whether the company can produce the product in large volume at a reasonable cost. By providing the money in stages that are conditional on the achievement of milestones, the investor puts in money only when key uncertainties about the business have been resolved, thereby reducing the amount of money that he risks losing.

Providing all the investment at one time also places the investor at risk of moral hazard by the entrepreneur.[27] Moral hazard is just a fancy term for actions that are not in the interest of the investor. Take a biotechnology entrepreneur as an example. Investors in scientific start-ups always risk putting their money behind entrepreneurs who are more interested in doing cutting edge science than they are in building businesses. So investors face moral hazard from entrepreneurs who could take the investors' money and use it to conduct additional scientific experiments instead of toward business goals. If the investor puts all his investment into a start-up at once, he is more vulnerable to the entrepreneur's moral hazard than if he doles out the money in stages, providing additional funding only if the entrepreneur has achieved agreed-upon milestones. Why? Because with a staged investment the entrepreneur has an incentive to do what the investor wants to get more money.

Staging is a powerful tool to protect investors, so most experts recommend staging; and most sophisticated investors in start-ups, like venture capitalists, stage their investments. So you probably assume that most angels stage their investments in start-ups. However, the reality is that business angels don't typically do this.[28] While researchers have used samples of only well-known and successful angels to investigate this question, making it difficult to address precisely, the data they have collected strongly suggest this conclusion. For instance, one study of angel investments in the United Kingdom found that funding was staged in only 21 percent of cases.[29]

Moreover, if staging is something that more sophisticated investors who better understand the investment process are more likely to do, then the typical business angel should be *less likely* than the angels surveyed in the above study to stage their investments. Therefore, the 21 percent figure for staging should be considered an upper bound on the frequency with which angels stage their investments. This lack of staging makes you wonder why so many "experts" on angel investing refer to the typical angel as a sophisticated investor who understands how to use financing tools to mitigate moral hazard and uncertainty problems in the financing of new companies.

ANGELS USE DETAILED, WRITTEN CONTRACTS LESS OFTEN THAN YOU MIGHT THINK

When people invest money in a company run by someone else, they always run the risk that the entrepreneur will take advantage of them. Because these investments are uncertain and entrepreneurs have more information about them than investors, investors are wise to be cautious and protect themselves against opportunistic entrepreneurs who are trying to gain personally at their expense. This is why many investors rely on formal contracts that outline the rights and responsibilities of the two parties, as well as terms of the deal, when they put money in private companies.[30]

For this reason, it is surprising to hear that angel investors don't always use formal contracts when they put their money into new companies. Some angels report that they still make handshake deals for investments of $20,000 to $30,000. In fact, in focus groups and interviews, several angels reported that they have made investments as large as $150,000 in unsecured debt with a handshake.

Moreover, business angels rely much less on written contracts to protect their interests than institutional investors, such as venture capitalists.[31] For instance, one researcher found that, on average, business angels spent only 2.7 percent of the amount of financing they provided to entrepreneurs on developing and writing the contracts used to govern their investments, as compared to 5.4 percent for venture capitalists.[32] In addition, a study of highly sophisticated business angels in California who made "Series A" investments in private companies for whom the legal work was done by the now defunct law firm, Brobeck, Phleger & Harrison showed that the angels spent significantly less on their legal fees than venture capitalists did for the same investments with the same law firm.[33]

So why don't angels use contracts to protect their investments in start-ups in the way that most institutional investors do? Research suggests three possible answers—one good, one not-so-good, and one that is either good or not-so-good depending on how you interpret it. The good reason is that they substitute their relationship with the entrepreneur and the person recommending the deal for the written contract. Studies show that written agreements are less common when angels know the person referring the investment to them and when they are located near the portfolio company.[34] So perhaps angels are just recognizing that contracts aren't as good a mechanism to control entrepreneurs as knowing who the honest ones are and interacting with them frequently to keep them truthful.

The reason that might-or-might-not-be-so-good is that angels use written agreements when the deals matter more to them. Research shows that the use of written contracts is associated with having a bigger equity share[35] and wanting more active involvement in the start-up.[36] So failing to use detailed written contracts might simply reflect a belief that the transaction costs are too high to make doing so worthwhile. If the angel isn't going to invest a lot of time or money, it might not be worth getting lawyers involved, given how much they cost.

On the other hand, these patterns might be interpreted as representing a failure of angels to pay attention to the details that are needed to protect their interests. Only when they have a lot of time or money at stake do they bother to get lawyers to write detailed contracts to protect their interests.

The reason that's not-so-good is that investors who know better use written contracts, but the naïve and inexperienced investors don't. Studies show that written contracts are used when investors have more investment and industry experience[37] and when they have invested in deals with other investors.[38] That is, angels don't use written contracts until they learn from experience that doing so is a good idea. Because a lot of angels don't have much investing experience, this suggests that a significant number of investors might fail to use the kinds of contractual protections that they should use simply out of ignorance.

FEW ANGELS USE THE TERM SHEET PROVISIONS THAT RECEIVED WISDOM SAYS THEY USE

Term sheets are documents that outline the financial, legal, and other terms under which investments will be made. For investments in private companies, they typically specify the valuation of the company, the type and price of the investment security, and other key terms of the agreement between the investor and the entrepreneur.[39] The provisions specified in a term sheet are thought to be very important because they make clear, and thus legally enforceable, the parameters of the agreement between the entrepreneur and the investor, and because they provide investors with the means to control the direction of the venture. As one observer explains, "One way angel investors protect their financial downside...associated with early-stage investments is by negotiating terms and conditions of an investment agreement or simple investment contract that allows the investors some degree of influence or control in decision making."[40]

Therefore, it is no surprise that the prevailing wisdom about angel investing is that angels use sophisticated term sheets to negotiate their agreements with entrepreneurs. Several observers explain that angel term sheets have become very similar to those used by venture capitalists (though, perhaps, with slightly less harsh terms).[41] In general, the typical angel term sheets are argued to include the following:

- Mechanisms to ensure that the entrepreneurs' incentives are aligned with investors' goal of creating a successful company, such as restrictions on the salary that entrepreneurs can be paid, and investment minimums for entrepreneurs.[42]
- Negative covenants (restrictions on what the entrepreneurs can do without permission from the investors), such as limits on the amounts that entrepreneurs can spend; the uses to which that money can be put; and requirements that entrepreneurs seek approval for major transactions.[43]
- Mechanisms to take action conditional on the achievement or non-achievement of objectives, such as the investors' right to purchase additional shares if the company fails to meet a milestone;[44] to repurchase the entrepreneurs' stock if they are fired or quit;[45] or to buy back shares with a cumulative dividend after a certain amount of time has passed, or a particular milestone has been achieved.[46]
- Control rights (the rights to control the direction of a company even if the investor does not have a voting majority of shares) and supra majority (the need to have more than just a simple majority to take action) terms that provide investors with a level of control over the venture that is disproportionate to their level of ownership.[47]
- Information rights (the right to obtain information about a company by receiving financial statements, attending board meetings or other means[48]) and strict financial reporting requirements to ensure that investors receive adequate information about what is happening with the ventures in which they invest.[49]
- Anti-dilution clauses that allow an investor to obtain a new share price following any additional investment that occurs at a lower price.[50]
- Liquidation preferences that give investors their money back first if the venture's assets are liquidated.[51]
- Board seats to increase investors' influence over the management of the company.[52]

The description of angel term sheets provided by many observers is very appealing. It gives the impression of great sophistication on the part of angel investors and shows a convergence between the approaches used by venture capitalists and business angels on techniques that are consistent with the tenets of finance theory. Moreover, because the professional investors are working off the same basic documents as the angels, the argument goes, it is easier to obtain a later round of investment from venture capitalists.

The only problem with all this is that it doesn't reflect reality. The limited research that we have on this question suggests that a great deal of angel investing does not involve the use of these types of term sheet provisions, and that angel term sheets are actually quite different from venture capital term sheets. For instance, even though as much as 90 percent of angel investments demand additional capital[53] and investors would like their positions not to be diluted down, angel investments generally do not contain anti-dilution clauses.[54] Moreover, research shows that angels are less likely to use anti-dilution protection than venture capitalists.[55]

Moreover, when angels do have anti-dilution provisions, the terms of their provisions are much more favorable to entrepreneurs than similar provisions used by venture capitalists. Anti-dilution can be accomplished by "full ratcheting," which lowers the price to the lowest previous price, or by a "weighted average," in which case the price is the weighted average of the new and previous price.[56] Although full ratcheting is more favorable to investors than weighted ratcheting, one study showed that full ratcheting protection was more common in venture capital investments than in angel investments.[57] Also, when business angels do use anti-dilution clauses they infrequently require the investor to "pay-to-play," whereas venture capitalists almost always require this provision.[58] (A "pay-to-play" requirement compels an existing investor to invest in a later financing round.[59])

Second, angels rarely reserve the right to take actions or change ownership conditional on the entrepreneur's achievement or non-achievement of milestones as venture capitalists do.[60] For instance, one study of investments by sophisticated business angels showed that in only 5 percent of angel investments did investors have a right to force bankruptcy or to veto management decisions; in only 2 percent of angel investments did angels have contingent board rights—rights to obtain control of the board under certain conditions—and in only 4 percent of cases were warrants at a lower valuation present.[61] (Warrants are the right to a company's shares or bonds at a specific price within a certain period of time.[62]) Another study showed that only 16 percent of angel investments permitted adjustment of the angel's share of ownership conditional on performance of the venture.[63] And a study of highly sophisticated business angels who made "Series A" investments in private companies for whom the legal work was done by the law firm of Brobeck, Phleger & Harrison showed that angel investments were statistically less likely than venture capital investments to have shares that were redeemable.[64]

Third, angel investment agreements are much less likely than venture capital investment contracts to include a liquidation provision.[65] For instance, one study found that only about half of the contracts written by sophisticated, accredited angel investors have a liquidation provision compared to the vast majority of venture capital contracts.[66] The study of highly sophisticated business angels whose "Series A" legal work was done by Brobeck, Phleger & Harrison indicated that angel investments were (statistically) less likely than venture capital investments to have liquidation preferences, showing those preferences in only 12 percent of angel-only deals compared to 58 percent of venture capitalist–only deals.[67]

Fourth, in most angel investments, the angel does not receive a seat on the board of directors.[68] In only 42.5 percent of angel funding rounds are board seats granted.[69] And, even in surveys of the most sophisticated business angels, only the very largest angel investments are sufficient to justify a board seat.[70] Studies of accredited, sophisticated business angels show that only between 15 and 37 percent of them sit on a board of directors.[71] Moreover, angels account for only about 18 percent of the board seats among companies that get both angel and venture capital funding.[72]

In short, the story about angel investors using sophisticated term sheets that are similar to those used by venture capitalists is at best referring to a handful of business angels, probably those who are part of organized angel groups (see Chapter 9 for more about these groups). For the typical angel, this story appears to be just that—a story, not a reflection of reality.

ANGELS ARE LESS LIKELY TO MAKE FOLLOW-ON INVESTMENTS THAN IS OFTEN CLAIMED

Are angels one-time investors or do they make follow-on investments? If you read much of what has been written to date on angel investing, you would probably believe that the typical angel investor makes follow-on investments. However, the data suggest the opposite. Many studies of sophisticated, well-known angels show that the typical angel invests in only a single round and relies on his or her early bets to achieve financial returns.[73] One study of angels in the United Kingdom found that angels provide follow-on money only 25 percent of the time.[74]

And Rob Wiltbank of Willamette University reports that accredited angel investors affiliated with angel groups and worth an average of $10.9 million, make follow-on investments in only 29 percent of the companies in which they invest.[75] Other studies show that even when start-ups get a venture capital round, only about 40 percent of angel investors follow on.[76] In fact, studies of sophisticated angel investors who are putting their money into high-growth ventures show that only 27 percent of angels *even write* contracts with portfolio companies that give them the right of first refusal to "follow on."[77]

Moreover, angels do not report that they set aside sufficient capital to invest in additional financing rounds. Although some observers note that angels typically set aside an equal amount for follow-on rounds as they put in for the initial round,[78] the angels who participated in Federal Reserve–sponsored focus groups indicated that reserve ratios need to be closer to two-to-one for each dollar of initial investment for angels to be able to follow on.[79]

ANGELS VERY RARELY CO-INVEST WITH VENTURE CAPITALISTS

A frequently made observation about angel investors is that they co-invest with venture capitalists. Venture capitalists, the argument goes, want to leverage the knowledge and expertise of angel investors.[80] The angels, in turn, want to attract more money to their portfolio companies; increase the odds of follow-on funding; take advantage of the venture capital firms' due diligence;[81] and earn the higher financial returns that venture capitalists tend to make.[82] However, angel-venture capitalist co-investment doesn't actually happen that often. Even among the most sophisticated accredited angel investors, backing the highest potential businesses, studies show that venture capitalist co-investment occurs in only about 21 percent of funding rounds.[83]

Venture capitalists don't invest in enough businesses for a high rate of co-investment to occur. Venture capitalist-business angel co-investment is most likely to occur at the seed and start-up stage of financing because very few angels can make investments of the magnitude necessary to participate in an expansion or later stage venture capital financing round, which calls for investments of as much as $10 million. In fact, making such an investment would even stretch many angel groups, which make an average investment per round of only $242,000.[84]

But there aren't enough seed and start-up stage investments by venture capitalists for many of those deals to involve venture capitalist-business angel co-investment. According to the National Science Foundation (NSF), only 612 companies received seed or start-up stage venture capital financing in 2004.[85] If business angels co-invest with venture capitalists in every one of these companies (a dubious assumption), only 1.1 percent of the 57,300 companies estimated to have received an angel investment that year would have received a co-investment from a business angel and a venture capitalist. Even if you assume that business angels co-invest with venture capitalists in all investments that the VCs make, including late stage ones, the maximum share of companies estimated to receive an angel investment that could also receive a co-investment from a venture capitalist is 4.5 percent.

It appears that many observers have overemphasized the amount of co-investing between business angels and venture capitalists because they have focused on a small number of angel investors who have made these co-investments and tried to generalize from their activities to all business angels. A more informative approach might be to recognize that very few business angel deals involve co-investment with venture capitalists and then to look at what makes some deals more appropriate for co-investment than others. While research on this question can only be suggestive—only samples of the best-known angels have been examined—there are some interesting patterns. Co-investment is more common when the venture is located further away from the angel investors.[86] It is also more common for investment rounds that are post-revenue, occur after the management team is in place, and involve raising a lot of money.[87] It is more common in industries with fewer fixed assets, higher book-to-market value, and greater volatility.[88] It is also more common when angel investors have less angel investment experience[89] and when portfolio company entrepreneurs have more start-up experience.[90]

VENTURE CAPITALISTS VERY RARELY FOLLOW ON ANGEL INVESTMENTS

Many authors of books and articles about angel investing frame the relationship between business angels and venture capitalists as a symbiotic one. Angels, the story goes, provide funding to high-potential companies, which then get follow-on funding from venture capitalists when the business reaches a stage of development at which its capital demands exceed the amount of money that angels can provide.[91] Once venture capitalists have made their investment, angels decrease their involvement and pass on their governance roles to the VCs.[92] As one author put it, "Business angels and venture capitalists clearly tend to serve different stages of firms and contrasting size categories of growth firms."[93]

The conventional wisdom is that venture capitalists make investments that follow on a significant portion of those made by business angels, as much as 12.7 percent of angel investments.[94] However, if you think about it for a minute, this number is impossible—unless *very few* angel investments are being made every year, far fewer than most observers (included the ones providing these numbers) claim. According to National Science Foundation, in 2004, 2,465 companies received a non–seed stage venture capital investment.[95] Even if *all* of these companies had previously received an angel investment (an unlikely scenario), this means that no more than 4.3 percent of the 57,300 companies that were estimated to have received angel money in the United States in 2004 are followed up with a venture capital investment.[96]

THERE IS NO EVIDENCE THAT GETTING AN ANGEL INVESTMENT INCREASES THE CHANCES OF GETTING A VENTURE CAPITAL INVESTMENT

The prevailing wisdom is that getting an angel investment will enhance your company's chances of getting VC money. The purported reasons are numerous:

1. Angels often bring the deals that they are considering to venture capitalists and encourage venture capitalists to co-invest in them.
2. Angel investors often work with venture capitalists, obtaining deal flow from those who believe that the businesses are too early for venture capital financing but who want the businesses to be developed and presented to them later.
3. Venture capitalists are more likely to invest in companies whose prior investors they respect, and many venture capitalists respect angel investors.[97]
4. Venture capitalists see an angel investment as a positive signal that makes them more likely to invest.[98]

So many people say (or at least imply) that receiving an investment from an angel increases a company's chances of receiving an investment from a venture capital firm that you'd think it was a proven fact. But it's not. All we have is a few studies that show an association between the receipt of an angel investment and the receipt of venture capital. For instance, one study of U.S. companies that received angel financing between 1994 and 2001 shows that the time it takes a company to receive a venture capital investment decreases with the number of angels who have invested in the company.[99] But as the expression goes, an association does not mean causation.

The association between the receipt of an angel investment and the receipt of venture capital can be very easily explained by reasons having nothing to do with the effect of the angels on the VC's decision to invest. If the average company that receives an angel investment has a better management team and is pursuing a more desirable business opportunity than the average company that doesn't receive this financing, then the company that gets the angel money might also get the VC money simply because the management team and business opportunity were attractive to both sets of investors.

Second, it's hard to know what to make of the numbers thrown around about the proportion of companies that get angel funding and subsequently obtain venture capital. For instance, one study found that 57.1 percent of firms that had received an angel investment also obtained a venture capital infusion, while only 10 percent of companies that had not received an angel investment received venture capital financing.[100] These numbers can't possibly be right. If no more than 2,500 companies receive post-seed stage venture capital investments every year, then no more than 4,400 companies could receive an angel investment for 57.1 percent of the firms that receive an angel investment to also get venture capital. However, estimates calculated from the data from the Federal Reserve Survey of Small Business Finances and the Entrepreneurship in the United States Assessment indicate that between 50,700 and 57,300 companies per year receive an angel investment.

Moreover, how do we get these numbers to jibe with the 10 percent of companies that do not get angel money but receive venture capital? Even if we take the smaller government estimates of the number of companies created every year—the roughly 600,000 new employer firms rather than the 2 million start-ups in general—and subtract the estimate of the number of companies that get angel money, we are left with 595,600 companies. If 10 percent of those companies received venture capital, then there would be 59,560 start-ups that were VC-backed but not angel backed every year! This can't be possible given the data which shows that VCs put money in less than 3,000 U.S. start-ups per year.

Even the idea that venture capitalists see an investment by the typical angel as a positive signal seems suspect. The typical, or median, angel-backed company, doesn't have a profile that would make it attractive to venture capitalists (more about this in the next chapter). Moreover, as Chapter 8 will discuss in greater detail, almost all of the investment performance of business angels is accounted for by a small handful of investors, and 40 percent of investors simply lose money. So it is not at all evident why the receipt of an investment from the *typical* angel would *cause* a firm's odds of getting venture capital to increase. Of course, it's possible that getting an investment from one of the handful of really successful angel investors could *cause* one's chances of getting venture capital to go up. But then we're not talking about something that would happen to very many businesses.

ANGELS DON'T USE SOPHISTICATED METHODS OF VALUATION

Equity investors must value the companies in which they invest because they provide cash in return for a portion of ownership. The exchange of money for shares of a business sets its value. For instance, if an entrepreneur gives a business angel 10 percent of his company to get $25,000, that means that 100 percent of the company must be worth $250,000. That is, the company's valuation is $250,000.

Because angel investors *must* value all companies in which they make *equity* investments, *how* they value those companies is an important aspect of angel investing. Many observers argue that angels engage in sophisticated approaches to valuing the companies in which they invest.

At first glance, a sophisticated approach makes sense. Valuation is a contentious issue—one of the two primary reasons that entrepreneurs and investors cannot agree upon the terms of an investment.[101] Moreover, a company's valuation has a direct effect on the investor's return. The higher the valuation, the more the company needs to be worth at the time the angel exits for the investment to generate a given financial return. And this relationship is nonlinear. For each percentage point increase in valuation, investors' expected returns go down by more than one percentage point.[102] Furthermore, if the valuation of a company is too high, the venture may be doomed to fail because additional investors won't provide capital (doing so often requires the earlier round investors to accept a reduction in the valuation of their investment).[103] And if the investors' reluctance to recognize the need to lower the valuation of their investment is overcome and additional funding can be obtained, the investors' expected returns will have to be reduced.[104] Finally, the valuations that investors are willing to accept should be related to the companies' risk. Investors should want higher returns for companies they perceive as riskier, so they should offer lower valuations for riskier businesses.

All of this points to claims by many observers that the typical angel screens deals on the basis of valuation[105] and considers a number of factors in valuing the companies in which he invests, including:

1. The expected value of the company when the investors try to sell it. (This, itself, is a function of the performance of the firm; the multiple on sales or earnings that exists in the industry; the company's exit strategy—IPOs have a higher multiple than acquisitions—and the strength of the IPO and mergers and acquisitions markets.)
2. The age of the company at the time of exit. (The greater the time to exit, the lower the valuation of the company because money has a time value.)
3. The degree of control the investors have. (Lesser control translates to a lower valuation.)
4. The amount of additional money that will be need to be raised and the corresponding dilution that investors will experience. (The greater the expected dilution, the lower is the valuation.)
5. The investors' discounting of the entrepreneur's financial projections. (The greater the discounting, the lower is the valuation.)
6. The quality of the management team and the investors' confidence in their ability to build the business. (The greater the quality, the higher is the valuation.)
7. The nature of the industry and the type of competitive advantage the firm has. (The better the industry and competitive advantage, the higher is the valuation.)
8. The stage of development of the venture. (The more developed the product or the more advanced the marketing effort, the greater is the valuation.)[106]

Given these points, you would think that business angels would have a good grasp of the principles of valuation and would devote a great deal of time and attention to the valuation of companies. While some angels do, a large number do not. In fact, many angels don't understand the basic process or terminology of valuation, confusing terms like pre- and post-money valuation.[107]

Some concrete evidence of the less sophisticated approach of business angels to valuation is their use of valuation tools. Most business angels do not use the venture capital method, which sets the post-money valuation (the post-money valuation is taken by adding the new amount of money to the pre-money valuation) equal to the terminal value of the business, raised to the power of the number of years to exit, divided by the required return on investment for that many years.[108]

Moreover, the evidence reported by many angels about how they value companies suggests that they do so in an informal, unsophisticated way, incorporating bits and pieces of information that they have gathered about the venture and subjectively negotiating the value of the companies in which they are seeking to invest. As one angel put it, "Negotiations were about ten minutes long. I liked it, and just went ahead with it."[109]

VALUATIONS OF ANGEL-FINANCED COMPANIES ARE LOWER THAN MOST PEOPLE BELIEVE

How much are companies worth at the time that angels invest in them? This question is important for both angel investors and entrepreneurs. The common view is that the typical start-up backed by angel investors is worth a fairly sizable amount of money. Experts have said that post-money valuations range from $250,000 to $10 million,[110] with an average valuation of between $2.5 and $4 million.[111]

However, these estimates are quite inaccurate because they reflect only the investments made by the most sophisticated and successful accredited angel investors. Basing estimates on just these investors is, of course, a flawed approach, akin to estimating the average salary of professional baseball players by looking only at the salaries of the players in the major league all-star game. If we look at the value of companies at the time that a *representative* sample of business angels invested in them, the numbers are much lower.

Very few companies that receive angel investments have a multimillion dollar net worth at the time of investment. As Table 5.1 shows, only 36.4 percent of angel investments were made in companies worth more than $1 million at the time of investment.

Other sources provide similar evidence. Data from the 2003 Federal Survey of Small Business Finances found that the average net worth of a company less than five years old that had received an informal equity investment in the past year was $324,000, while the median net worth was $58,000. (The average net worth of all companies that had

TABLE 5.1. Value of the Businesses Receiving Angel Investments
at the Time of Investment

Value of the Business at the Time of Investment	Share of Angel Investments
Less than $50,000	42.4%
Between $50,001 and $100,000	9.1%
Between $100,001 and $500,000	6.1%
Between $500,001 and $1,000,000	6.1%
More than $1,000,000	36.4%

Source: Created from data contained in the Entrepreneurship in the United States Assessment and Reynolds, P. 2004. *Entrepreneurship in the United States Assessment.* Miami, FL: Florida International University.

received an equity investment from a business angel in the previous year was $2.5 million, but the average age of those businesses was 16.5 years old and only 15 percent were less than ten years old, making it difficult to interpret the net worth information on the companies that had received angel investments in the past year.)

Of course, it's possible that the valuations angels place on the companies is much higher than their net worth would suggest. We can calculate the valuation of the typical company that received an external equity investment in its first year of operation using data from Kauffman Firm Survey (KFS), a survey of a representative sample of new companies started in 2004. The KFS data show that the valuation of a typical firm that was started in 2004 and received an external equity investment in that year was $171,000 (but the average was $1.4 million). In short, the valuation of the typical external equity-backed start-up company is much lower than is commonly believed, probably because most of the information about valuation comes from the most highly valued companies.

ANGELS DON'T CAREFULLY TARGET MAJORITY OWNERSHIP

Related to the issue of valuation is the issue of ownership because valuation is set by the share of ownership taken in return for the cash invested. The percentage ownership taken by angels is important because it affects control; the more of a company an angel owns, the more he can affect the direction of the company. It also affects the angel's return, particularly given the potential for such investments to be diluted down over subsequent investment rounds. Moreover, the share of ownership taken by a business angel is a source of conflict between entrepreneurs and angels, with studies showing that it is one of the top two reasons entrepreneurs and investors fail to agree on investment terms[112] and one of the most difficult things for entrepreneurs and angels to negotiate.[113]

Some observers explain that angels seek majority ownership to influence the development of the venture and earn a reasonable rate of return on their investment, despite the dilution that occurs if the venture receives several rounds of financing.[114] As one angel said, "I prefer that investors as a group have control, certainly control if a downside contingency occurs."[115] In particular, owning a lot of the company facilitates obtaining a board seat, which helps investors to monitor and guide the development of the company.

Given the importance of percentage ownership taken by business angels, your intuition might be that business angels carefully calculate their percentage of ownership to ensure that they have majority ownership of their portfolio companies. However, this turns out not to be the case. Angels rarely use complex formulas for figuring out how much ownership to take.[116] In fact, studies have shown that they are much less likely than venture capitalists to employ the venture capital method of calculating ownership.[117] Instead angels have been found to rely largely on gut feel.[118]

Moreover, in practice, business angels rarely come close to majority ownership in their portfolio companies. For instance, one study of twenty-five business angels in Canada found that in only one case did the angel have majority ownership.[119] Most studies show that angels who invest in the initial financing round of a start-up collectively acquire between 20 and 35 percent of the company in which they are investing.[120] For example, in a study of 1,377 companies in which angels invested between 2000 and 2004, the Center for Venture Research at the University of New Hampshire found that the angels took an average of 20.4 percent ownership of the portfolio companies.[121] The 2003 Federal Reserve's Survey of Small Business Finances showed that the first owner of companies less than five years old that received an informal equity investment in the previous twelve months owned 70 percent of their companies after the investment occurred. Even the study of highly sophisticated business angels who made "Series A" investments, for which the legal work was done by Brobeck, Phleger

& Harrison, showed that after angel-only rounds were completed, the average founder still owned 62 percent of his company.[122]

These numbers should be taken with a grain of salt because they are based on convenience samples of sophisticated business angels—except the Fed data—and might not apply to the typical angel. However, they do point out the fallacy of the argument that angels seek enough ownership to affect the development of the ventures in which they invest. In fact, one study showed that individual angels each averaged owning only about 4.2 percent of the companies in which they invested,[123] too little to ensure that they affect the direction of the company, particularly after their initial investment is diluted down.

Why are angels willing to invest if they cannot get enough ownership to influence the development of the business? Several reasons are possible. First, owning a small share of the company increases the alignment of the entrepreneur's goals with those of the company. Because the entrepreneur owns a lot of the company, he is motivated to make the company a success. Second, angels are not placed in the position of having to take control of the companies if the entrepreneurs do not lead them successfully.[124] This is important because angel investors don't like stepping in and replacing CEOs, and they do so at a much lower rate than venture capitalists. Third, a low level of ownership facilitates the raising of additional capital. If angels take too much of a company, then later stage investors will be deterred because the entrepreneur will not have enough shares to offer them.[125] Fourth, a low level of ownership facilitates the involvement of other investors. And the presence of peer investors is necessary to confirm the results of due diligence and the valuation of the company.

Too much should not be made of the average ownership share taken by business angels in return for their investments because the share taken varies greatly across angels and portfolio companies. Data from the 2003 Federal Reserve Survey of Small Business Finances indicates that the share of ownership held by the first owner of a firm less than five years old after an informal equity investment ranges from 11 to almost 100 percent. This variance begs the question: if the goal of angels to obtain majority ownership of the companies in which they invest does not determine the percentage ownership taken by business angels, what does? Research identifies several factors:

- The stage of the investment: angels receive a greater portion of ownership for investing in early rounds, 3 percent more, on average, for investing in a first round, according to one study.[126]

- The size of the investment: angels' ownership share increases with the dollar value of the angel investment.[127]
- The co-investors: angels' ownership share is higher when they co-invest with venture capitalists—4 percent more, on average, according to one study.[128]
- The development of the company: angels' share of ownership is higher in pre-revenue companies than in post-revenue companies and is lower if there is a complete management team in place at the time of their investment.[129]
- The industry: angels' share of ownership is higher if the industry in which the company operates is more volatile.[130]
- The entrepreneur they are backing: angels' share of ownership is lower if the entrepreneurs being financed have previously started companies.[131]

KEY FACTS TO REMEMBER

Median size of an angel investment	$10,000
Proportion of angel funding in the form of debt	40.2 percent
Proportion of sophisticated angel investments that use common stock	40 percent
Proportion of sophisticated angel investments in which convertible debt is used	6.7 percent
Proportion of angel investments in which funding is staged	<21 percent
Proportion of sophisticated angel investments in which the investor can force bankruptcy or veto management decisions	5 percent
Proportion of sophisticated angel investments that include contingent board rights	2 percent
Proportion of sophisticated angel investments that include warrants at a lower valuation	4 percent
Proportion of angel investments that involve co-investment with VCs	< 1.1 percent
Proportion of angel-backed companies that receive a VC follow-on investment	< 4.3 percent
Proportion of angel-backed companies worth more than $1 million at the time of angel investment	36.4 percent

Valuation of the typical one-year-old firm that has received an external equity investment	$171,000
Individual angel's share of ownership of the typical angel-backed company	4.2 percent

IN CONCLUSION

To understand angel investing, we need to understand the nature of the deals that angels strike with entrepreneurs. And if we believe the conventional wisdom, then we don't understand angel investing very well. Much of what has been written about the nature of angel deals is not correct for the typical angel deal. The typical angel deal involves a much smaller investment with a greater proportion of debt than many people realize. The financial instruments that are used are less sophisticated than many of the articles and books on angel investing would have us believe. When equity is involved, it is not always the convertible preferred stock that many observers talk about. In fact, the purchase of common stock is far more common than many people think, and the use of convertible debt by angels is downright rare. Staging of investment is infrequent, co-investment with venture capitalists is uncommon, and follow-on investments are few and far between.

Some angels still make investments in start-ups without a written contract, and when they write contracts, their agreements are simpler than those used by venture capitalists. Contrary to the popular opinion that the typical angel uses a standard venture capital term sheet, the typical angel investment term sheet lacks many of the clauses common in venture capital agreements: angels rarely get board seats, tend not to have liquidation provisions, infrequently reserve the right to take actions if entrepreneurs fail to meet milestones, and tend not to have anti-dilution protection. Angels don't use the venture capital tools for valuing early stage businesses and tend to own too small a percentage of the companies in which they invest to affect the companies' development. In many ways, the typical angel deal might be best characterized as the provision of a bit of money in return for a bit of the company under pretty generous terms, in the hopes that the one-time investment will have been placed in a winner. That, of course, leads us to the topic of the next chapter: Who gets angel money?

SIX

Who Gets Angel Money?

THE DESCRIPTIONS OF the companies that receive angel money have taken on mythic proportions. Angels, it seems, are looking for everything: a high-growth market, a profitable business, an experienced team, a proprietary competitive advantage, a good business model, a well-written business plan, strong financial projections, the right financial structure, excellent exit options, and a high rate of return, among other things. Take the following example of what angels are purported to be looking for that I downloaded from one Web site:

WHAT DO ANGEL INVESTORS LOOK FOR?

1. High growth potential, e.g., expected ROI to be at least 30% and greater than 5 times money over expected holding period.
2. Experienced, strong, cooperative management team in place. Management should have sales experience in the targeted market segments.
3. Well-defined and analyzed segmented market—large or fast growing.
4. Clear and complete marketing plan including details on distribution channels, positioning, marketing, promotion, and sales, strategies, and staffing needs.
5. Clear and detailed competitor analysis, e.g., why we can beat them.

6. Aggressive market approach with unique selling proposition.
7. Understandable proprietary technology.
8. Well structured, complete business plan with executive summary.
9. Financial projections (i.e., P&L, Balance Sheet and Cash Flow) with explanatory notes and assumptions.
10. Board or Advisory position offered/available for investors.
11. Staged investment based on milestones.
12. Debt or preferred shares convertible to common if pre-revenue stage.
13. Sales start no later than the first equity injection/conversion.
14. Positive cash flow within 12 months.
15. Financial buffers to carry company six months under worst-case scenario.
16. Detailed budget and milestones.
17. High quality outside advisors.
18. Substantial investment by management and controlling owners.
19. Investor exit options within three to five years.
20. Downside protection, where appropriate.
21. Deal sizes $200K to $2.0 million.
22. Clear plan for use of funds with impact analysis for higher and lower funding, where appropriate.
23. Plan for subsequent financing rounds until company is self-supporting with cash flow.
24. Reasonable, justifiable valuation.
25. Below market cash compensation to management pre-profit.[1]

And this is the list my editor would let me reproduce because it was the short one! Some books and articles about angel investing go on for pages upon pages about the characteristics that angels are looking for, listing well over 100 different things that angels want. Before you get discouraged and think that angels are only interested in a very special group of companies that are nothing like the company that you've started, and certainly before you fork over $77 for a CD that will tell you all the things that angels are looking for,[2] let me be the first to tell you not to worry. Angels invest in plenty of companies that don't meet these criteria. In fact, the typical company that receives an angel investment has relatively few of the characteristics described in most articles or books on angel investing.

So what types of companies are angels *really* putting their money into? What, if any, characteristics do the founders of those companies have in common? Let's take a look.

THE EXPERTS DISAGREE ON WHAT ANGELS ARE LOOKING FOR

Before we look at the types of entrepreneurs and companies that angels actually finance, we have to figure out what angels really want. The introduction to this chapter was misleading in one important respect. By giving you one list of criteria that experts say angels want, I gave the impression that angels actually agree on their preferences. But it turns out that this is not the case. In one fascinating study, thirty-five business angels (who, in this case, were defined as high net worth individuals who invest in high-potential new companies) were asked to look at a single investment opportunity and explain what factors would affect their decision to invest or not invest. While the angels all agreed that the investment opportunity was not a good one, there was very little agreement on why, even though the angels were looking at exactly the same business opportunity. No two angels identified the same reason for rejection. Even at the more aggregate level of categories of reasons, there was little agreement. Of the rejections, 36 percent were because of the entrepreneur or management team, 25 percent were the result of the marketing strategy, and 25 percent were because of the financials.[3]

The results of surveys of angels on the criteria that matter to them are little better at showing agreement. Table 6.1 shows the top ten investment criteria identified by business angels participating in three different studies.[4] Even when the wording of the three questionnaires is changed slightly to *make them more likely to agree*, only three of seventeen criteria make the top ten in all three studies. And even then, the rank orderings of the overlapping items are quite different.

It's hard to believe that there is a set of criteria that make companies appropriate for angels when there is so little agreement between angels on what those criteria are. Because these criteria are so different from angel to angel, either you have to believe that the expert whose list you've chosen to follow is right and the others are wrong, or you have to conclude that these lists of what angels want aren't too helpful. For those of you who paid money to get access to the Web sites, books, and CDs with "the list," you might want to see if you can get your money back.

TABLE 6.1.   Top Ten Investment Criteria of Business Angels

Criterion	Van Osnabrugge and Robinson Ranking	Hill and Power Ranking	Sudek Ranking
Enthusiasm of the Entrepreneur	1		3
Trustworthiness of the Entrepreneur	2		1
Sales/Revenue Potential of the Product	3		5
Expertise of the Entrepreneur/Quality of the Management	4	1	2/6
Degree to Which Entrepreneur is Liked	5		
Growth Potential of the Market	6	2	7
Quality of the Product	7		
Perceived Financial Rewards for the Investor/Return on Investment	8	7	8
Presence of a Niche Market	9		
Track Record of the Entrepreneur	10		
Proprietary Nature of the Product/Competitive Protection		3	10
Size of the Market		4	
Presence of Barriers to Entry		5	9
Nature of the Competition		6	
Industry the Venture is in		8	
Stage of Company Development		9	
Potential Exit Routes			4

Source: Created from information contained in Von Osnabrugge, M., and Robinson, R. 2000. *Angel Investing: Matching Start-up Funds with Start-up Companies—The Guide for Entrepreneurs, Individual Investors, and Venture Capitalists.* San Francisco: Jossey-Bass; Hill, B., and Power, D. 2002. *Attracting Capital from Angels.* New York: John Wiley; and Sudek, R. Angel investment criteria. 2007. *Journal of Business Strategy,* 17(2): 89–104.

WHAT'S A HIGH-GROWTH COMPANY TO A BUSINESS ANGEL?

Business angels are looking for high-growth companies, right? Everyone agrees—angels are looking to finance businesses with significant sales potential and reject businesses that have too little chance to grow.[5]

Thus, even if angels don't agree on all the criteria for what makes a business angel-appropriate, it appears that they agree on something. But alas, the evidence of this turns out to be less clear than it looks. While everyone agrees that angels are looking for businesses with "significant sales potential," they disagree on what that term means.

One survey of business angels indicated that "significant sales potential" means that the business will generate $1,000,000 in sales five years after starting;[6] another study found that two thirds of business angels would require a business to have projected sales in five years of at least $5 million for them to consider investing.[7] Other experts say that businesses have to have $10 million in sales after five years to be appropriate for angel investment.[8] The Angel Capital Association (ACA) sets a higher bar, saying that a company needs to reach at least $15 million in revenues in three to seven years to be angel fundable.[9] Still other angels indicate that for a business to be interesting to them it needs to project at least $20 million in sales in five years.[10] Yet another expert says that a company has to project $25 million in revenue in five years to be interesting to angels,[11] while Tech Coast Angels, a California-based angel investment group, writes on its Web site that it looks for businesses with the potential to create at least $50 million in annual revenues.[12] Successful and experienced business angel Bill Payne pushes the bar even higher, saying that a venture "must have" projected sales of $100 million in year five for him to invest.[13]

In short, everyone *agrees* that businesses have to have "significant sales growth potential" to be interesting to angels, as long as significant sales growth means achieving between $1 million and $100 million. In other words, angels are looking for either the 9.2 percent of U.S. start-ups that reach $1 million in sales in six years, or the 0.03 percent of businesses that reach $100 million in sales in that time period, or something in between. Not exactly agreement, do you think?

INDUSTRIES IN WHICH ANGELS INVEST

What industries do angels want to invest in? This should be easy to figure out because everyone *knows* that angels invest in a small number of high-tech industries that have large and rapidly growing markets, and that they shy away from retail and personal service industries. As one set of authors put it, "Business angels in the United States and Canada prefer investing in high technology and manufacturing ventures."[14]

Or as another set of authors writes, "We have consistently identified a strong preference for technology-related ventures."[15] Survey after survey of convenience samples of known angel investors indicates that the majority *prefer* to invest in high-technology companies, primarily in information technology and the biomedical arena.[16] In fact, the experts claim that only a small minority of angel investments—perhaps 15 percent—are made in all nontechnology businesses (e.g., manufacturing, real estate, construction, and retail) combined.[17]

(Business angels, the argument goes, are interested in technology businesses because they are more scalable[18] than banks, restaurants, and retail businesses, which rarely reach a level at which they can grow faster than their capital needs.[19])

Some experts also argue that certain industries are *inappropriate* for angels. They say that consumer products companies are no good because they are marketing intensive and require access to shelf space. Businesses selling commodity products are said to be inappropriate because the companies selling them cannot differentiate themselves, yet lack the scale to compete on price. Businesses in slow-growth industries are no good because competition for customers is intense and new companies are not able to survive such strong competitive pressures.[20] Businesses in small markets are considered inappropriate because the businesses would have to capture a large share of the market to have enough sales to succeed.[21]

In particular, several experts explain that personal service businesses are inappropriate for angel investors because these businesses sell at a low multiple; require rapid growth to generate enough revenue to be sold at a good price; lack economies of scale and require significant employment growth to increase revenues; rarely have intellectual property to protect against imitation by others; give employees tremendous control over investors; and lack assets to sell off in the event of failure.[22]

Several observers say that angels *seek* businesses that are not capital intensive, break even quickly, have low overhead, don't require expensive market testing, have little inventory, and have customers that pay in advance (or suppliers that provide credit).[23] They claim that angels look for businesses that are projecting good margins[24]—at least 15 percent before tax[25]—and reject low margin businesses, which have little room for error.[26]

However, the *actual* investments made by business angels don't fall into the narrow set of industries that the experts say angels prefer.[27] When researchers conducting the Entrepreneurship in the United

States Assessment asked a representative sample of angel investors about the businesses they had backed over the previous three years, they found that angels put their money into a very wide range of industries, including things you might not think of, such as barbershops and wineries, and they aren't biased toward high technology. Moreover, the data show that the statement that angels don't invest in personal services or retail businesses is just plain wrong: 25 percent of angel investments go into retail businesses, and 12.5 percent of angel investments go into personal service businesses.

And these numbers aren't an artifact of the exclusion of investments by "friends" from the angel investment category. The numbers are pretty similar for external equity investments (remember that these are investments made by angels and by friends of the entrepreneur, but not by his family members).

The Entrepreneurship in the United States Assessment isn't the only source that shows this pattern. The numbers provided by the Census Bureau on all companies aged five-and-under that received external equity investments from 1997 to 2002 show that most of them aren't the high-tech, computer-related businesses that we tend to read about. In fact, the Census data show that more external equity investors put their money into retail businesses than put their money into information-based companies. As Figure 6.1 indicates, the information sector, which includes software companies, accounts for only 6.8 percent of the recipients of external equity investments, whereas the retail trade sector accounts for 8.3 percent of them.

Contrary to the argument that angels avoid capital-intensive businesses, external investors actually prefer them. Statistical analysis that I conducted on the Census data shows that there is a strong *positive* relationship between an industry's degree of capital intensity and the proportion of companies in the industry that receive external equity investment. (The rank correlation, or degree to which the ranking of the industries on the two numbers move together, is 0.51; a correlation of 1.00 indicates a perfect match, in which the ranking of the two numbers move in exactly the same way.)

Business angels do not restrict their investments to high-margin industries, as many observers say they do. The industries that many observers *say* are popular with business angels are not particularly high-margin industries, and many of the industries with the highest profit margins are not ones that most observers *say* angels tend to invest in. Moreover, there is no observable statistical association between the profit margin of an industry and the proportion of firms

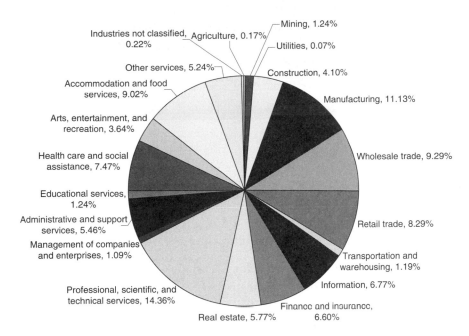

FIGURE 6.1. Industry Distribution of New Companies Founded Between 1997 and 2002 that Received External Equity Investment. *Source*: Created from data contained in a special tabulation of the Survey of Business Owners of the U.S. Census.

aged five-and-under that have received an external equity investment. That is, angels don't appear to be picking high-margin industries at any greater rate than low-margin ones.

One argument that is often made about business angels is that they focus their attention on industries similar to those selected by venture capitalists. (In fact, the Angel Capital Association even measures industry the same way as the venture capital industry, using PriceWaterhouseCoopers MoneyTree™ sector definitions rather than the industry definitions used by the federal government.) But this isn't true. What many observers fail to realize is how few companies are actually started in the industries in which venture capitalists tend to operate. Table 6.2 shows the number of start-ups founded in 1996 in these industries. Even taking a very inclusive view of the MoneyTree™ sector definitions when matching them to the Census Bureau's industry definitions, we can see that fewer than 14,000 companies were started in the industries in which venture capitalists have tended to make investments. It is *literally impossible* for business angels to finance the number of companies per year that they are argued to finance and also invest in just those high-technology industries that venture capitalists favor.

TABLE 6.2.   Number of New Single Establishment Businesses Founded
in 1996 in Industries in Which Venture Capitalists Have
Tended to Invest

Industry	Number of Start-ups
Medicinals and Botanicals	23
Pharmaceutical Preparations	49
Diagnostic Substances	8
Biological products, Except Diagnostics	17
Electronic Computers	51
Computer Storage Devices	16
Computer Terminals	9
Computer Peripheral Equipment, Not Elsewhere Classified	85
Calculating and Accounting Equipment	14
Office Machines, Not Elsewhere Classified	10
Telephone and Telegraph Apparatus	44
Radio and Television Communications Equipment	65
Communications Equipment, Not Elsewhere Classified	20
Electron Tubes	11
Printed Circuit Boards	85
Semiconductors and Related Devices	109
Electronic Components, Not Elsewhere Classified	178
Storage Batteries	7
Magnetic and Optical Recording Media	26
Electrical Equipment and Supplies, Not Elsewhere Classified	39
Search and Navigation Equipment	24
Measuring and Controlling Devices, Not Elsewhere Classified	256
Laboratory Apparatus and Furniture	8
Environmental Controls	15
Process Control Instruments	35
Fluid Meters and Counting Devices	7
Instruments To Measure Electricity	47
Analytical Instruments	32
Optical Instruments and Lenses	28
Surgical and Medical Instruments	115
Surgical Appliances and Supplies	99
Dental Equipment and Supplies	58
X-Ray Apparatus and Tubes	11
Electromedical Equipment	24

Industry	Number of Start-ups
Ophthalmic Goods	18
Radiotelephone Communications	606
Telephone Communications, Except Radio	597
Telegraph and Other Communications	36
Cable and Other Pay TV Services	202
Computer Programming Services	4,560
Prepackaged Software	1,271
Computer Integrated Systems Design	1,190
Data Processing and Preparation	460
Information Retrieval Services	1,302
Computer Facilities Management	106
Computer Rental and Leasing	73
Computer Maintenance and Repair	614
Commercial Physical Research	816
Testing Laboratories	322
Total	13,798

Source: Created from data contained in a special tabulation of the Survey of Business Owners of the U.S. Census. (These industries are measured at the four-digit SIC code level.)

In short, angels don't appear to focus on high-technology, high-margin, low capital-intensity industries that experts say that they do. So what do they focus on? Let's take a look.

ANGELS TEND TO INVEST IN INDUSTRIES THAT THEY KNOW

One of the myths about angel investing is that typical angels recycle money from old, declining industries into new, high-growth ones. As a result, they don't care that much about understanding the industries in which they invest and don't necessarily put money into the same industries in which they work. As one observer wrote, "Compared to venture capitalists, business angels tend to be less concerned about knowing the industry in which the firm competes."[28] Or as another author said, "Although institutional investors will invest less often in industries they don't understand or have experience in, angel investors are more involved in industries they don't have direct experience in."[29]

However, the data belie this argument. The evidence indicates that angels tend to invest in industries they know and reject those they do not understand because information about an industry gives them confidence and mitigates their perceptions of risk.[30] Stated another way, software people invest in software companies, retail people invest in retail businesses, and real estate people invest in real estate businesses because they see investments in the industries that they know as less risky than investments in industries that are new to them.[31]

The data from the Entrepreneurship in the United States Assessment shows that business angels have an average of 9.2 years of experience working in the industries in which they invest. Moreover, other studies show that the number of years of experience that angel investors have in the industry in which the investment was made *is positively correlated* with their returns on the investments.[32]

The industry distribution of angel investments raises an important question about how angels could be responsible for recycling money from old industries to new industries. If angels focus their investments on industries that they know (which the data show); if high-performing start-ups are concentrated in high-technology-intensive industries (which the data show); and if angels make most of their investments locally (which the data show), then how do angels in places with a lot of old economy companies transform their local economies *and* make money from angel investing at the same time? If the angels in these places invest in new industries, like biotechnology and computer software, their performance will suffer because they lack experience in those industries. But if they invest in old industries, like steel and autos, their performance also will suffer because young companies in those industries tend not to perform very well. So are angels in these old economy places just philanthropists who are willing to earn a low return on investment to make their communities better places or are they not really transforming their local economies as the experts claim they are?

ANGELS' INDUSTRY PREFERENCES MIRROR THOSE OF FRIENDS-AND-FAMILY INVESTORS

Many observers claim that angel investors focus their investments on a narrower set of high-growth, high-tech industries than other types of informal investors. However, the data don't indicate that angels invest in a *narrower* set of industries than friends-and-family investors. Although angels are less likely than friends-and-family investors to invest in construction, professional and technical service, administrative support, and accommodation and food businesses, they are more likely than friends-and-family investors to invest in wholesale trade, utilities, information, finance, insurance, and real estate businesses. In short, angels don't seem to be any more focused on particular industries than friends-and-family investors.

Data from other sources also is consistent with this pattern. The Global Entrepreneurship Monitor data show that over recent years, 42.5 percent of the angel investments were made in consumer products, 35 percent were made in business services; 20 percent were made in transformative industries, and 2.5 percent were made in extractive industries. In comparison, 43.2 percent of friends-and-family investments were made in consumer products, 15.8 percent were made in business services, 33.6 percent were made in transformative industries, and 7.4 percent were made in the extractive industries. Thus, these data show that angels are more likely than friends and family to invest in business services and are less likely to invest in extractive and transformative industries, but that angel investments aren't "narrower" in industry scope than those of friends and family.

Moreover, in comparison to venture capitalists, business angels are much less industry specialized.[33] The data show that from 1990 through 2004, 81 percent of all venture capital dollars were invested in just five industries: computer hardware, computer software (including the Internet), semiconductors and other electronics, communication, and biotechnology, and 73 percent of recipient companies operated in these industries.[34] Thus, business angels invest in a much wider range of industries than venture capitalists, who *are* concentrated in the high-growth, high-tech sectors of the economy.

START-UPS THAT RECEIVE ANGEL FUNDING ARE OLDER AND MORE DEVELOPED THAN CONVENTIONAL WISDOM SUGGESTS

The conventional wisdom is that business angels invest in new companies at the earliest stages of their development and differ from venture capitalists precisely because they make most of their investments at the seed and start-up stage.[35] A quick glance at some of the books and articles about angel investing shows the following claims:

- Angels prefer to invest at the seed or start-up stage, and most angel investments occur at those stages.[36]
- Many angel investments are made in companies that are less than one year old, and most occur in companies that are less than two years old.[37]
- Most of the companies that receive angel money are less than one year old at the time of first financing.[38]
- Most of the companies that receive angel investments do not yet have revenue.[39]

Once again, however, the data from the Entrepreneurship in the United States Assessment show a different pattern. A whopping 64.6 percent of investments made by angel investors are cash flow positive, and almost half of the businesses (48.4 percent) are viewed by the investors as being "established companies" at the time of investment (see Table 6.3). Only 35.5 percent of angel investments are made in the pre-revenue companies that angels are believed to invest in. And this is not a function of the businesses to which angels lend money as opposed to buying shares. The numbers are very similar if we restrict the examination to companies that receive an equity investment from business angels.

Similar patterns are seen in the data from the 2003 Federal Reserve Survey of Small Business Finances. Only 15 percent of the small businesses that received an angel investment in the previous 12 months were less than 10 years old. Moreover, the odds that an informal investment is an angel investment increase with the age of a business. The Fed data show that only 2.3 percent of the informal equity investments received in the previous 12 months by small firms less than five years

TABLE 6.3.   The Status of Businesses Receiving Angel Investments at the Time of the Investment

Business Status at the Time of Investment	Share of Angel Investments
No Revenue	35.5%
Positive Cash Flow	16.2%
Established Company	48.4%

Source: Created from data contained in the Entrepreneurship in the United States Assessment and Reynolds, P. 2004. *Entrepreneurship in the United States Assessment.* Miami, FL: Florida International University.

old were angel investments, but 7.4 percent of the informal equity investments in all small businesses were angel investments.

What about venture capitalists? Do angels make earlier stage investments than venture capitalists? The answer is yes, but not by as much as many people think. The National Science Foundation reports that in 2004, 612 of the 2,578 companies that received venture capital were either at the seed or the start-up stage at the time they received the investment.[40] That is, 23.7 percent of venture capital deals occur at the seed or start-up stage. Data from the Entrepreneurship in the United States Assessment indicates that 35.5 percent of angel investments occur at the seed or start-up stage.[41]

PORTFOLIO FIRM CHARACTERISTICS

What do the companies that angels put their money into look like? This is a question that many entrepreneurs, business angels, and policy makers would like to have answered. Entrepreneurs want to figure out whether their companies fit the "angel investment profile." Angels want to see whether they are targeting similar kinds of companies as other angel investors. And policy makers want to know whether angels are financing the high-potential, job-creating start-ups that they are believed to support. The answer to the question might surprise you. The kinds of businesses that *most* angels invest in don't look all that impressive.

The 2003 Federal Reserve's Survey of Small Business Finances shows that the typical business less than five years of age that received an informal equity investment in the previous year had sales of only $200,000, employment of seven, and profits of $14,000. For businesses of any age (the average age was 13.3 years), the numbers for the typical firm were sales of $435,000, employment of seven, and profits of $7,500. Moreover, a study of companies financed by informal investors in Canada showed that angel-backed companies had revenues only 16 percent higher, on average, than companies financed by friends-and-family investors.[42]

A surprisingly large number of angel-backed businesses are home-based businesses. Data from a special tabulation of the Survey of Business Owners, conducted by the U.S. Census, indicates that 9 percent of new employer firms with external equity investment are home-based,[43] whereas the data from the Kauffman Firm Survey show that 17.7 percent of the businesses that received such an investment in their first year of operations operated out of someone's home.

Even though many observers argue that companies need to have a proprietary competitive advantage to receive an angel investment,[44] the data from the Kauffman Firm Survey indicate that the founders of one out of every five businesses that received an external equity investment in their first year of operations (19.2 percent) *don't believe* that their businesses have a competitive advantage of any kind.

Many experts explain that angels are seeking to invest in companies that have a patent, trade secret, or other proprietary competitive advantage that can serve as a barrier to competition.[45] However, the reality is that many companies get angel financing even if they have no intellectual property to speak of. The data from the Kauffman Firm Survey indicate that only 14.1 percent of the businesses that received an external equity investment in their first year of operation have a patent; only 15.5 percent have a copyright; and only 33.3 percent have a trademark.

Companies that make products and sell them to other businesses are more likely to receive angel investments. The data from the Kauffman Firm Survey shows that 69.1 percent of businesses that received an external equity investment in their first year of operation provide a product whereas 66.7 percent provide a service. In contrast, only 52.8 percent of all start-ups responding to the survey make a product while 82.8 percent provide a service.

The Kauffman Firm Survey data also indicate that 56 percent of sales of companies that received an external equity investment in their first year of operation went to businesses while only 39.7 percent of sales went to consumers. By comparison, only 46.6 percent of the sales of all start-ups that responded to the survey go to businesses while 48.8 percent go to individuals. Similarly, data from the Survey of Business Owners indicate that 50 percent of the young employer companies that have received an external equity investment sell to businesses while only 38.4 percent sell to consumers.

CHARACTERISTICS OF THE OWNERS OF COMPANIES THAT RECEIVE EXTERNAL EQUITY INVESTMENTS

What do the entrepreneurs who get angel money look like? From several sources we can piece together a description of the demographics of the founders of businesses that receive external equity investment.

By-and-large, this description indicates that the individuals who receive external equity investments look different from their typical description in the media.

The Demographics of Who Gets Angel Money:
A Caution for Policy Makers

One of the striking things about books, articles, blogs, and Web sites on angel investing is an absence of some very basic demographics from their copious descriptions of the characteristics of the entrepreneurs who get angel money. These sources tend not to say anything about the race or gender of the entrepreneurs that angels finance. Perhaps this omission is accidental—the authors don't think race and gender are very interesting—or perhaps it is intentional because the numbers on race and gender suggest that women and minorities are under-represented among the entrepreneurs who receive external equity investments.

Male-led businesses are much more likely than female-led start-ups to get external equity investments.[46] Data from the Census Bureau's Survey of Business Owners showed that only 11 percent of the firms that were five years old or younger and had received external equity investments had a female primary owner[47] compared to 25 percent of all businesses of the same vintage.[48]

Minorities are also underrepresented among the founders of companies that receive external investment.[49] Only 3.8 percent of businesses that have received external equity investments have a Hispanic primary owner compared to 6.5 percent of all businesses of the same age, and only 1.4 percent of those businesses have a Black primary owner compared to 4.5 percent of all businesses of the same vintage.[50]

The patterns are similar for brand-new firms. The Kauffman Firm Study indicated that 90.4 percent of the primary owners of the businesses that received an outside equity investment from a non-relative in their first year of operation were White and 3.6 percent were Black. In contrast, 84.6 percent of the primary owners of all businesses begun in 2004 were White and 7.5 percent were Black.

These patterns suggest an important caution to policy makers who are thinking of providing a stimulus to angel investing. Any efforts to increase the total number of companies that receive angel funding without targeting women and minority entrepreneurs would likely benefit White men disproportionately. While this might occur just because White men are more likely to start companies that need external capital, this is beside the point for elected officials. Measures of which entrepreneurs benefited from an angel investment stimulus will show a greater percentage increase for White male entrepreneurs than other categories, which won't look good politically. Perhaps this is why the race and gender of the entrepreneurs who receive angel money aren't discussed very much. That information isn't going to help make the case to elected policy makers for angel investment subsidies.

It's Middle-Aged Entrepreneurs Who Receive Most of the Angel Investments

The popular perception is that angels favor young entrepreneurs who are developing the latest, new, new thing. This suggests that companies led by twenty-something-year-old entrepreneurs are the most likely businesses to get angel money—or at least get a large portion of it. However, again the popular perception is at odds with reality. The data from the Census Bureau's Survey of Business Owners shows that middle-aged entrepreneurs receive most of the external equity investments made in this country. As Table 6.4 shows, over two thirds of the entrepreneurs whose businesses had received an external equity investment and were less than six years old in 2002 were between the ages of 35 and 54 years, and only 0.05 percent were less than 25 years old. Moreover, young entrepreneurs are actually *less* likely to get angel money than other age groups. The proportion of entrepreneurs 25 and older that received an external equity investment is forty times as large as the proportion of entrepreneurs under 25 that did so.[51]

TABLE 6.4. Age Distribution of the Primary Owners of Businesses with External Equity Investment

Age Category of the Primary Owner	Share of Businesses Receiving External Equity Investment
Under 25	0.05%
25 to 34	9.92%
35 to 44	33.40%
45 to 54	34.43%
55 to 64	17.07%
65 and Over	5.13%

Source: Created from data contained in a special tabulation of the Survey of Business Owners of the U.S. Census.

Education Matters

One of the surprising things about the entrepreneurs whom angels back is how educated they are. Even though most experts don't write that angels screen potential investments for educated founders, and few angels report that founder education is an important selection criterion, the data show that founder education has a large effect on the odds that a business will receive an external equity investment. As Figure 6.2 shows, almost two thirds of the primary owners of the businesses that have received an external equity investment have a college degree or greater education, a much higher proportion than is the case for start-ups in general.

Similar patterns can be seen in other surveys. The Kauffman Firm Survey data show that 57.4 percent of the primary owners of the businesses that received an external equity investment in their first year of operation had a college degree or more education, compared to 50.6 percent of the founders of all businesses started in 2004.

Angels Are Interested in Experienced Entrepreneurs

Many studies show that the entrepreneurial and industry experience of the team approaching angels for money is an important factor in the angels' investment decision.[52] Business angels are said to prefer

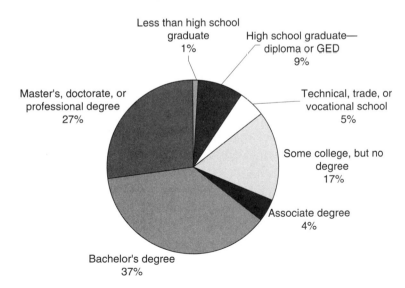

FIGURE 6.2. Distribution of the Highest Level of Education of the Primary Owners of Businesses with External Equity Investment. *Source:* Created from data contained in a special tabulation of the Survey of Business Owners of the U.S. Census.

experienced entrepreneurs and to reject investment opportunities when the founders don't have enough entrepreneurial experience. In fact, several studies show that the entrepreneur's track record at creating successful start-ups is one of the most important factors in attracting angels to their investments.[53] The data from the Kauffman Firm Survey supports this position, showing that 60.2 percent of the primary owners of businesses that have received an external equity investment have started at least one prior business.

Business angels are also looking for entrepreneurs with experience in the industry in which they are starting their businesses.[54] As one angel said, "The team should have industry experience and be able to execute its business plan."[55] In fact, one expert advised would-be angels, "In evaluating the management, consider above all whether the entrepreneur and her team possess direct experience in the industry of the proposed venture."[56] The data from the Kauffman Firm Survey are consistent with this view. Almost 89.3 percent of the entrepreneurs who founded a business that received an external equity investment in its first year of operation had at least one year of work experience in the industry in which the business was started, and 50.6 percent had more than ten years of experience.

You Don't Need a Team to Get Angel Money

While the data support the received wisdom about entrepreneurial experience, they don't support the commonly held view that angels tend to back companies founded by a "balanced founding team"—a team made up of people with complementary skills.[57] In fact, the conventional wisdom that you need a team at all to get external equity is probably mistaken. The Kauffman Firm Survey finds that 39.4 percent of the new businesses that receive an external equity investment in their first year of operation are founded by only one person. Moreover, "teams" of entrepreneurs that get such financing are fairly rare. Only 33 percent of new ventures that get an external equity investment in their first year of operation are founded by three or more people.[58]

Invested in the Business

Another misperception about angel investing appears to be the belief that angels won't finance businesses unless the founders have a significant financial and personal investment in the business.[59] Founder investment of time and money, the argument goes, ensures that the entrepreneur is committed to the development of the business.[60]

However, the data show that the founders of businesses that get external equity are far less invested in those businesses than is commonly believed. A surprisingly large number of entrepreneurs obtain such financing with no or minimal equity investment of their own. The data from the Kauffman Firm Survey reveal that in 25.5 percent of the external-equity-financed businesses in which the founders had put in money, the primary owner-founder's combined investment was less than $10,000. The founders of these companies aren't on the hook for the business's debt, either. Only 29 percent of the owners of companies that received external equity had to pledge personal assets to secure loans for their businesses.[61]

The patterns are similar for the founders' investment of time. Many of the founders of businesses that have received external equity financing are not dependent on the businesses for their income. According to data from the Census Bureau's Survey of Business Owners, for only 54.8 percent of the companies less than six years old that received an external equity investment was the business the founder's primary source of income. Moreover, the founders of young companies that have received an external equity investment don't put a great deal of time into their businesses. According to data from the Census Bureau, in 32.6 percent of the businesses with external equity five years old or less, the founder worked less than twenty hours per week on the business, and in *half* of the businesses, the founder worked forty hours per week or less.

The Personal Qualities of the Entrepreneurs

Many books and articles about angel investing concentrate on the personal characteristics that angels look for in the entrepreneurs they back. While not all of the books and articles focus on the same characteristics, you'll come up with the following list (or one a lot like it) if you put together the characteristics identified by different authors. Business angels are said to seek entrepreneurs that display these traits:

- Passion[62]
- Persuasiveness[63]
- Confidence[64]
- Perseverance[65]
- Leadership[66]

- Self-Awareness[67]
- Vision[68]
- Flexibility[69]
- Honesty[70]
- Openness to Others[71]
- Team Orientation[72]
- Coachability[73]

Before the entrepreneurs among you start trying to figure out whether you have these characteristics, it's important to point out that there is no scientific evidence that angels actually *select* entrepreneurs to finance on the basis of these characteristics. In fact, even the argument that they do is dubious. Earlier we presented a list of seventeen factors that angel investors consider in making their investment decisions that came from combining the top ten factors identified in the research conducted by Sudek, Osnabrugge, and Robinson, and Hill and Powers. At most, only two of the psychological attributes that angels are purported to look for—passion, which could be the same thing as entrepreneurial enthusiasm, and honesty, which could be the same thing as trustworthiness—make the list.

Moreover, it is hard to see how these criteria could differentiate business angels from other types of investors in start-up companies. After all, what type of investor—or anyone for that matter—wants to support a passionless, unpersuasive, unconfident, visionless, dishonest, closed-minded, self-centered, uncoachable entrepreneur who is lacking in perseverance, leadership, self-awareness, and flexibility? If you're an entrepreneur and that list describes you, I'll bet that even your parents won't finance your company.

KEY FACTS TO REMEMBER	
Proportion of angel investments made in retail businesses	25 percent
Proportion of angel investments made in personal service businesses	12.5 percent
Sales of the typical business less than five years old with an informal equity investment	$200,000
Employment of the typical business less than five years old with an informal equity investment	7

Proportion of businesses that received an external investment in the first year of operation that have a patent	14.1 percent
Proportion of businesses that received an external investment in the first year of operation that have don't have a competitive advantage	19.2 percent
Proportion of businesses that received an external equity investment in their first five years of operation whose primary owner is female	11 percent
Proportion of businesses that received an external equity investment in their first five years of operation whose primary owner is Black	1.4 percent
Proportion of businesses that received an external equity investment in their first five years of operation whose primary owner is between the ages of 35 and 54	67.8 percent
Proportion of businesses that received an external equity investment in their first five years of operation whose primary owner has a college degree or more education	64 percent
Proportion of businesses that received an external investment in their first year of operation whose founders have at least one year of work experience in the industry	89.3 percent
Proportion of businesses that received an external investment in their first year of operation whose founders have started at least one prior business	60.2 percent
Proportion of businesses that received an external investment in their first year of operation that were started by three or more people	33 percent
Proportion of the companies that received an external investment whose founders had to pledge personal assets to secure a loan	29 percent
Proportion of the companies that received an external investment in their first year of operation with a combined founder investment of $10,000 or less	25.5 percent

(*continued*)

(*continued*)

Proportion of businesses that received an external equity investment in their first five years of operation that are the primary owner's main source of income	54.8 percent
Proportion of businesses that received an external equity investment in their first five years of operation on which the primary owner works twenty hours per week or less	32.6 percent

IN CONCLUSION

The typical start-up that receives financing from an angel investor doesn't look like the mythical business that the media makes it out to be. In fact, it's hard to even know what that mythical business is because angels disagree much more about the characteristics that they are looking for than most observers report. In particular, the consensus that angels finance "high-growth" businesses masks a complete lack of agreement on what a "high-growth business" is.

Despite the often repeated statement that angels differ from friends-and-family investors because they focus on high-tech businesses in large, high-margin, low capital-intensity industries, the data on the actual investments made by angels reveals that they invest in as wide a range of businesses as friends and family and put money into the retail and personal service businesses that experts say they won't finance. In reality, angels invest in the industries in which they have experience.

The companies that receive external equity investments are older and more developed than is commonly believed. They are not particularly high performing and include a surprisingly large number of home-based businesses and a surprisingly small number of companies with intellectual property. But there are some differences between companies that receive external equity and companies that do not. Two of the major distinctions are the tendency to provide a product rather than a service and the tendency to sell to businesses rather than to consumers.

The entrepreneurs who receive external equity financing also look different from the picture that is often presented in the media. They are older, more educated, less likely to be part of a team, and less heavily invested in their businesses than is commonly portrayed. And—policy makers take note—they are disproportionately White men. But they probably don't differ from other entrepreneurs on the basis of the psychological characteristics that angels are said to consider heavily in their investment decisions.

SEVEN

How Does the Angel Investment Process Work?

Business angels finance only some of the companies they could potentially invest in. So understanding how angels learn about deals and why and how they select some for further investigation and funding is important for entrepreneurs, angels, and policy makers. Knowing the patterns in the angel investment process helps entrepreneurs to raise money, angels to make investment decisions efficiently and effectively, and policy makers to make good policy.

While many authors have provided descriptions of the angel investment process, the standard discussion is airbrushed to show that angel investors are careful decision makers who make wise choices about which companies are worthy of their investment of time and money. Unfortunately, this description doesn't reflect the reality of how the angel investment process actually works. This chapter describes the angel investment process like it really is. Rather than recounting the stories told by the angels and the experts who often rationalize a very messy process, it relies on the evidence. And the picture it presents is very different from what you may have read elsewhere. To see what I mean, take a look at the data.

DEAL ORIGINATION

Let's start with how angels hear about potential investment opportunities. The standard explanation is that many entrepreneurs get in contact with angels by networking.[1] Most angels, this argument holds, generate deal flow proactively by attending events, speaking to groups of entrepreneurs, writing articles or books, creating Web sites, meeting with service providers, and otherwise networking.[2] However, this explanation reflects more of the tendency for business books to provide practical advice whenever possible, than it does the actual deal origination process. (It's hard to tell your readers that their chances of getting their business ideas in front of angels are very slim if they don't already know the business angels and don't have any friends or family members that know them.)

While some entrepreneurs find angels by networking, it happens a lot less often than the experts tell you. Most angels don't invest in businesses referred to them by professional service providers, like lawyers and accountants.[3] Few angels proactively search for deals,[4] and they rarely get them through electronic networks or other organizations.[5] Instead, most angels get their deals passively from their friends and family, with one study showing that 57 percent of the investments made by business angels came from one of these two sources.[6]

Many angels do not accept unsolicited deals but only accept referrals from people they know and trust,[7] in some cases screening deals on the basis of whether they know the entrepreneur or the person who introduced him.[8] Even if an angel will consider a deal brought to him by someone other than a friend or family member, research shows that the probability of an investment occurring is lower than for a deal referred by a friend.[9] It might not give you a warm and fuzzy feeling to learn that your chances of getting an angel investment depend a lot on whether you or your friends and family already know some business angels, but that's reality. At least if you know this, you can gauge how much time you want to spend on the networking activities that many experts recommend. While those activities might increase your chances of getting angel money, they won't increase them as much as received wisdom suggests. And you might be better off devoting your scarce time to something else.

DEAL EVALUATION

Once angels learn about investment opportunities, they need to evaluate them, either explicitly or implicitly, before investing. So how do angels evaluate potential deals? The typical answer is carefully and thoughtfully. But the reality is a lot messier.

High Return Expectations?

One of the myths about angel investing is that typical angels seek opportunities that offer a high rate of return to compensate them for the risk of investing in start-up companies.[10] The standard description has angels looking for deals that offer a clear path to achieving a good financial rate of return and rejecting those that don't offer a return commensurate with the risk involved.[11] However, in reality, many angels don't pay attention to potential returns when making their investment decisions, and when they do, they don't have the high return expectations that most observers think that they have.

Many Angels Don't Consider Expected Returns

Many observers claim that the typical business angel pays careful attention to the potential returns from investing in private companies. Take, for example, the following statement made by one expert: "Reading the financial section thoroughly...they do their own calculations, trying to discern how much money can be made."[12]

However, many angels do not consider expected financial returns when making their investment decisions and instead look for companies they believe will be successful, assuming that they will make money if the company succeeds. For instance, one angel who participated in focus groups on angel investing sponsored by the Federal Reserve explained that he does not start out with a return expectation but rather a hope that the entrepreneur will build a successful company.[13]

More quantitative data also support the view that most angels don't focus on expected returns when making their investment decisions. In fact, one study showed that only 32 percent of business angels *even calculated* an expected financial return on their last investment.[14]

Even among angels who *do* consider expected returns, many of them don't care as much about financial returns as other types of investors, perhaps because they don't have a fiduciary responsibility for other people's money, like venture capitalists.[15] And angels think more about nonfinancial factors than VCs. Studies show that as many as half of all angels accept lower financial returns than institutional investors because they derive other types of benefits from investing in private companies, such as the opportunity to be involved with a growing business, to create local jobs, or to achieve a social goal.[16]

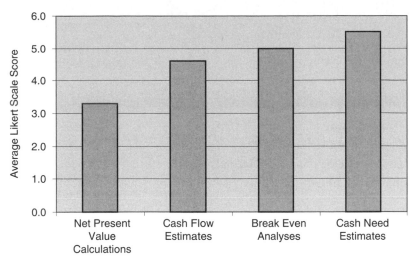

FIGURE 7.1. Importance of Different Evaluation Tools to Business Angels. *Source:* Created from data contained in Wiltbank, R. 2006. *At the Individual Level: Outlining Angel Investing in the United States.* Downloaded from www.willamette.edu/~wiltbank/AtTheIndividualLevel7.pdf.

Many Angels Don't Calculate Net Present Value

When angels use financial analysis tools to evaluate potential investments, they tend not to look at net present value calculations but instead focus on measures of the ventures' financial performance. (Net present value calculations estimate how much an investment is worth today, given information about the timing of cash inflows and outflows and the desired rate of return.) In fact, as Figure 7.1 shows, one study of angel investors found that they consider net present value calculations to be the *least important* analysis tool and calculation of the ventures' cash needs to be the *most important*.[17]

Angels Have Low Investment Multiples

Many observers claim that typical angels expect to earn a high multiple on their investments in private companies. (Returns on angel investments are often expressed as a multiple of the invested capital—an "X" times return.[18]) Although one author writes, "Most angels hope to quintuple their money in five years,"[19] others say that angels target returns of ten times, twenty times, or even thirty times their invested capital.[20]

These higher return expectations make angel investing sound exciting and sophisticated—which may be the reason they are so frequently

TABLE 7.1.   Proportion of Angels with Different 10-year Expected
Investment Multiples

Ten-Year Expected Return	Share of Angel Investments
20 Times Invested Capital	21.2%
10 Times Invested Capital	24.2%
5 Times Invested Capital	12.1%
2 Times Invested Capital	18.2%
Between 1 and 2 Times Invested Capital	3.0%
Amount of Capital Invested or Less	21.3%

Source: Created from data contained in the Entrepreneurship in the
United States Assessment and Reynolds, P. 2004. *Entrepreneurship in the
United States Assessment.* Miami, FL: Florida International University.

presented—but they don't jibe with the data. The majority of angels
don't expect to earn ten, twenty, or thirty times their money. As Table
7.1 shows, the typical (median) angel investor expects to earn five times
his invested capital, and only 45.4 percent of angel investors expect to
earn a ten times or higher return, with 21.3 percent of angel investors
not expecting anything more than the return of their invested capital.

Moreover, the return expectations of business angels are actually quite similar to those of friends-and-family investors. Analysis of
the data from the Entrepreneurship in the United States Assessment
reveals that there is no (statistical) difference between the expected
returns of angel investors and other types of informal investors. Given
that other studies have shown that financial rewards are less important
to business angels than to venture capitalists,[21] it appears that angels
are more like friends and family than venture capitalists when it comes
to the amount of money that they expect to make from their investments in start-ups.

Angels Expect Lower Rates of Return than Is Commonly Believed

By combining the expected investment multiple with the expected
time to exit, you can measure the investment's expected rate of return.
(The rate of return is an important measure of financial performance
because a given investment multiple is better if the time to achieving
that return is shorter, and it is worse if that time horizon is longer.) Of
course, to figure out the expected return for an investment portfolio,
you need to consider the proportion of investments that will generate

those returns, which, according to the Angel Capital Association, is only one-in-ten for angel investments.[22]

Many observers say that typical angels target as much as a 100 percent per year rate of return on their investments.[23] The logic is that if only one-in-ten angel investments succeeds (returns any money at all) and all investments are of equal size,[24] then an investors needs to target a return on each of his investments of 112 percent per year to earn a higher return on his whole portfolio than he could get by putting his money into a mutual fund that matched the Standard & Poor's 500 (11.2 percent per year return over the decade ending when this book was written). (If a smaller proportion of angel investments succeed than the one-in-ten rate that most observers claim, then the rate of return target needs to be even higher.)

However, the expected rate of return on the typical angel investment is nowhere near 112 percent per year. The data from the Entrepreneurship in the United States Assessment show it to be approximately 23 percent for a representative sample of angel investors. That is, given the expected success rate and time horizon for angel investments, the typical angel expects a rate of return that is less than he could earn by putting his money into a stock market index fund.

The Myth That Angels Make Thoughtful Investment Decisions

Many observers claim that angels make their investment decisions carefully and thoughtfully. According to the typical explanation, angels sift through a large number of deals, carefully evaluating them on key parameters and selecting only the best ones. Typical angels are said to consider carefully an entrepreneur's business plan, looking at how well written and realistic it is.[25] And they are believed to consider thoughtfully the assumptions behind the pricing, salaries, sales, and other numbers.[26]

Typical angels are also said to evaluate the market opportunity carefully, considering its size and the reasons why potential customers would be willing to buy the company's product or service. They are believed to examine the company's business model, considering how the business will make money,[27] the profit margins on the product or service,[28] the power that suppliers have over the company,[29] and any regulatory issues that it faces. They are thought to examine whether the business has a competitive advantage and, if it does, what that advantage is,[30] as well as the strength of barriers to imitation and the business's unique qualities (e.g., technology, people, products).[31]

Typical angels are also said to evaluate a venture's management team, identifying the key decision makers in the company and examining how they make decisions.[32] They are also thought to consider the entrepreneur's knowledge of the market, decide whether the management team has the expertise to build the business,[33] and identify any needed skills that the founders lack.[34] Typical angels are said to look at the financial, career, and physical backgrounds of the founders and management team.[35] They are believed to look at how much money the founding team has invested in the business[36] and are thought to evaluate whether they can trust the entrepreneur.

Finally, typical angels are said consider the company's exit strategy[37] and the valuation of the company suggested by the entrepreneur.[38]

However, in actual fact, many angels do not make decisions this carefully. First, several business angels report that they do not engage in a very scientific process to evaluate new ventures. As one business angel said, "It's about 70 percent just gut feeling and 30 percent financial analysis."[39] Another business angel said that investing involves "putting your finger in the air and hoping that the wind is blowing in the right direction."[40]

Second, studies confirm that angel decision making is subject to a number of errors and biases. One study of 124 business angels found that they engage in representativeness—the tendency to generalize from a single example rather than look at patterns of data—and overconfidence in making investment decisions.[41] Angels' decisions also are very much dependent on the timing of their meetings with entrepreneurs. For instance, if the angels recently have had a successful exit, then the probability of their investment is higher than under other circumstances.[42] Angels' decisions are also swayed by the personal qualities of the entrepreneurs seeking money.[43] For instance, several studies report that one of the primary reasons that angels don't invest in new ventures is that they don't like the entrepreneur[44] or the personal impression that he makes.[45] Finally, efforts by an angel to get to know an entrepreneur during the due diligence process leads to the creation of a social relationship between the two parties that increases the odds that investor will finance the business.[46]

Third, angels often make investment decisions without gathering adequate information. One study found that only 15 percent of business angels do "extensive" research on the sector in which a company they are evaluating for investment operates.[47] Other authors report that many angel investors tend to make very fast decisions on the basis of executive summaries of business plans and without detailed due diligence.[48]

Fourth, most business angels make their decisions on their own, an approach that has been shown to lead to poor decisions about investing in new companies. Approximately 84 percent of angels make their investment decisions without input from others, relying primarily on their own judgment rather than that of co-investors. Moreover, the average angel investor talks to fewer people about a prospective investment than the average venture capitalist and makes investment decisions in only two-thirds the time.[49]

Fifth, business angels often make their investment decisions on the basis of how involved they can become with the companies in which they invest;[50] they are more likely to invest in businesses that want their assistance than those that don't, even when the businesses that don't want their assistance offer better potential financial returns than those that do.[51]

The Myth That What Business Plans Say Matters a Lot to Business Angels

Many observers argue that an entrepreneur's business plan is important to getting financing from business angels and that having a weak business plan is one of the main reasons that angels reject potential investments.[52] Angels, the argument goes, want to see a business plan that clearly lays out the business opportunity,[53] shows whether the entrepreneur is making realistic assumptions,[54] demonstrates an accurate understanding of what it takes to build a business,[55] provides sufficient information for the angel to make an investment decision,[56] explains the value of the venture opportunity,[57] shows the entrepreneur's professionalism,[58] and demonstrates how much effort the entrepreneur is putting into the development of the business.[59]

However, the reality is that business plans are less important to business angels than most experts suggest. One study sampled accredited angel investors who appear in the database of a consulting firm because they have made the kinds of angel investments in high-growth companies that many people write about; the findings showed that 35 percent would make an early stage angel investment *without* looking at the entrepreneur's business plan.[60] Other studies show that 25 percent of angel investors would invest without seeing a business plan first.[61] If 25 to 35 percent of business angels would invest in start-ups without seeing a business plan, then business plans can't be as important to angel investors as many observers say.

Moreover, some business angels indicate that business plans are not very important because the information those plans contain is too inaccurate to be useful[62] and because the financial plans presented by entrepreneurs are invariably positive.[63] As one angel explains, "At this stage detailed financials are not worth the paper they are written on."[64] In short, it appears that the importance of business plans to angels has been overemphasized.

The Myth That Angels Conduct Extensive Due Diligence

Most books and articles explain that conducting due diligence is an important part of angel investing and that business angels invest a great deal of time in this activity. As one observer writes, "To judge the viability of a prospective early-stage direct investment, the veteran investor will require numerous face-to-face meetings with the entrepreneur; thorough reviews of the business plan; interviews with management, customers, suppliers and competitors; and counsel from relevant industry experts."[65]

In conducting due diligence, angels are said to investigate many different aspects of the business opportunity and the entrepreneur pursuing it. This includes evaluating the entrepreneur's knowledge of markets, customers, and technology; his capabilities to generate sales, manage a company, and develop products; his integrity, commitment, and passion,[66] and his goals for the company.[67] It also includes evaluating the market (its size, growth rate, concentration, pricing, segmentation, and customer preferences); the company's business model, product or service, marketing plan, strategy, technology, intellectual property position, and stage of development. Finally, it includes evaluating the company's financial records, financial projections, valuation, capital requirements, and exit strategy.[68]

A composite of how different authors have described the prototypical way that angels do this is as follows:

1. Look at the entrepreneur's business plan.
2. Meet with the entrepreneur.
3. Talk to other potential investors, industry contacts, employees of the company, and its customers and suppliers.
4. Scope out competitors.
5. Talk to patent attorneys and other subject matter experts.
6. Show the product or technology to technical experts and potential customers.
7. Check out references.
8. Conduct background checks.[69]

However, the reality is that most angels conduct very little due diligence. Studies show that the typical angel spends about twenty hours on due diligence for a potential investment.[70] Because approximately one third of the due diligence effort is spent on the market and customers, one third on the technology, 22 percent on the competition, and 12 percent on references,[71] this means that the typical angel spends 6.6 hours on the market and customers, 6.6 hours on the technology, 4.4 hours on the competition, and 2.4 hours on reference checking.

The amount of due diligence that angels conduct is significantly less than that of venture capitalists.[72] One study showed that 89 percent of venture capitalists, but only 50 percent of angels, conducted "extensive" due diligence. Moreover, only 2 percent of venture capitalists but 20 percent of angels performed *no* due diligence on investments that they made.[73]

Business angels also are much less likely than venture capitalists to meet with entrepreneurs in whose companies they are considering investing. Only one third of business angels, compared to two thirds of venture capitalists, met more than five times with the entrepreneurs in whom they were considering investing. And one study showed that the average angel meets with an entrepreneur 5.4 times before investing compared to 9.5 times for venture capitalists.[74]

Business angels also conduct relatively little reference checking. Between 54 and 66 percent of angels get no references other than those the entrepreneurs provide[75] compared to only 6 percent of venture capitalists. And only 8 percent of business angels talk to more than two references, leading to an average of one non-entrepreneur-supplied reference for investments made by angels as opposed to 4.2 for investments made by venture capitalists.[76]

The Myth of Selectivity

The received wisdom is that typical angels are very selective investors. They are thought to receive a large number of business plans from interested entrepreneurs and to winnow them down, carefully selecting the 4 or 5 percent that meet their investment criteria. They then meet with the entrepreneurs, discuss the opportunities with them, conduct due diligence, and invest in 1 or 2 percent of the business opportunities that were initially presented to them.

While this pattern may be true for a small number of business angels, particularly those who are part of organized angel groups, the typical angel is not that selective. The Federal Reserve Survey of Small

Business Finances provides information on the number of companies that sought informal equity financing and the proportion that subsequently received it. Of those that tried to raise this money, the Federal Reserve researchers found that one third were successful.[77] Of course, that's good news for entrepreneurs. It means that they are much more likely to get money from angels than received wisdom suggests.

The Myth of the Active Investor

Most people think that angels are active investors in start-ups. This view is understandable given the description of angel investing that is provided in most books and articles.[78] Take the following statement in one book: "Business angels generally prefer more personal and active involvement in their investments than venture capitalists."[79] Or consider another expert's view: "Angels like to be involved in their companies beyond sitting on an advisory board or board of directors."[80] Still another observer wrote, "It requires significant time commitments since the investments are more active than passive."[81]

While some angels are indeed active investors, most are not. As Chapter 5 indicated, a minority sit on the boards of the companies in which they invest. Moreover, most business angels don't have time to get actively involved with their portfolio companies. Unlike venture capitalists, whose job is investing in start-ups, most business angels have full-time jobs at the same time they make angel investments. In fact, as we saw in Chapter 3, only 34.6 percent of business angels are retired or out of the labor force.

Also, when surveyed by researchers, business angels don't report spending much time working with their portfolio companies. One observer writes that angel investors spend as little as one hour each week on their investments, while a survey of angel investors revealed that only one third of angels were active, hands-on investors.[82]

In fact, when measured on a per venture basis, angels spend very little time on the companies in which they invest, too little to be considered anything close to active investors. One study of accredited angel investors found that they spend an average of twelve hours per week on investing in start-ups, of which only 30 percent is spent on businesses in which they have already invested. This works out to 3.6 hours per week on post-investment involvement with portfolio companies. But because the average investor in this study was invested in 5.16 companies at a time,[83] each angel averaged 41.9 minutes per week per venture! And given that the angels reported that the number one aspect of their involvement was monitoring the venture's financial performance, it is hard to see how average angels could be considered actively involved in helping the entrepreneurs in whose businesses they have invested.

Moreover, it is even hard to find a subset of angels who provide much assistance to the businesses in which they invest. A study by Rob Wiltbank of Willamette University indicates that the third of angels *most involved* with portfolio companies spent only twenty-eight hours per week on their ventures. This level of involvement leaves just 8.4 hours, on average, for post-investment involvement, spread across 5.16 ventures, or one hour and thirty-eight minutes per week per business.[84]

At the other end of the spectrum, the angels don't even spend enough time to take a weekly phone call from their portfolio companies. The bottom third of the sample in Wiltbank's study spent only two hours per week on their ventures.[85] That translates to a little under seven minutes per week of post-investment involvement per venture!

The patterns aren't that different if we look at what happens within angel groups. My experience with the Northcoast Angel Fund in Cleveland, Ohio, is that only about one-quarter to one-third of the members attend the group meetings, hear the entrepreneurs pitch the deals, and vote on prospective investments. An even smaller proportion of the members, probably closer to 10–15 percent, participate in due diligence on the companies in which the fund has invested. A still smaller percentage is involved in sitting on the boards of portfolio companies or in getting involved with helping the entrepreneurs build their companies. Whether these estimates are exactly right or not, the fact remains that the vast majority of the members of at least one angel fund should be considered passive investors who provide little assistance to the companies in which they invest. In short, it is hard to see how typical business angels—or for that matter, even the most involved third of business angels—are actively involved in the ventures they back.

The Myth of the Value-Added Investor

The standard view of angel investing holds that business angels provide a great deal of value to the companies in which they invest. This value, the argument goes, comes from angels' experience building successful companies, differentiates angels from friends and family, and justifies the relatively high cost of capital thought to be paid for this source of funds.[86] As one observer said, "Most investors bring much more to the table than their checkbook."[87]

Angels are reported to give business advice; provide contacts from their networks to help find strategic alliance partners, suppliers, customers, management talent, and potential board members; help entrepreneurs to structure their businesses financially and raise more money from follow-on investors; provide information about the market; assist with strategy and the development of business plans; and even provide direct operational assistance.[88] Take, for example, the following statement about the assistance that angels provide to their portfolio companies: "These investors add value beyond the money that they invest by helping to develop products and/or services and by providing advice."[89]

All of this provides a good story about angels being value-added investors. Of course, it's a story written from the angels' point of view. And it seems unlikely that most angels would 'fess up to adding little value to their portfolio companies if you asked them. Moreover, a great deal of research in psychology suggests that angels probably *believe* that they add value, even if they don't, because the act of doing something for others is almost always believed by the helper to be helpful, even when it is not. So if we want to know whether angels are adding value to the companies in which they are investing, we need to do something more than just ask angels: "Are you adding value to your portfolio companies?" or "Do you bring more than money to the companies in which you invest?"

The data don't make a very good case for the typical angel adding much value to the companies in which he invests. (Remember that this is the *typical* angel; there are certainly some value-adding angels out there.) To begin with, the typical angel doesn't spend enough time on the average portfolio company to add much value. Even if the typical angel provides very sage advice, it is hard to see how much help anyone can provide in forty-two minutes per week when some portion of that time is spending monitoring the investment through the review of monthly or quarterly financial statements. After all, monitoring the performance of their investments, not assisting the entrepreneurs, is the most frequent activity that angels engage in after making their investments. And let's not forget that one third of angels are only giving 7 minutes to each venture per week. That third doesn't even seem to have enough time to provide adequate monitoring, let alone add value.[90]

Moreover, we have some evidence that the approach of angels to their portfolio companies is less about helping others than controlling them. At least one study shows that the typical business angel is high in the psychological trait of need for dominance and wants to control how his money is used.[91] This suggests that typical angels probably are spending a good portion of the time devoted to their average portfolio company trying to find out what is happening with their money and trying to direct the entrepreneurs they have funded on how to use those funds.[92]

Second, the type of assistance that business angels typically provide to their portfolio companies is not the same as the type of assistance that the business angels themselves perceive as the most important. Figure 7.2 shows the *frequency* of different types of post-investment involvement by angels alongside data from the same survey on the *importance* of these different types of post-investment involvement. This figure clearly shows that average accredited angels don't focus their attention on the very activities they see as most valuable to their portfolio companies.

Third, what the angels perceive as the most important forms of assistance to their portfolio companies aren't the things that the entrepreneurs they back view as most important. For instance, one study found that the CEOs of start-up companies believe the most useful benefit provided by angels is advice, followed by contacts.[93] However, as Figure 7.2, shows, angels believe that providing advice is only

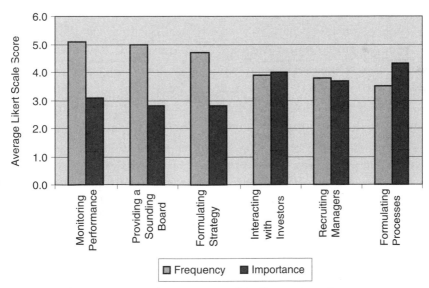

FIGURE 7.2. Importance and Frequency of Different Post-Investment Activities. *Source:* Created from data contained in Wiltbank, R. 2006. *At the Individual Level: Outlining Angel Investing in the United States.* Downloaded from www.willamette.edu/~wiltbank/AtTheIndividualLevel7.pdf.

the sixth most important thing that they do, less than two-thirds the importance of formulating processes in the organization, something that entrepreneurs don't see as very important at all.

Fourth, many angels who are willing to provide assistance actually lack the skills and capabilities to do so. Many business angels *believe* they provide important contacts to entrepreneurs by introducing them to potential executives who can fill out their management teams, to C-level managers at prospective customer firms, and to other investors who can provide additional capital.[94] However, the data don't support the position that the typical angel has a valuable enough Rolodex to help entrepreneurs build a management team or raise additional money. And studies show that venture capitalists are much more likely than business angels to be able to help entrepreneurs with these things.[95]

In fact, the typical angel doesn't help his or her portfolio companies to obtain additional capital. In a convenience survey of the highest quality business angels—those who are successful entrepreneurs involved with angel groups and worth, on average, in excess of $10 million—only a minority (29 percent) indicate that their investments received follow-on investment from anyone, and in only 12.7 percent of cases did the businesses backed by these very high-quality business angels have a follow-on investment from a venture capitalist.[96] It goes without saying that if such high-quality business angels have such a low follow-on investment rate, the typical business angel's follow-on investment rate is almost certainly even lower.

Finally, business angels are not a very good source of support for taking a company public. They are much less likely than venture capitalists to know the investment bankers who do this; and companies are rarely able to go public after investments solely by business angels.[97]

Fifth, typical business angels falsely believe that they have more experience at running companies than other types of informal investors and that this experience allows them to help entrepreneurs to manage their companies effectively.[98] While some angels no doubt have very valuable experience and probably help their portfolio companies a great deal, the *typical* angel does not. He has no more entrepreneurial experience than the typical friends-and-family investor. So why should his advice be more valuable than the advice offered by mom and dad?

Some observers have argued that even if business angels have no more experience than other investors, they are a valuable source of assistance because they don't charge for their help. Because angels are investors, the argument goes, they don't demand high fees or salaries in return for their advice, like consultants or employees do. But this argument is deceptive because angels aren't giving away their advice for free; they are being compensated with shares in the company (or interest on a loan). Leaving aside the fact that angels sometimes receive salaries for working for their portfolio companies or fees for serving on their boards and focusing only on the return on their investments, their advice can be pricey. An angel investment can cost the entrepreneur a lot more money than he would pay by the hour to consultants or to management talent in the form of salary.

In some cases, the angels' lack of capabilities and skills doesn't just keep them from helping entrepreneurs; it actually ends up hurting them. The angels with little entrepreneurial experience—the doctors and lawyers and ex-bankers—are sometimes not passive enough. They invest at the wrong price and under bad terms, and that makes the companies that they back unattractive for later investors. They might even get board seats, not because they think they can help the companies but because it gives them control or is ego gratifying. While on the board, they give advice that is ill-thought-out and ends up holding back the development of the companies.

So, on average, is the help provided by angels worth it? We don't really know because no one has ever looked at the performance of comparable companies that receive and don't receive angel money. But we can get a sense of how much value angels would need to add to companies to make their assistance worth the cost. As we saw in Chapter 5, angels take between 20 and 35 percent of the companies in which they invest. If we take the information about the probability that new companies reach particular levels of sales six years after being started, we can estimate how much more likely to grow to particular sizes companies have to be for angel investing to be worthwhile.

Angels often say that their assistance can make the difference between having a $10 million company and a $100 million company in five to six years. So, taking this statement as a baseline, we can calculate the expected value of owning between 65 and 80 percent of an angel-backed company versus owning 100 percent of a non-angel-backed company. If angels take 35 percent of the companies in which they invest, then they need to make companies 3.2 times more likely to achieve $100 million in sales rather than $10 million in sales in six years; and if they take 20 percent of the companies, then they need to make companies 2.6 times more likely to achieve the $100 million mark. Anything short of this level of improvement and, on average, entrepreneurs would be better off without angel money. So, when you are thinking of taking money from angels, ask yourself the question: How much more likely do I think the odds will be that their involvement will make my company worth more than $10 million five to six years from now? If the answer is "not much" then you probably shouldn't take the money.

IN CONCLUSION

Collectively, we have an inaccurate image of how angels make investment decisions. The process is typically presented as more rational, more financially oriented, and more sophisticated than it actually is. In reality, the typical angel passively waits for investments to come to him through friends and family and then conducts a much more subjective and much less financially driven evaluation than received wisdom suggests—a process that is very much prone to decision-making biases.

In addition, many angels don't consider expected financial returns when deciding which companies to fund, and those who do tend to expect lower investment multiples and rates of return than is commonly believed. Many angels pay very little attention to what business plans say, in some cases not even caring if the entrepreneurs whose businesses they are considering financing have a business plan. And they spend far less time on due diligence, and conduct it in a far less detailed manner, than most observers believe.

Finally, once they invest, angels are a lot less active and add a lot less value than received wisdom suggests. A minority of angels sit on the board of the companies in which they invest. The average high net worth, accredited angel group member spends only 41.9 minutes per week on each of his portfolio companies. The value added by the typical angel isn't that high, in contrast to the story told (perhaps not surprisingly) by the angels themselves. Finally, the advice and assistance offered by angel investors is not cheap, especially when they take a substantial portion of the equity in their portfolio companies in return for their money and help. We have no evidence—and I am bracing myself here for an onslaught of criticism from my angel friends here—that the value angels add is greater than the cost of their assistance. So before you assume that the angels' self-reported value-added is valuable, you might want to consider how much worse off you would be without it.

Next, we turn to a topic perhaps *the* topic—of significant interest to angels, entrepreneurs, and policy makers. How well do angel investments perform?

EIGHT

How Well Do Angel
Investments Perform?

E VERYONE WANTS TO know how well the typical angel investment performs. Current angels want to benchmark their coun-
terparts. Prospective angels want to decide whether or not
to make angel investments. Entrepreneurs want to gauge what angel
investors are looking for in their investments. And policy makers want
to set policies toward angel investing.

So how does the average angel investment perform? The impression that you get from reading the typical magazine or newspaper article is that angels do quite well. But that's because most authors focus
on the extremely rare, blockbuster successes like the angel investment
in Google and imply that the typical angel investment does almost
as well.

However, in reality, successful angel investing is quite rare. Data
from a number of sources show that business angels invest in few companies that achieve high rates of growth and invest in fewer still that
go public or get acquired. Even when angels exit their investments successfully, the valuations of those companies are not that high, and the
returns from their investments, particularly when adjusted for opportunity cost, are far from extraordinary. To show you what I mean, let's
take a closer look at the numbers.

FEW ANGEL INVESTMENTS END
IN POSITIVE EXITS

For a venture to be attractive to angels, it needs to create value for equity holders, not just cash flow.[1] Therefore, angel investors are looking for companies that plan for one of two types of exit strategy: an initial public offering (IPO) or an acquisition by another company.[2] So how often do these exits occur?

Angels Have Few Exits via IPO

On average, the best financial returns for investors in start-up companies are garnered from investments in companies that go public. Unfortunately for those of you who want accurate information on this question, most observers believe incorrectly that a high proportion of angel-backed companies go public. For instance, a study by Colin Mason and Richard Harrison indicates that 7.6 percent of angel investments end in an IPO.[3] (While Mason and Harrison's data is for the United Kingdom, many observers have taken this proportion of IPOs to be true in the United States as well.) However, data from Jay Ritter of the University of Florida—the man the academic finance community calls "Mr. IPO" for the wealth of data he has collected on initial public offerings—shows how implausible this rate is. Ritter's effort to count every company that went public in the United States from 1980 through 2006 shows that, on average, 264 companies go public in the United States every year (see Figure 8.1). Even if every company that goes public has received an angel investment—a highly implausible scenario—there could be only 3,474 companies per year that receive an angel investment if angel investments have the IPO rate shown by Mason and Harrison. As you may remember from Chapter 2, estimates from the 2003 Federal Reserve Survey of Small Business Finances show that approximately 50,700 companies per year get angel money. And estimates from the data in the Entrepreneurship in the United States Assessment indicate that 57,300 companies get angel money each year. (Because the smaller the number of companies that get angel financing, the higher the ratios of IPOs and acquisitions to angel-backed companies are, I use the lower Federal Reserve Survey estimate as a conservative way to show that the estimates of the rate of IPO and acquisition for angel-backed companies are overstated. The numbers are even more extreme if I use the estimate of the number of angel-backed companies from the Entrepreneurship in the United States Assessment.)

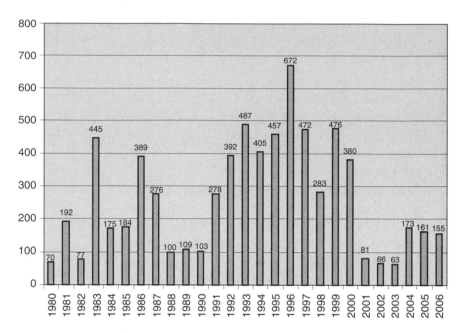

FIGURE 8.1. Number of Initial Public Offerings per Year from 1980 through 2006. *Source:* Created from data contained in Ritter, J. 2006. Some Factoids about the 2006 IPO Market. Downloaded from http://bear.cba.ufl.edu/ritter/New%20Folder/IPOs2006Factoids.pdf. (Excludes certain categories of specialized IPOs, such as IPOs with a price of less than $5.00 per share, partnerships, auction companies, real estate investment trusts, banks and savings and loans, unit offers, and closed-end funds.)

The numbers are even smaller if we consider that a sizable share of initial public offerings involves companies in which angels are believed not to invest. According to Ritter, 24 percent of the IPOs from 2000 through 2006 have been related to buyouts.[4] A substantial number of the others are foreign companies and older companies—businesses well in excess of ten years old. Because angels tend not to invest in buyout-related IPOs, companies founded in other countries, or older companies that go public, over the 2000 through 2006 period, the number of companies that angels would likely have backed and went public was closer to 100 businesses per year. At this rate of angel-backed IPOs, the data from Mason and Harrison would suggest that only 1,316 companies get angel financing every year, much too small a number for their IPO rate to be plausible.

If 100 angel-backed companies go public each year, that yields an IPO rate of between 0.17 and 0.2 percent of the companies financed by angels, depending on whether the Federal Reserve data or the Entrepreneurship in the United States Assessment data are used to estimate the number of angel-backed businesses.

Exit via Acquisition

Most exits from angel investments are not through initial public offerings; they are through sales of companies to other companies.[5] The prevailing wisdom is that a large portion of angel-backed companies are acquired. For instance, Colin Mason and Richard Harrison estimate that 26.1 percent of angel investments end in an acquisition or trade sale.[6] This number doesn't seem plausible. To start with, even the Band of Angels, perhaps the country's most successful group of angel investors, reports that only 17.5 percent of its investments have ended in an acquisition.[7] And it is hard to believe that they would be below average on this key metric.

In addition, Harrison and Mason's numbers don't jibe with data from the U.S. Census and the Federal Reserve. Combining the estimates from the Federal Reserve on the number of companies that get an investment from a business angel every year with Harrison and Mason's proportion of angel investments that end in an acquisition, we get an estimate of 13,233 angel-backed companies that are acquired every year. However, estimates based on data from the Census Bureau's Longitudinal Establishment and Enterprise Microdata file—our government's best longitudinal database of businesses—show that only about 7,000 small businesses are acquired each year. Moreover, only 69 percent of these are thirteen years old or less. Therefore, approximately 4,800 small U.S. businesses less than fourteen years old are acquired annually.[8] That is, the number of small businesses less than fourteen years old that are acquired every year in this country is about one-third the size of the estimate of the number of angel-backed companies that are acquired annually derived from Harrison and Mason's data.

Furthermore, the estimate of 4,860 small, young businesses acquired every year that is derived from Census data might be too high. In 2001, Thomson Financial Securities reported that there were 4,044 mergers and acquisitions worth $5 million or more of businesses of *any* age that were not foreign acquirees, leveraged buyouts, or divestitures.[9] Given the proportion of U.S. businesses less than fourteen years old, using Thomson's data, the number of small young companies that are acquired every year for $5 million or more is closer to 2,800.

But how many of these companies received angel financing? We don't really know, but we do have data that allow us to make some guess-timates. Because the Inc. 500 companies are the kind of growth companies that many observers say angels seek, the proportion of acquired Inc. 500 companies that received angel funding might give us an idea of that proportion. *Inc.* magazine reports that only 17 percent of the acquired Inc. 500 firms ever received an angel investment. At this proportion of angel investment, approximately 475 of the 2,800 small young companies acquired every year for $5 million or more would have been backed by angels. Stated differently, 0.9 percent of the 50,700 companies that estimates based on Federal Reserve data indicate are financed by angels each year and 0.8 percent of the 57,300 companies that estimates based on data from the Entrepreneurship in the United States Assessment show are backed by angels annually are acquired for $5 million or more.

Another guesstimate comes from considering the ratio of IPO to acquisition exits for venture capitalists. While the guesstimate based on this ratio has to assume that angels and venture capitalists have the same ratio of IPOs to acquisitions, that assumption might not be bad. Many observers argue that angels seek follow-on investment from venture capitalists and that, for companies that exit successfully, angel financing is often a stage in the process of financing that involves venture capitalists at some point before exit. Therefore, very few angel investments will result in an IPO or acquisition without ever having received venture capital. If this is true, then the ratio of acquisitions to IPOs for venture capitalists will also be true for business angels. The ratio of venture capital–backed companies that were acquired to venture capital–backed companies that went public averaged 6.7 from 2001 through 2006.[10] Given the earlier estimate of 100 angel-backed IPOs every year, this ratio suggests that approximately 670 angel-backed companies are acquired every year. Stated differently, the Federal Reserve Survey estimate of the number of angel-backed companies suggests that 1.3 percent of companies that receive angel financing are acquired, whereas the estimate based on the Entrepreneurship in the United States Assessment suggests 1.2 percent.

In short, somewhere between 0.17 and 0.2 percent of angel investments end in an IPO, while somewhere between 0.8 and 1.3 percent end in an acquisition, depending on the source of data used for the estimate. How does the rate of IPO and acquisition of angel-backed companies compare to the rate of IPO and acquisition among venture capital investments?

The National Venture Capital Association, the trade association of the venture capital industry, reports that from 2001 through 2006, venture capitalists had 2,286 liquidity events—1,988 mergers and acquisitions and 298 IPOs.[11] That translates to an average of 381 liquidity events per year, of which 331 are mergers and acquisitions and 50 are IPOs. Because venture capital exits do not occur at the same time as the investments, we need to match the exits to the investments made earlier. Venture capitalists often target a five-year exit window, suggesting that the 2001–2007 exits should correspond to the 1996 to 2002 investments. If we look at data that the National Science Foundation gathered from various sources on the number of companies receiving venture capital investments between 1996 and 2002, we see that an average of 3,634 received venture capital every year over that period.[12]

But the late 1990s were a venture capital bubble, so the number of investments made in that period might be much higher than normal. We can get a more conservative estimate of the average number of companies receiving venture capital money every year if we take the average from 1990 through 2004, which the NSF data show to be 2,450 companies per year.[13] If we put these numbers together, we see that venture capitalists invested in an average of 2,450 companies per year and had an average of 331 exits through mergers and acquisitions and fifty exits through IPO. That is, venture capitalists had an IPO in about 2 percent of their investments and an acquisition in approximately 13.5 percent. So venture capitalists have between 10 and 11.8 times as high a proportion of IPOs among their investments as do business angels, and between 10.4 and 16.9 times as high a proportion of acquisitions. That should give you pause for thought when you hear the frequently discussed myth that business angels' investments perform better than those of VCs.[14]

THE GROWTH OF START-UPS

While it is possible for an investment by a business angel to perform better than the company in which the investment is made, the performance of investments made by business angels tends to be highly correlated with the performance of the companies in which they invest. Therefore, it is useful to consider how well companies perform in industries that angels are thought to prefer. Even if angels pick the biggest winners in these industries, it is difficult to see how they could be making a lot of investments in high-growth companies, given the small number of companies founded every year in these industries. Table 8.1 summarizes the distribution of companies in different industries that angels are reported to favor (measured at the three-digit SIC

TABLE 8.1.   Share of Start-ups Achieving Different Levels of Six-Year Sales for

Industry	Number Started in 1996	Number that Achieve $50 million + in Sales by 2002	Portion with <$100,000 in Sales in 2002	Portion with $100,000–$499,000 in Sales in 2002
Industrial Inorganic Chemicals	33	0	3.03%	12.12%
Plastics Materials and Synthetics	35	1	0.00%	8.57%
Drugs	97	2	2.06%	10.31%
Soap, Cleaners, and Toilet Goods	139	0	5.76%	16.55%
Paints and Allied Products	60	0	3.33%	13.33%
Industrial Organic Chemicals	31	2	3.23%	12.90%
Agricultural Chemicals	37	0	0.00%	8.11%
Miscellaneous Chemical Products	80	1	3.75%	7.50%
Farm and Garden Machinery	82	1	4.88%	14.63%
Construction and Related Machinery	204	0	5.88%	18.63%
Metalworking Machinery	583	0	10.63%	20.24%
Special Industry Machinery	321	0	5.30%	20.56%
Engines and Turbines	16	0	6.00%	36.00%
General Industrial Machinery	216	0	4.17%	16.67%
Computer and Office Equipment	185	3	5.41%	10.81%
Refrigeration and Service Machinery	108	1	6.48%	14.81%
Industrial Machinery, Not Elsewhere Classified	1,768	2	12.56%	23.47%
Electric Distribution Equipment	36	0	2.78%	11.11%
Electrical Industrial Apparatus	117	0	2.56%	22.22%
Electric Lighting and Wiring Equipment	84	0	4.76%	14.29%
Household Audio and Video Equipment	68	0	8.82%	22.06%
Communications Equipment	129	1	3.10%	11.63%
Electronic Components and Accessories	425	7	5.88%	9.18%
Misc. Electrical Equipment and Supplies	92	0	6.52%	11.96%
Motor Vehicles and Equipment	322	2	2.80%	15.22%

Portion with $500,000–$999,000 in Sales in 2002	Portion with $1,000,000–$4,999,999 in Sales in 2002	Portion with $5,000,000–$9,999,999 in Sales in 2002	Portion with $10,000,000–$49,999,000 in Sales in 2002	Portion with $50,000,000–$99,999,999 in Sales in 2002	Portion with $100,000,000+ in Sales in 2002
0.00%	24.24%	3.03%	6.06%	0.00%	0.00%
5.71%	14.29%	2.86%	8.57%	0.00%	2.86%
6.19%	22.68%	6.19%	9.28%	2.06%	0.00%
8.63%	15.11%	3.60%	2.88%	0.00%	0.00%
8.33%	15.00%	3.33%	3.33%	0.00%	0.00%
9.68%	25.81%	6.45%	0.00%	6.45%	0.00%
10.81%	10.81%	0.00%	2.70%	0.00%	0.00%
13.75%	25.00%	0.00%	8.75%	1.25%	0.00%
4.88%	18.29%	2.44%	3.66%	1.22%	0.00%
8.82%	16.67%	2.45%	7.35%	0.00%	0.00%
8.58%	11.15%	1.89%	0.69%	0.00%	0.00%
5.61%	14.95%	1.87%	0.62%	0.00%	0.00%
0.00%	6.00%	6.00%	12.00%	0.00%	0.00%
8.33%	17.59%	1.85%	1.39%	0.00%	0.00%
6.49%	12.43%	2.16%	4.86%	0.54%	1.08%
6.48%	16.67%	2.78%	0.93%	0.93%	0.00%
9.33%	9.39%	0.79%	0.23%	0.00%	0.11%
13.89%	19.44%	2.78%	0.00%	0.00%	0.00%
11.11%	15.38%	1.71%	0.85%	0.00%	0.00%
8.33%	16.67%	4.76%	4.76%	0.00%	0.00%
2.94%	7.35%	0.00%	1.47%	0.00%	0.00%
2.33%	16.28%	1.55%	9.30%	0.00%	0.78%
8.24%	21.41%	1.88%	3.76%	0.24%	1.41%
6.52%	19.57%	3.26%	1.09%	0.00%	0.00%
6.21%	16.77%	6.21%	5.28%	0.31%	0.31%

(continued)

TABLE 8.1. (*continued*)

Industry	Number Started in 1996	Number that Achieve $50 million + in Sales by 2002	Portion with <$100,000 in Sales in 2002	Portion with $100,000– $499,000 in Sales in 2002
Aircraft and Parts	86	0	2.33%	18.60%
Ship and Boat Building and Repairing	323	1	6.19%	26.32%
Motorcycles, Bicycles, and Parts	37	0	2.70%	21.62%
Miscellaneous Transportation Equipment	100	0	2.00%	14.00%
Measuring and Controlling Devices	214	0	5.14%	20.09%
Medical Instruments and Supplies	307	3	6.84%	14.98%
Photographic Equipment and Supplies	50	0	8.00%	20.00%
Telephone Communications	1,203	7	5.90%	11.72%
Telegraph and Other Communications	36	0	2.78%	8.33%
Radio and Television Broadcasting	615	1	6.50%	15.45%
Cable and Other Pay Television Services	202	4	9.41%	13.37%
Communications Services, Not Elsewhere Classified	408	2	5.15%	15.93%

Source: Created from data contained in a Special Tabulation of the Business at the three-digit SIC code level.)

code) by level of sales achieved six years after starting. Across all of the industries shown in Table 8.1 only forty-one of 8,849 companies achieved more than $50 million in sales by the end of their sixth year of operations, and many of those forty-one companies might not have been backed by angels.

An examination of more fine-grained definitions of the industries that many people say business angels favor (industries measured at the four-digit SIC code level) yields very similar results. In the computer programming services industry, for instance, only seven of the 4,560 companies started in 1996 reached $50 million or more in

Portion with $500,000–$999,000 in Sales in 2002	Portion with $1,000,000–$4,999,999 in Sales in 2002	Portion with $5,000,000–$9,999,999 in Sales in 2002	Portion with $10,000,000–$49,999,000 in Sales in 2002	Portion with $50,000,000–$99,999,999 in Sales in 2002	Portion with $100,000,000+ in Sales in 2002
6.98%	10.47%	3.49%	2.33%	0.00%	0.00%
7.43%	6.81%	0.93%	1.86%	0.31%	0.00%
5.41%	13.51%	5.41%	2.70%	0.00%	0.00%
10.00%	12.00%	5.00%	5.00%	0.00%	0.00%
8.88%	18.22%	2.80%	1.87%	0.00%	0.00%
9.12%	16.61%	3.58%	2.28%	0.98%	0.00%
6.00%	8.00%	4.00%	0.00%	0.00%	0.00%
4.57%	6.23%	1.00%	1.16%	0.17%	0.42%
5.56%	2.78%	0.00%	0.00%	0.00%	0.00%
6.67%	8.46%	1.14%	1.30%	0.16%	0.00%
2.97%	5.94%	1.49%	0.99%	1.49%	0.50%
4.90%	8.33%	2.45%	1.23%	0.49%	0.00%

Information Tracking Series of the U.S. Census. (These industries are measured

sales at the end of their sixth year. In semiconductors, only six of the 109 companies founded in 1996 reached this level of sales, while in the prototypical prepackaged software industry, only five of the 1,271 businesses in the 1996 cohort reached $50 million or more in sales by 2002. In short, while some companies in the industries that angels are said to prefer achieve the desired $50 million or more in sales in six years, these amount to just a handful of the companies started in the United States every year, and some portion of these companies don't get financed by business angels. Therefore, it's just not possible for angels to back a large number of high-growth start-ups every year.

THE VALUE OF ANGEL-BACKED
COMPANIES AT EXIT

We don't have any direct evidence of the value of angel-backed companies at the time of exit, but we can estimate how much better than average angels would have to be at picking companies to have exits of the kind of value the anecdotes suggest they have.

Let's start by looking at the overall numbers. Using data from Pratt's Stats, we can figure out the median multiple on sales for mergers and acquisitions that occurred in the United States between 1996 and 2002. This turns out to be 0.68 times one-year sales. The first thing we should note is that the *typical* multiple on sales for companies that are acquired is significantly *lower* than the rule of thumb for screening angel deals recommended by the Angel Capital Education Foundation in its Power of Angel Investing seminars, which is one times the pro forma revenues in year five.[15]

Next, we can use data from Pratt's Stats and the U.S. Census Bureau to calculate the value in 2002 (around the target point when angels want to exit) of the typical surviving new business founded in 1996. The data show that the value in 2002 of the typical start-up company founded in 1996 and still alive in 2002 is *only* $204,000. That is, the typical start-up is not worth enough to meet angel investors' criteria at the time they exit the business—not by a long shot.

But in all fairness to the experts on angel investing who have written about this topic before, angels don't invest in the typical start-up, and as Table 8.2 indicates, the value of six-year-old businesses varies across sectors. So we are probably better off looking just at the specific industries that angels are said to prefer to get a sense of the value of the typical company in which they might invest six years after founding.

Of course, in doing that, we need to pay attention to an important caveat. There can't be as many of these high-value companies as received wisdom suggests because once we focus on the industries in which angels are thought to concentrate their efforts, we are now talking about a very small number of companies. With that caveat in mind, let's look industry by industry at the value of the *typical* surviving six-year-old company.

Because the number of observed exits in some industries is too small to provide proper estimates of the value of acquisitions, we can estimate the median value of start-up companies at the end of their sixth year for only some industries. Two patterns emerge from these data. First, in most industries, the value of the typical surviving start-up is

TABLE 8.2. Value of the Typical Surviving Start-up Company by
           Primary Industry Sector

Sector	Number of Start-ups in 1996	Value of a Typical Six-Year-Old Firm
All Sectors	510,654	$204,000
Agriculture, Agricultural Services, Forestry, Fishing	11,412	$177,000
Mining	1,554	$459,000
Construction	67,384	$123,000
Manufacturing	23,545	$222,000
Transportation, Communications, Utilities	24,160	$294,000
Wholesale Trade	34,209	$322,500
Retail Trade	102,706	$111,000
Finance, Insurance, Real Estate	43,975	$399,000
Services	198,524	$222,000

Source: Calculated from data contained in Pratt's Stats and a special
tabulation of the Business Information Tracking Series of the U.S. Census.

less than $1 million. Second, some of the industries with the highest
value companies, such as depository institutions and wholesale trade
in durable goods, are not ones that most observers say angels tend to
invest in.

If we look at industry defined more precisely (at the four-digit
SIC code level), we begin to see a few industries in which the value
of the typical company at the time that angels target their exits is rea-
sonably large. For instance, as Table 8.3 shows, the typical surviving
semiconductor start-up is worth $11.2 million at the time an angel
would target exiting, the typical pharmaceuticals preparations company is worth $9.3 million, and the typical surgical preparations start-
up is worth $3.4 million. But the number of start-ups founded in these
industries each year is very small. In short, except in a very small subset
of industries, the typical start-up tends not to be worth very much
money at the time angels tend to target their exits. Either angels make
just a small handful of investments or they must invest in a lot companies for which the median value at the time of exit is not very high.

Some readers might argue that the price-to-sales ratio used in
this analysis is too low because companies that are acquired by public

Industry	Value of a Typical Six-Year-Old Firm
Computer Peripheral Equipment, Not Elsewhere Classified	$ 1,545,000
Computer Programming Services	$ 666,000
Prepackaged Software	$ 1,158,000
Computer Integrated Systems Design	$ 738,000
Data Processing and Preparation	$ 600,000
Information Retrieval Services	$ 2,865,000
Computer Related Services, Not Elsewhere Classified	$ 453,000
Printed Circuit Boards	$ 615,000
Semiconductors and Related Devices	$11,190,000
Electronic Components, Not Elsewhere Classified	$ 3,180,000
Electromedical Equipment, X-ray Apparatus and Tubes	$ 855,000
Pharmaceutical Preparations	$ 9,270,000
Surgical Preparations	$ 3,420,000
Radio Telephone	$ 468,000
Other Telephone Communications	$ 525,000
Radio and Television Broadcasting	$ 2,842,500
Communications, Not Elsewhere Classified	$ 450,000
Radio and Television Apparatus	$ 3,180,000
Miscellaneous Publishing	$ 603,000

Source: Calculated from data contained in Pratt's Stats and a special tabulation of the Business Information Tracking Series of the U.S. Census. (These industries are measured at the four-digit SIC Code level.)

companies or go public are valued at significantly more than the median multiple on one-year sales for that sector or industry.[16] While it is true that the value of exits through IPO are higher on average than the value of exits through acquisition, the inclusion of information on exits through IPO won't change the numbers by very much. Very few companies go public—fewer than 300 companies every year—and less than half of them are new companies founded in the United States.

Moreover, the price of companies that go public is not as high as many people think. One study shows that from 1996 to 2005, the typical multiple for companies that went public was only 1.5 times one-year sales.[17] Another study, this one for 1980 to 1997, showed that a median price-to-sales multiple on an IPO was 1.29.[18] A third study showed that the median price-to-sales multiple on an IPO for 1993 to 2000 was only 1.43.[19]

Furthermore, the lower multiple used in the analysis presented above will not affect the estimates of the *median* value of start-ups at the time angels target their exit from them. Because the median is the *typical* value, changing the value of the highest estimates, which is what adjusting the numbers for those that go public does, will not change the median. In fact, even the *average* value would not change very much if we adjusted for the higher IPO multiple because these multiples aren't that much higher than the acquisition multiple, and there are very few businesses that exit through initial public offering.

There are only twenty-seven four-digit industries (out of 677) in which companies founded in 1996 went public over the following six years. Therefore, there are only twenty-seven industries in which the estimate of the value of the typical business based on acquisition multiples *can be* incorrect because the higher valuation of the companies that went public is not included, and in these industries, the proportion of companies that went public is very small. Moreover, even in these twenty-seven industries, the value of the companies that went public affects only the estimates for the largest businesses in each industry because the typical company that went public between 1993 and 2000 had sales of $89.6 million,[20] something that fewer than 500 companies founded in the United States in 1996 managed to achieve over the time horizon that angels target.

RETURNS ON ANGEL INVESTMENTS

So far in this chapter, I have only suggested that angels probably don't make as much money from their investments in start-ups as traditional wisdom suggests because far fewer of the companies that they back get acquired or go public, and the value of those companies at the time of exit is lower than most people believe. But I haven't addressed directly the question of the returns to the typical angel investment. That's because we have no good data with which to address it.

However, the absence of good data hasn't stopped many authors from claiming that the returns to typical angel investments are quite high. And many angels believe that these returns are large. One survey of business angels revealed that 42 percent thought that angel investing was the *most* lucrative form of investing possible.[21]

To estimate the returns on angel investing, many sources simply speculate or focus on a few, very successful investors, such as the Band of Angels. But take a look at how inaccurate the estimates of the returns from angel investing are by drawing inference to the investment performance of the typical angel investor from this group. Since the founding of the Band of Angels in 1994, 4.6 percent of its portfolio companies have gone public. If the average angel in the United States had the same IPO rate on his portfolio, then the 50,700–57,300 companies that are estimated to receive an angel investment every year would result in between 2,332 and 2,636 angel-backed IPOs annually, a number between 8.8 and 10 times the number of total IPOs that occur annually and between 23.3 and 26.4 times the estimated number of angel-backed IPOs that occur each year! Clearly, the Band of Angels is far from the typical angel investor, and drawing any conclusions about angel investing from the investment performance of this group is very inaccurate. It's akin to looking at Barry Bonds's home run record to draw conclusions about how many home runs the average major-leaguer will hit in his career.[22]

Unfortunately, we don't have any information on the performance of angel investments for a representative sample of angel investors. The best we have is data from the Federal Reserve's Survey of Consumer Finances on the value of a typical *informal equity* investment held by an American household in 2004, which was $79,300 with a cost basis of $47,327. Thus, the multiple on a typical *informal equity* investment held by an American household in 2004 was approximately 1.7.

These data, of course, have one big problem. They offer no information on the length of time that the investments were held, making it impossible to calculate the rate of return on them.[23] A multiple of 1.7 on an investment held for one year is a whopping 70 percent per year return, but the same multiple on an investment held for eight years or more is below what you would earn in most mutual funds that invest in public equities.

Because we have no studies of the performance of angel investments for a *representative* sample of angel investors, we need to look at data on unrepresentative samples, which makes figuring out the numbers quite tricky. The best data we have from a non-representative sample are those on the investment performance of business angels who are affiliated with angel groups, collected by Rob Wiltbank of Willamette University.[24]

Before we look at what the data say about performance of angel investing, it is important to understand the limitations of Wiltbank's data. The angels Wiltbank surveyed are far from typical. Because they are affiliated with angel groups, all of them are accredited investors. Moreover, they represent the cream of the crop of angels. They have an average net worth of $10.9 million (which, according to the IRS Statistics of Income, puts them in a league with only 123,000 U.S. households), and they made investments in start-ups that averaged a whopping $191,000. A full 85 percent of them had at least three years of entrepreneurial experience, and the average angel in the sample had founded 2.7 companies and had been an entrepreneur for 14.5 years.

Moreover, participation in Wiltbank's study was voluntary, which almost certainly makes the typical investment performance he reports overstated.[25] Why? Think about your willingness to fill out a survey that gathers information about something that you are very successful at versus one that gathers information about something that you are not so good at. If you're human, you're going to be more likely to fill out the survey about something you're good at. (No jokes here from the cynical among you who think business angels aren't human beings.) Therefore, Wiltbank's survey almost certainly includes a much larger proportion of successful angel investors than unsuccessful ones, biasing the reported performance numbers upward.

But even if the survey includes only the most successful angels among an already highly successful sample, the results are useful. If the performance of the typical angel in the sample isn't very good, then we have strong evidence that angel investments typically generate low returns.[26]

Rob Wiltbank examined the investment returns of 539 angel investors from 86 angel groups who had made 3,097 investments, from which they had experienced 1,137 exits. Some investments made money. In fact, the average investment in the sample (mean investment) generated a profit of $295,000 on an investment of $191,000 in 3.52 years.[27] But before you start thinking that this is evidence that the returns to angel investments are good, consider the following:

First, this is the average return for the best possible group of angels— high net worth, accredited investors affiliated with angel groups—and includes some of the superstars of angel investing—people like Luis Villalobos and John May. Moreover, the returns are based on investments made by only 13 percent of the sample contacted, and those who didn't answer the survey probably had lower returns than those who responded.

Second, even these highly successful angels lost money on more than half (52 percent) of their investments. In fact, the typical (median) angel investment made by this sample of very experienced and successful angels was a loser; it involved an investment of $50,000 that returned $40,000 or 80 cents on the dollar. Moreover, only 7 percent of the investments accounted for three quarters of the financial returns.[28]

Third, many of the investors lost money on their entire portfolio. The data show that almost 40 percent did not get back the money they put into angel investments. And the top 10 percent of investors generated half the financial returns.[29]

Fourth, the rate of return is overstated because it fails to take the opportunity cost of the angel's time into consideration. Angel investing isn't passive, like putting money into a mutual fund, a venture capital limited partnership, or a hedge fund. So a complete comparison of returns to angel investing should look at the portion of the angel investor's return that is financial, after taking into account the cost of his time.

We can figure this out by looking at the data from Wiltbank's study because he also measures the amount of time the average angel spends per week on his investments (12 hours).[30] Over the 3.52 years that it takes the average angel investment to reach an outcome, positive or negative, the average angel spends 2,196 hours on his investments. Because the respondents in Wiltbank's sample had an average of 5.16 investments, that's 426 hours per venture.

Given the average number of hours put in by an accredited angel to generate the average return, the opportunity cost of the angel's time is $129,520. That is, the angel gave up the opportunity to earn $129,520 in income to generate the financial return from angel investing, money that could have been earned if the angel had invested the money passively.[31]

To get a fair estimate of the financial return from angel investing, we need to subtract this opportunity cost from the amount earned on the typical angel investment. If we do that, we can see that the average angel earns $165,480 on a 3.52 year investment of $191,000[32] or an annual rate of return of 19.2 percent. While this number is high, it is worse than other alternatives available to the very wealthy investors in the study. For instance, the investors could have put their money into one of many venture capital limited partnerships, which, as an asset class, had an average ten-year return of 26.9 percent—and a 41.5 percent return for early stage investments.[33]

Proportion of angel investments that end in an IPO	0.17 to 0.2 percent
Proportion of angel investments that end in acquisition	0.8 to 1.3 percent
Number of companies founded annually that reach $50 million in sales in 6 years in industries that sophisticated angels say they favor	41 companies
Valuation of the typical surviving start-up at the time that angels target exiting	$204,000
Multiple on the average informal equity investment held by a U.S. household	1.7
Proportion of investments of highly successful angels that return less than the capital invested	52 percent
Average annual rate of return on angel investments for high net worth business angels associated with angel groups willing to discuss their investments, adjusted for the opportunity cost of the angel's time	19.2 percent

IN CONCLUSION

A large number of books and articles have made reference to the small number of spectacularly successful angel investments, such as those in Google or the Body Shop, giving the impression that the returns on angel investments are very good. However, the reality is that very successful angel investing is quite rare and that the typical angel investment does not perform as well as the typical investment in other asset classes. Most of the information about the performance of angel investments—whether the proportion of angel investments that end in IPOs or acquisitions, the growth or value of the types of companies that angels are said to invest in, or the returns to capital invested in start-up companies—overstates the performance of the typical angel investor. Careful estimates constructed from hard data about IPOs and acquisitions suggest that less than one-quarter of one percent of all angel investments end in an IPO and less than 1.5 percent of all angel investments end in an acquisition.

Moreover, angel investors cannot make investments in a very large number of high-growth companies in the industries in which they are said to invest because the *total* number of companies that reach high-growth sales targets is very small. For instance, the total number of companies founded in 1996 that achieved the often referred to angel sales target of $50 million within six years of founding in thirty-seven high-tech industries that angels are said to prefer is forty-one (out of a total of 8,849 start-ups) or 0.5 percent of the companies founded in those industries.

The value of angel-backed companies at exit is unlikely to be as high as received wisdom suggests because, six years after founding, the typical start-up company is worth far less than most people believe. The median multiple on sales for an acquired company in the United States is only two thirds the size of the multiple that the Angel Capital Education Foundation considers a rule of thumb for screening angel deals. Moreover, the typical surviving U.S. start-up is worth only $204,000 six years after starting, and there are few industries in which the typical start-up is worth the sums of money that many observers of angel investing believe angel investments should be worth at the time of exit.

The returns on investments made by angel investors are not very high. Even the cream of the crop of angel investors—people with a net worth of $10.9 million, who are members of an angel group, have founded an average of 2.7 companies, have been entrepreneurs for an average of 14.5 years, and are willing to talk about their experiences investing in start-ups—earn a 19.2 percent per year rate of return once the opportunity cost of their time is considered. That rate is significantly lower than the average rate of return on investments in other asset classes that angels can invest in.

NINE

What Are Angel Groups?

THIS CHAPTER EXAMINES a recent development in angel investing: the emergence of organized angel groups (efforts that
combine the start-up investment activities of multiple accredited investors in a coordinated way).[1] The oldest of these angel groups
is believed to be the Band of Angels in Silicon Valley, which began in
1994 with twelve members and, in 2006, had 105 members and $7.2
million invested in twelve companies.[2]

The newness of angel groups means that they are essentially unex-
plored in other books on angel investing, even though they are a unique
form of investing in private companies. As this chapter will show, angel
groups are very different from individual angels. All members of angel
groups are accredited investors, making group members wealthier
than the unaccredited investors who make up 79 percent of all business
angels. Moreover, angels in groups differ from individual angels on a
variety of dimensions, including their demographics,[3] the amounts of
money they provide, the industries they favor, their preference for debt
and equity instruments, the terms of their contracts, their tendency to
get follow-on investment from venture capitalists, their expected and
actual rates of return, and so on. In fact, angel groups may be more
like venture capital firms than like individual angels. These differences
make angel groups important for entrepreneurs, angels, and policy
makers to understand.

THE ANGEL GROUP NUMBERS

Observers estimate the number of angel groups in the United States to be between 125 and 300 groups.[4] About half of all known angel groups have banded together to form a trade association called the Angel Capital Association (ACA) to help facilitate information exchange and to develop policy related to angel investing.

Much of what we know about angel groups comes from surveys of the membership of the ACA, which may or may not accurately represent the typical angel group. But information on the ACA members is the best data we have on angel groups. So it's helpful to see what it shows.

Angel group members are clearly a minority of all business angels operating in the United States. In 2006, the groups that participate in the Angel Capital Association were composed of 5,632 angel investors.[5] As we saw in Chapter 2, there are approximately 261,500 unaccredited investors and 69,500 accredited investors who made an angel investment in the United States between the beginning of 2001 and the end of 2003. Thus, members of angel groups that compose the ACA account for only about 8.1 percent of accredited angel investors, and 1.7 percent of all angels. Even if we assume that the ACA accounts for only half of all angel groups, the percentage of angels that belong to angel groups is very small.

In 2006, the 128 groups that were the members of the Angel Capital Association made 947 investments in 512 companies, providing start-ups with a total of $228.8 million.[6] Because we don't know what portion of angel groups are members of the Angel Capital Association, we cannot know for sure how this compares to our estimates for overall angel investing activity. However, if we again make the assumption that the members of the ACA account for half of all angel groups in the United States, then angel groups make approximately 1,900 investments totaling $457.6 million in 1,024 companies every year. These estimates would suggest that angel groups accounted for 1.8 percent of the companies receiving angel investments, and 2 percent of the dollar value of angel investments.

These numbers aren't that high in comparison to other types of investors in start-ups. In 2002, the latest year for which the data are available, small business investment corporations (SBICs) made 4,004 investments in 1,979 companies, providing $2.7 billion. Of this total, $842 million was placed in 730 companies that were less than two years old. In fact, from 1994 to 2002, SBICs averaged making $1.03 billion in seed stage investments every year.[7] Thus, SBICs make more investments to more companies and provide more money than angel groups. They might even make more seed stage investments (although we lack the data on the stage of investment by angel groups to know).

WHERE ARE THE GROUPS?

While some observers give the impression that angel groups have sprung up everywhere, using breathless statements like "there are angel groups in nearly every U.S. city now,"[8] the reality is that angel groups have emerged primarily in certain areas, and many cities do not yet have an angel group, at least not one that has joined the ACA. In particular, these groups are much more prevalent in east and west coast cities than in cities in other parts of the country.

Moreover, angel groups from different places are different from each other. Groups from California, for instance, tend to have more members, finance more companies per year, and are more likely to have committed funds—funds that must be invested in some of the companies that present to the group—than angel groups from other states. Angel groups from metro areas in which more technology invention tends to occur have more members and different presentation formats from angel groups in other areas. And angel groups from places with a lot of external investment activity in prior years tend to have more entrepreneurs present their business ideas at each group meeting.

WHAT DO ANGEL GROUPS LOOK LIKE?

Angel groups come in a lot of shapes and sizes: Some are manager led, while others are member led. Some involve the pooling of funds by investors; others are composed of investors who invest separately in companies. Some are formally organized; others are informally structured. Below, I describe some of the important differences between angel groups and some characteristics of the groups that tend to be related to these differences.

The Age of Angel Groups

Most angel groups are not very old. The median age of an angel group that is a member of the Angel Capital Association is only three years old, and the average age is only 4.2. Only 27 percent of these groups were established before 2000 and only 7.2 percent were established before 1997.[9]

However, focusing on the young age of the average angel group can be deceptive because angel groups of different ages tend to differ on other dimensions as well. For instance, older angel groups have significantly more members, finance more companies, and are structured differently from younger groups.

The Size of Angel Groups

The Angel Capital Association's survey of its members showed that the average group has 47.6 members (median of 37) and 0.7 staff (median of 0). However, the number of active angel investors in these groups tends to be much smaller. According to the Center for Venture Research at the University of New Hampshire, 62 percent of angel group members do not invest in a given year.[10] And estimates from the ACA data indicate that approximately 17.5 percent of angel group members invest in each deal.[11]

Angel groups tend to be small because large groups are difficult to manage.[12] Moreover, they are generally open to only a small number of people, with new members found through referrals by existing members[13] and membership limited to accredited investors to minimize disclosure requirements.[14]

Despite the small average size, groups differ a lot on this dimension. For instance, the Angel Capital Association's survey of its members in 2007 found that the smallest group had only three members, while the largest had 280, and the number of staff working for the groups ranged from zero to seven.

Older angel groups tend to be larger than younger angel groups, with a one-year increase in group age corresponding to an increase of 5.3 investors. In addition, being located in California adds 31.4 members to the average size of angel groups. On the other hand, angel groups that are found in technology-intensive locales tend to be smaller, as are angel groups that are required to invest in the state in which they are domiciled, and angel groups that seek to invest in companies within a four-hour drive of their location. Those groups that are required to invest within the state in which they are domiciled have 18.6 fewer investors than other angel groups and angel groups that prefer to invest within a four-hour drive of their location have 25.2 fewer investors.

The Magnitude of the Investment Effort

The average angel group has the founders of 24.1 companies present their business ideas (2.48 companies presenting at an average of 9.7

meetings), and invests in 3.8 companies every year. The average angel group invests $241,528 per investment round.[15]

As with the size and age of angel groups, the average numbers for investment activity is a bit deceptive because the magnitude varies considerably across groups. For instance, among the angel groups that are members of the ACA, the number of companies funded in the previous year ranges from 0 to 19; the number of group meetings that take place annually varies from 0 to 52; and the number of companies presenting per meeting ranges from 1 to 20. Moreover, while some groups make investments in excess of $1 million per round, 20 percent make investments of $150,000 or less.

What explains these differences in investment activity? One factor is whether the group is domiciled in California. Angel groups located in California fund 4.1 more companies per year than angel groups located elsewhere. Another factor is the age of the angel group. For each year they get older, angel groups fund an additional 0.6 companies annually. A third factor is the location where the group invests. The requirement that the angel group invest in the state in which the group is domiciled and the preference for investing in companies located within a four-hour drive of the group's home both are associated with a lower likelihood of making small investments. A fourth factor is the past history of external investing in the region. The more external equity investing that occurred in the group's metro area in the past, the more companies tend to present at each group meeting.

Stage of Investment

Contrary to what many observers think, the seed stage is not the stage at which most angel group members want to invest. In fact, slightly more angel groups that are members of the ACA express an interest in early stage investing than express an interest in the seed stage, with 82 percent wanting to invest at the early stage and 80 percent wanting to invest at the seed and start-up stages. Much smaller numbers express an interest in expansion stage (35 percent), and late stage (10 percent) investing.[16]

But like many other aspects of investing, angel groups differ significantly on the stages of investment at which they like to invest, and the interest in different stages is related to other characteristics of angel groups. For instance, angel groups that like later stage investing tend to have more committed funds than groups that like earlier stage investments, and groups that like expansion stage investing tend to charge members higher dues than other angel groups.

Source of Funds

Angel groups need money to cover their costs. Although some angel groups use a portion of their committed capital, organize events, and raise sponsorships to cover their expenses, membership dues are the primary source of funding for most groups.[17] In general, these dues are fairly modest. Among members of the Angel Capital Association, annual dues average $992 per member (the median is $750).

However, there are significant differences across groups in the magnitude of member dues, which range from $0 to $6,000 per year. Moreover, a variety of group characteristics are related to the size of membership dues. Angel groups that are organized as nonprofit mutual benefit corporations or as limited liability companies charge significantly higher dues than angel groups taking other legal forms. Those angel groups that require investments to be made in companies in the same state as the group pay significantly lower dues than angel groups without this requirement (perhaps because these groups are more likely to receive some sort of state funding to defray their operating costs). Finally, members of angel groups that like expansion stage investment pay higher dues than members of other groups.

Legal Form

Although many angel groups are organized as limited liability companies or limited partnerships,[18] these groups actually take on a variety of different legal forms. Just less than half of the groups that compose the Angel Capital Association (48 percent) are for-profit entities.

The many angel groups that are set up as nonprofit organizations generally are structured this way for one three reasons. First, the group is part of a broader economic development effort and can more easily obtain government or foundation support if it is not a commercial entity. Second, the angels that compose the group want to invest as individuals and simply need an entity to organize their meetings and other activities. Third, the group wants to have an unlimited number of members, and nonprofit organizations are not limited in their membership size.

In terms of legal form, 35 percent of the groups are limited liability companies; 28 percent are nonprofit mutual benefit corporations; 8 percent are S or C corporations; and 29 percent have a different or no legal form.

These differences in legal organization are related to other differences among angel groups. Angel groups set up as corporations tend to have more members than other angel groups, while those groups that are established as limited liability companies tend to have more meetings and higher dues. Finally, groups that are organized as nonprofit mutual benefit corporations are less likely to have committed funds than other angel groups.

Funds or Networks

Angel groups differ in their organizational structure. Some are set up as investment funds while others are just networks of people who see the same deals. Angel groups also differ in their use of committed funds and in their use of sidecar funds (individual investments made in conjunction with the investments of the group).

Angel Networks

The vast majority of angel groups—77.4 percent of those in the ACA—are set up as networks.[19] In many cases, angel networks are configured as nonprofit organizations because the organization itself is just a mechanism for managing the collective activity of meeting and looking at deals.

Angel networks are less structured than angel funds. They are usually member led, with leadership of the group rotating across members or with a lead member farming out to others some of the key tasks, such as due diligence or screening.[20]

Within the general category of angel networks, groups vary in their formality: there is the social tie model, the informal group model, the loosely organized group model, and the formally organized group. The social tie model of angel network is the most informal of all angel groups. It involves people who know each other socially and get together in a quasi-social setting to consider deals but invest alone on a case-by-case basis.[21]

This type of group typically has no legal structure and tends to be very small. Its deal flow tends not to be organized; the angels in it typically learn about potential deals from their friends and pass the potential investments on to others they know well and who are interested in financing that type of company. This process of deal exchange is typically reciprocal, with people exchanging information on deals with others who are willing to exchange information with them. Investments tend to be small in magnitude, and deal terms tend to be informal and unsophisticated.

The next level up in organization is the informal group, which involves a set of investors who get together regularly at a country club or other setting to discuss deals. An example is the Margarita Club in Denver, a group of three angel investors who get together to drink margaritas and evaluate deals.[22] In informal groups, the individual angels source deals and bring them to the attention of the other group members. The deal flow for these groups depends largely on what its members have heard about through their other activities; there are no formal submissions or presentations. The members tend to evaluate the ventures alone and decide whether to invest as individuals. Investment terms tend to be informal and unsophisticated. The main difference between the informal group and the social tie model is a permanent group of members and regular meetings at which investments are discussed.

Loosely organized groups are the next step up the hierarchy of organization. Examples include the Colorado Springs Investor Group and the Loosely Organized Retired Executives (LORE) in Pennsylvania.[23] With loosely organized groups, the network exists independently of its members but its organization is limited. The groups are unlikely to have professional management, and screening and due diligence are led by volunteers. The group itself might have a Web page, deals might come to the group as opposed to the individual members, and the deals might be presented to the group of investors collectively,[24] but members decide on their own whether to invest and how much money to put into a company.[25] Usually a member must champion a deal to move it toward investment because each member invests as an individual. And the group typically needs to form a separate limited liability company for each investment so the members can invest together.[26] Because loosely organized groups tend to be member-led and have little support, they are subject to the problems of burnout and group management.[27]

The most organized angel network is the formally organized group. With this model, the network has a formal legal organization that is independent of its members. The organization typically has a physical location, a Web site where entrepreneurs can learn about the network and submit deals, a budget for managing the investment process, and some sort of staff to support the members. Usually the group has regularly scheduled meetings with formal presentations by entrepreneurs. It might require a fee to join, which pays for marketing and program organization.[28] The members of these groups tend to evaluate deals, conduct due diligence, and make investments together.[29]

Some angel networks are organized under a pledge model in which each member commits to investing a certain amount of money—typically between $50,000 and $150,000 over a several year period[30]—in the ventures that the group looks at.[31] For example, at Tech Coast Angels, members agree to attend half the meetings, participate in at least two due diligence efforts, and make $50,000 worth of investments in at least two deals per year.[32]

Several factors are related to the tendency for an angel group to have committed funds. The first is that the group is domiciled in California. Angel groups in California are 43.8 times as likely as those located outside the state to have committed funds. The second is the legal structure of the group. Groups that are set up as nonprofit mutual benefit corporations are less likely to have committed funds whereas groups set up as limited liability companies are more likely to have them. The third is the set of other organizational characteristics of the group. Being member led, making later stage investments, and having sidecar funds are all positively related to having committed funds.

Angel Funds

The minority of angel groups—roughly 8.1 percent of the members of the ACA—combines investor money into a pool of funds to invest jointly in start-ups.[33] For example, the Northcoast Angel Fund in Cleveland, Ohio, is an angel group composed of 99 members who have each put $25,000 into a fund that is used to invest in new companies.

Angel funds are usually independent legal entities that manage the process of deal sourcing, deal evaluation, due diligence, and investment. With a fund, the members of the group invest a fixed amount of money and then participate in evaluating deals, conducting due diligence, and making investments. The decisions about which companies are asked to present, which companies move forward to due diligence, and which companies are funded are made by votes of the members. Because the fund itself makes the investments in portfolio companies out of the collective funds contributed by the members, the investors in the fund cannot opt out of specific investments.[34]

Some angels believe there is a trend toward the use of the fund structure because it allows greater involvement of passive investors who do not have the time or expertise to select target companies or manage angel investments.[35] However, other angels see the fund model as having a major drawback. The group members have to tie up their money because it is difficult to cash out. When the fund exits an investment profitably, the proceeds often go back to the group rather than to the individual members.[36]

Some angel groups, particularly those set up as funds, have side-cars—a mechanism for individual angels to invest in the chosen start-ups alongside the group. The data shows that 21 percent of groups have sidecars,[37] and 14.5 percent of groups are set up as networks with sidecars.[38] Other than being more likely to be set up as funds, angel groups with sidecars differ from other angel groups in several ways. They tend to be more organized and have more employees and more meetings. They are also more likely to have committed funds than other angel groups.

Manager Led

Approximately 59 percent of angel groups are member led, and 41 percent are manager led. Manager-led angel groups differ from member-led groups in several important ways. They have more employees and, hence, are more expensive to run.[39] They tend to be more formally organized because the manager and other staff conduct basic screening of deals, prepare entrepreneurs for presentation, organize logistics, manage communications with the members, and help with due diligence.[40] Manager-led groups are also more likely than member-led ones to have regularly scheduled meetings, a formal organization, and a budget. Angel groups organized as funds are more likely to be manager-led because the fund is an entity that needs professional management.[41]

In manager-led groups, the manager typically is compensated through a combination of salary, other incentives, and carried interest (profits from the investments).[42] One study of angel groups found that 42 percent of compensated group leaders received some portion of the carry.[43] Because the manager of an angel group cannot receive any of the "carried interest" if the group is legally structured as a nonprofit corporation, manager-led groups tend to be for-profit entities.[44]

Investment Region

While the average angel group makes primarily local investments in start-up companies, angel groups differ significantly in their view of what is an acceptable investment region. About 36 percent of the Angel

Capital Association's groups want to make investments within a four-hour drive of the group's location; the rest are willing to make investments anywhere. Approximately 21 percent of angel group members of the ACA are restricted to investing in the state in which the group is domiciled; the vast majority can invest in any state.

The geography of angel group investments is related to other characteristics of the groups. Those that want to make investments in companies that are within a four-hour drive of the group's location tend to have fewer meetings and are less likely than other groups to make small investments—less than $150,000 per round. Similarly, angel groups that are restricted to investing in their home state have fewer members and lower dues, and are less likely than other groups to make investments smaller than $150,000 per round.

Co-Investment

Another important aspect of angel group investing is co-investing. Some observers believe that co-investing among angel groups, and between angel groups and venture capitalists, is increasing because co-investment permits greater investment diversification across geography, industry, and technology, and it permits investment to be made in companies that demand more capital than any single angel group can provide.[45]

The concept of co-investment is very popular among the groups that make up the Angel Capital Association;[46] 98 percent of ACA groups want to co-invest with other angel groups, and 82 percent want to co-invest with early stage venture capitalists.[47] The amount of co-investment with venture capitalists actually undertaken by angel groups is somewhat smaller than the desired amount but is substantial nonetheless. Almost three-fourths (72 percent) have co-invested with VCs.[48]

ALONE OR TOGETHER?

Individual angels can choose to invest alone or as part of a group. So why do angels make the choice to go one way or another? Some reasons are obvious. Unaccredited investors invest alone because they don't have the choice to invest as part of most angel groups. But what about accredited investors? Why do some invest alone and others join groups? Let's take a look at the reasons the angels give.

Angels join groups for a variety of reasons. First, they do so to get access to deals. As individuals, angels often have poor deal flow. They hear about deals through some unsystematic means, such as a passing comment from a friend or an e-mail from a service provider who also does work for a company in need of capital.[49] By joining a group, angels can increase the number of deals from which they can choose[50] because it is easier for entrepreneurs to find angel groups than to find individual angels.[51]

Moreover, participation in angel groups helps angels to find better quality deals. The screening process of many formal groups allows angels to concentrate their time and attention on only the highest quality deals. And seeing deals in groups allows deals to be viewed in a form that allows for better comparison of the information provided by the entrepreneurs. One angel explained that group investing facilitates high-quality deal flow because the group's screening committee ensures that only viable deals are presented, and makes sure that the investors have adequate information about the companies on which to make decisions.[52]

Second, angels join groups because group investing allows them to take advantage of each other's expertise. Angel groups can pool the knowledge and expertise of different angels, allowing them to evaluate deals and monitor portfolio companies more effectively than they can as individuals.[53] One angel who participated in the Fed-sponsored focus groups gave the example of his group in which a small number of scientists and biomedical executives provide the expertise that allows the rest of the group to invest in biomedical ventures.[54]

By being part of a group, angels can verify the accuracy of their own judgment about the potential of new companies. In a group investment setting, angels need to convince other angels to support investments before they can be made. The process of convincing others to support an investment provides validation of the investment opportunity. In fact, because the people championing an investment to a group of angels are putting their reputations on the line, they may even conduct better due diligence than they would just to satisfy themselves. In describing how investing in a group helps him to verify his judgment, one angel said, "Investing together let's you pitch an idea to someone to see if you can generate the same enthusiasm in another stranger. It's a great validation."[55]

Finally, being part of a group facilitates learning. Less experienced angels can learn how to be better investors from more experienced angels,[56] and because the group is made up of people with different knowledge and skills, angels can learn about technologies, industries, or deal terms with which they are not familiar.[57]

The third reason angels join groups is to improve the efficiency of their investment activity. Groups can achieve greater economies of scale in due diligence and administrative support.[58] They can also more efficiently manage deal flow, prescreening, and due diligence because they can hire staff to help take care of these tasks.[59] Groups can also standardize term sheets, investment processes, and approaches to negotiation, which allows them to spend less time and money on each deal.[60]

Fourth, angels join groups to pool resources. By investing with others, angels can make investments that they otherwise might not have enough capital to make on their own. As one angel explained, "Sometimes it's dictated by size. I might personally put a million bucks in an angel deal but if it was 10 million bucks I'd want it to be part of a group."[61] In addition, by combining financial resources, angels can make larger investments,[62] which is valuable because better deals sometimes require larger amounts of capital.[63] Furthermore, by pooling their capital, angels can create stronger negotiating positions with entrepreneurs, strike better terms for their investments,[64] and have more influence with entrepreneurs and venture capitalists.[65] As one angel explained, "You are more likely to get crushed by venture capitalists in a later round if you invest as an individual because networks can get a stronger term sheet with anti-dilution provisions and so on."[66]

By combining financial resources, angel groups can diversify across investments.[67] The individual angels can invest the same amount of money but spread it across a greater number of companies; this is important because angels need to make between ten and twelve investments across different industries and technologies to manage their risk effectively.[68]

By combining human resources, angel groups can assemble the manpower to conduct more due diligence.[69] Angels typically have a day job, so they often do not have time to do everything necessary to evaluate and monitor their investments. The opportunity to work as part of a team saves the angels "wear and tear" in due diligence by allowing them to divide up the work. Angels can also amortize the cost of due diligence over a larger investment by investing as part of a group. Because there is a limit on the amount of money that angels can justify spending on due diligence—X percent of their prospective investment—the pooling of funds means that angels can spend more money to conduct due diligence.[70]

The benefits of the division of labor that comes from participation in a group are enhanced in managed angel networks where professional staff members do some of the work on behalf of the angels. For instance, in many networks, the managers conduct some of the due diligence on potential portfolio companies, contacting technical advisors and writing summaries of their evaluations for the angels. One angel network even has a local law firm and law school collaborating to provide due diligence to the angel investors at no cost. One angel group manager in Philadelphia explained the benefits of group investing in terms of the effort demanded of angels. She said, "We're a managed angel network. My partner and I drive the due diligence. My partner and I write a due diligence summary. We distribute that to the membership."[71]

Fifth, angels join groups for social reasons, such as the opportunity to get together with their friends or to network with other angels.[72]

Sixth, angels join groups to have the option to invest individually or as a member of a group. Because some investments might be better made by an individual angel and others by a group of angels, this flexibility is advantageous. It is also advantageous because it allows the angel to obtain the benefit of knowledge sharing in the deal evaluation phase and still make an individual investment if the group passes on a company the angel thinks is worthy of investment. Furthermore, this option allows the angel to deflect requests for financing away from himself personally and maintain relationships with the entrepreneurs, even if not making an investment in their companies.[73]

Seventh, angels join groups to provide more value to portfolio companies than they can as individuals. Angel groups increase the odds that portfolio companies will get follow-on funding by deepening the capital pool. They also increase the odds that the companies will get money from venture capitalists because angel groups are seen as more professional than individual angels.[74] Finally, angel groups can provide more post-investment expertise to their portfolio companies because they have a deeper knowledge base.[75]

Why Do Angels Invest Alone?

Angels also have a number of reasons for investing alone. First, some angels, particularly "super angels" invest alone because they have such a large personal financial capacity that they do not need to pool their capital with other people to make angel investments. As one angel explained, "Sometimes you'll find an individual who thinks that their resources are equal to or above the group. They just think they don't need that capacity."[76]

Second, some angels invest alone because they want to minimize the cost of investing and do not want to pay for the administrative overhead that comes from investing as part of an organized group.[77]

Third, some angels invest alone because they do not want others to know about their investment capacity or preferences. These angels are often afraid that if this information were made public, they would be overwhelmed by requests for money.[78]

Fourth, some angels invest alone because they began investing before angel networks came into vogue and aren't familiar with the group investment model. Others don't have the option to invest in a network because few other angels live or work near them.[79]

Fifth, some angels invest alone because they cannot do the kinds of deals they want to do as part of a group. This might mean doing the small deals that angel groups avoid because of high transaction costs[80] or it might mean doing deals in which the angel can become involved in an operating capacity with the portfolio company.[81] When people want to get heavily involved with a small number of portfolio companies, they are more likely to invest alone because that model is not conducive to investing alongside others.[82]

Sixth, some angels invest alone because groups have drawbacks as investment vehicles. Angel groups sometimes make poor decisions because groups of people are subject to decision-making biases[83] and are prone to a herd mentality.[84] Their decisions can be swayed by group dynamics, just like the decisions of any other group.[85] For instance, angel group decisions sometimes depend less on the merit of the venture than on horse trading between different members of the group. Or decisions depend on the members' evaluation of the due diligence team and not the venture itself.[86] And single individuals can kill deals that they don't like with negative analysis, particularly if they are responsible for conducting due diligence.[87]

Angel groups also raise a variety of governance issues not present with individual investments. For instance, if an angel group invests in a company and gets a board seat, who should occupy that seat? And if a particular person represents a group on the board, should that person be compensated for that role? Moreover, the person who occupies the board seat is often the person who championed the venture most vigorously. This means the board member's reputation is at stake with the other members of the group; as a result, he may not provide accurate information to the group on the development of the venture.

Finally, angel groups sometimes trend toward disorganization. They can lack leadership as people become burned out by the process of running the group. The attention of the participants can wane as members lose interest.[88] And the groups can lack continuity as annual turnover in some groups reaches 10 to 20 percent of members.[89]

THE ANGEL GROUP INVESTMENT PROCESS

Angel groups tend to have standard processes that they follow to figure out which companies to invest in. The Director of the Band of Angels, Ian Sobieski, describes the process at that group as follows: "Each month there are about ten deals referred from the members. We invite them in and they give a small pitch to a subset of angels and [we] make a decision about what three we should invite to the full Band of Angels dinner meeting. Three come each month, based on preliminary screening, and get 20 minutes to present at a dinner at which 70 people attend. The following week we have a lunch on three separate days, two hours for each company, at which time people can ask detailed questions, really dig into the company and try to get to understand it better."[90]

Not only do angel groups tend to have standardized investment processes but these processes also display patterns about how groups source deals, evaluate them, select businesses in which to invest, and manage their investments. Prospective angels, entrepreneurs, and policy makers need to understand these patterns if they are to grasp the role of angel groups in the entrepreneurial finance system in this country.

The Concept of the Investment Funnel

Angel groups are selective in choosing the businesses they will fund. This selection does not occur at once but takes places through a process in which businesses are winnowed out at successive stages. At each point in the process, the group members typically look for problems with the venture (e.g., the wrong exit strategy, valuation that is too high, incomplete management team) and eliminate those that show the greatest number of problems or the most severe deficiencies. Many angel groups think of this process as a funnel that begins with the initial screening of executive summaries, followed by evaluation by a screening committee, moving to presentation to the membership and the selection of companies for due diligence, followed by evaluation of the results of due diligence and the negotiation of a term sheet, moving to post-investment assistance and monitoring, and culminating in an exit.

Sourcing Deals

Angel groups source deals in a variety of different ways. Common methods include obtaining referrals from service providers and venture capital firms; participating in investment forums, networking events, and university programs; and using Web sites to capture unsolicited deals.[91] The last mechanism is particularly important in distinguishing angel groups from individual angels; putting up a Web site to solicit deals is much more effective for groups than for individuals because of the higher volume of deals that the former can evaluate, which lowers the per-deal cost of maintaining the site.[92]

Screening Deals

The typical angel group employs a two-stage screening process. The group first screens submissions for ventures that "have a prayer of being funded." Deals that are outside the industry preference or investment criteria of the group are eliminated at this stage. In many of the more organized angel groups, this initial screening is conducted by a group leader, staff member, or a committee of investors.

The initial screening is not an in-depth evaluation and generally involves a quick read of the executive summaries of the submitted business plans. Most business opportunities do not make it through this evaluation phase, with different studies showing rejection rates of between 63 and 91 percent.[93]

The difference in the selectivity depends, at least in part, on how the groups learn about the opportunities. In some groups, the pool of potential deals will have been created by open submission (entrepreneurs who see the group's Web site, know one of its members, or are directed to the group by a third party). In other groups, this pool is limited to submissions sponsored by group members.[94] The former set of groups tends to be much more selective at the initial screening stage because they have many more submissions, and submissions of more varying quality.

From among the deals that fit the group's criteria, the screeners take a more careful look at the opportunities to identify those that would be most appealing to the group's members. This evaluation stage generally does not involve an in-depth examination of the company, with one study showing that investors spend only about ten minutes considering each business.[95] In some cases, the screeners talk to the entrepreneurs and try to evaluate their skills and abilities; in other cases, the screeners evaluate only the business plan itself. Key criteria considered at this stage are who referred the deal; the attractiveness of the opportunity; the quality of the business plan; and the strength of the management team,[96] particularly its start-up and industry experience.[97] On the basis of this evaluation, some of the businesses are eliminated and other businesses move to the presentation stage.[98]

Presentations by Entrepreneurs

Some angel groups move immediately from the screening stage to presentations to the overall membership of the group; others first have entrepreneurs present to a smaller committee. In the groups that have presentations to a smaller committee, the presentations range in length from five to forty-five minutes and include question and answer time. In some cases, the entrepreneurs are asked to present their business opportunities in a standard format to make it easier for the committee to evaluate the different businesses. In other cases, they are allowed to present in a freer format. In some groups, technical experts are brought to the screening committee presentation to give feedback to the investors.[99] Typically, ventures progress from the committee to the overall membership of the group if the committee votes in favor of that action, with the threshold for a positive vote ranging from a simple majority to unanimous agreement.[100]

Presentations by the entrepreneurs to the overall membership of the angel groups, which typically occur at regularly scheduled weekly, monthly, or quarterly meetings, generally take the form of a short presentation followed by a question and answer period.[101] A survey of the groups that belong to the Angel Capital Association showed that the average presentation time is 21.1 minutes (median of 20 minutes) and the average question and answer period is 16.1 minutes (median of 15 minutes).

However, angel groups allow entrepreneurs very different amounts of time to present their business ideas and permit very different amounts of time for them to answer questions posed by angels. The ACA's membership survey indicates that different groups allow entrepreneurs between five minutes and three hours to present their business opportunities and between zero and ninety minutes to answer questions.

Moreover, the length of the presentation and question and answer periods are related to other characteristics of the angel groups. For instance, angel groups in California give entrepreneurs more time, an additional 24.4 minutes over what angel groups in other states allow. Angel groups set up as nonprofit mutual benefit corporations have presentations that are 16.9 minutes shorter than angel groups in some form of for-profit configuration or with no legal structure at all. Finally, angel groups led by managers have shorter presentation times—7.9 minutes less than non-manager-led groups.

The Decision to Go to Due Diligence

After the presentations, the members of angel groups typically decide whether to conduct due diligence on the companies.[102] Usually, this decision is made in real time, immediately after the entrepreneur presents. In many groups, the entrepreneur is asked to step outside after the question and answer period is over while the group discusses the opportunity and makes a decision on whether to conduct due diligence.[103] In some cases, that decision is made individually, with interested investors given the option of pairing off with entrepreneurs to conduct due diligence.[104] In other cases, the group votes on whether to conduct due diligence collectively.[105] Some groups poll their members to make sure there is enough interest to meet the level of investment needed by the entrepreneur before beginning due diligence.

Once companies present, the odds are good that they will make it to due diligence. Different studies show that between one third and 55 percent of companies that are screened by angel groups make it to this next step.[106]

The Due Diligence Process

Once the decision is made to conduct due diligence, the group either assigns responsibility for that activity to one of its members or a staff person or asks for volunteers among the members.[107] Once in the due diligence process, the angel groups investigate the entrepreneurs, market, product, technology, intellectual property, financials, and anything else they think is important in determining whether the business has the potential to be successful.

The due diligence phase varies in selectivity across angel groups, with different studies indicating that between 18 and 76 percent of companies make it from due diligence to a financing event.[108] Some angel groups are positively disposed to companies that make it to due diligence and only reject companies at this stage if they find a glaring problem they did not expect to see, such as a problematic agreement already in place, an inconsistency in the background of a management team member, insufficient intellectual property protection, or evidence of money being used for inappropriate purposes. Other groups rank different business opportunities using the information they gather during the due diligence process and then eliminate all but the top scoring businesses.

The Decision to Invest

After due diligence is conducted, the typical angel group due diligence team prepares a report and presents it to the group's membership.[109] After the due diligence report is presented, group members generally have the opportunity to ask questions of their colleagues on the due diligence team to understand better the opportunity they are being asked to fund. Following the discussion of the due diligence report, the angel group members typically are asked to decide whether to invest in the company.

In some groups, the members decide as individuals; in other groups a vote is taken to determine whether the group should invest. For groups whose members decide whether to invest individually, there is often an effort to get several angels to support the venture, especially when the companies need more money than a single investor can provide alone. In these groups, the angels who are interested in investing in the company often e-mail each other back and forth, talk to each other on the phone, and have side conferences. This process allows the angels to persuade each other of the value of the venture as well as to gather additional information about it. Some angels join the bandwagon to invest and others drop out as this process unfolds over time. The search for information and efforts to persuade other angels to join in generally continues until a deadline is imposed—usually the date of the company's financing round.[110]

The process of making an investment decision is different in groups that make collective decisions. For these groups, the due diligence team generally needs to convince other group members to support the investment or it will not occur. Thus, the investment decision depends largely on the persuasiveness of the due diligence team and the presence of a champion or champions who work to garner support for the venture. Typically, the champion examines the venture very carefully and continues to gather information even after deciding personally to make an investment. Because the champion needs to convince others to make an investment on the basis of his evaluation, he usually wants to make sure that he has strong evidence to support his decision.[111]

After the presentation by the due diligence team and the discussion of what it found, the groups that make collective investment decisions then vote on the investment. The decision rule for what constitutes a positive vote generally ranges from a simple majority to unanimous consent. If the decision is positive, the group then moves to the negotiation of a term sheet.[112]

If the investment decision is negative, the members of an angel group sometimes continue the relationship they have established with the entrepreneur and continue to coach him. Sometimes, investment decisions are negative because the company is not yet ready for an investment but might be ready in six months or a year. For this reason, the group might maintain its ties to the entrepreneur so they can consider investing in the venture at a later time.[113]

KEY FACTS TO REMEMBER

Proportion of companies receiving angel investments that are funded by angel groups	1.8 percent
Proportion of angel investment dollars provided by angel groups	2 percent
Median age of an angel group	3 years
Median size of an angel group	37 members
Number of companies that present to the average angel group every year	24.1
Number of companies receiving investment by the average angel group every year	3.8
Proportion of angel groups that like early stage investments	82 percent
Proportion of angel groups that like seed/start-up stage investments	80 percent
Proportion of angel groups that operate as networks	77.4 percent
Proportion of angel groups that are member led	59 percent
Proportion of angel groups that want to make investments in businesses within a 4-hour drive of group's location	36 percent

After the investment closes, the group moves into the post-investment phase. This phase involves both monitoring and assisting portfolio companies. The form that this monitoring and assistance takes varies substantially, depending on whether the group invests collectively. When the group invests as a set of individuals, the angels typically assist and monitor the portfolio companies on their own. But when the group invests collectively, it generally assigns someone or asks for a volunteer to represent the group. That individual typically meets regularly with the portfolio company management to help with business issues that arise and to check on the performance of the venture. If the group's investment warrants a seat on the board, that individual typically occupies the board seat and reports back to the group's membership.[114]

IN CONCLUSION

A recent development in angel finance is the formation of groups of angel investors who invest together in a coordinated way. While these groups are emerging in a large number of states and cities, they are not emerging equally quickly everywhere, raising important questions about why and how they form.

Angel groups are a unique form of angel finance. Their members tend to be accredited investors, which makes their investment processes very different from those of individual angels. In particular, angel groups tend to have standardized approaches to investing, are more selective, and employ more sophisticated terms than individual angels.

However, angel groups also tend to vary significantly, with their age, size, location, legal structure, organizational structure, stage of investment preference, and source of funding all related to different characteristics of these groups. Therefore, understanding the differences among groups is crucial to understanding angel investing in this country.

Finally, not all angels join groups, which makes it important to understand why some angels join groups and others do not. Angels join groups to get better access to deal flow, to take advantage of the expertise of others, to improve their investment efficiency, to pool resources, to get together with friends and network with others, to have the option to invest alone or with others, and to increase the value that they can add to their portfolio companies. Angels invest alone because they don't need to pool capital with others, to minimize the cost of investing, to avoid letting others know their investment capacity or preferences, to continue an approach that they used before angel groups emerged or that work better where they live, to do the kinds of deals that groups don't do, or to avoid the problems that occur when angels invest in groups.

In short, while angel groups account for a small minority of all angel investors, the companies that receive angel capital, and the amount of angel investment made every year, they are an important subset of angel investors for entrepreneurs, policy makers, and angels themselves to understand.

TEN

How Do the Best Angels Invest?

A s with most types of investing, performance at angel invest-ing is highly skewed—a few people make almost all the money. And this pattern is what makes most discussions of angel investing uninformative. The standard approach is so focused on glo-rifying business angels that it misses this essential point and draws its advice and conclusions without differentiating the best investors from the average.

Of course, as you by now realize, the typical angel is not a good role model. Just like most investors in the stock market, most angels are ill-informed, and they pay the price for that ignorance in terms of inferior financial returns. So following what the *typical* angel does will lead you down the road to poor performance.

However, once you accept the fact that *most* business angels are nothing special and do nothing special, you can learn what it takes to be a successful angel investor. By paying attention to the differences between the professional investors and the fools, you can identify the key parameters for financially successful angel investing.

Before we get into the differences between typical angels and suc-cessful ones, I need to show you that there are dimensions on which we can identify the successes. One of them is membership in a long-established angel group, like the Band of Angels. Since the group's founding in 1994, 4.6 percent of the companies in which it has invested have gone public. That might not sound like a lot, but it's an IPO hit rate at least 23 times as high as that of the typical angel!

Differences between the Band of Angels and the typical angel exist on other dimensions as well. The Band of Angels makes money from angel investing, which separates its members from the 40 percent of high net worth angels associated with angel groups who lost money on their angel investment portfolios![1] Moreover, the average internal rate of return on angel investments across people associated with angel groups is much lower than the Band of Angels' internal rate of return of 55 percent,[2] and those people probably have higher returns than individual angels.

If the typical investor is doing something different from the members of the Band of Angels, then knowing what those differences are is likely to help you to be a financially successful angel. So what makes the best of the best the best? Let's take a look.

FINANCIALLY SUCCESSFUL ANGELS ARE ACCREDITED INVESTORS

In Chapter 2, I showed you that the vast majority of angels are unaccredited investors. This means that the *typical* angel is unaccredited. However, most *financially successful* angels are accredited investors. So wealth is by no means a predictor of who is an angel, but it *is* a predictor of who is a *successful* angel. So why are rich people better at making angel investments than other angels? There are several reasons, which I list from least important to most important.

- First, entrepreneurs can do several things differently when raising money from accredited investors that they can't do when raising money from unaccredited investors. For instance, when money is raised from unaccredited investors, the number of investors is limited to thirty-five, but there is no limitation on the number of investors when money is raised from accredited investors. In addition, entrepreneurs must show that unaccredited investors are sophisticated investors who can judge the risk of investing in private companies. Finally, additional disclosure is necessary to raise money from unaccredited investors.[3] (This reason isn't so important because most entrepreneurs don't raise money from more than thirty-five distinct investors, and the cost of the additional disclosure isn't that high.)
- Second, accredited investors have more money, which enables them to make more, and larger, investments and makes them more likely to have contacts with venture capitalists and strategic investors who can finance additional stages of the

development of private companies. Although there are no data to show angel investments by size of investment for both accredited and unaccredited investors, these data are available for all informal investments. As Figure 10.1 shows, accredited investors account for the majority of large (greater than $100,000) informal investments made in the United States.

The rub, of course, is that accredited investors make up the minority of business angels. So if only some of the accredited investors are successful angels, then only a minority of people making angel investments are the people who truly make money at this activity.

- Third, and most important, accredited investors can band together in investment groups much more easily than unaccredited investors. And, as the previous chapter points out, angel groups tend to make better investments than individual angels because groups:
  - Have access to more due diligence capability.
  - Allow investors to provide larger amounts of money and demand better terms on investment contracts.

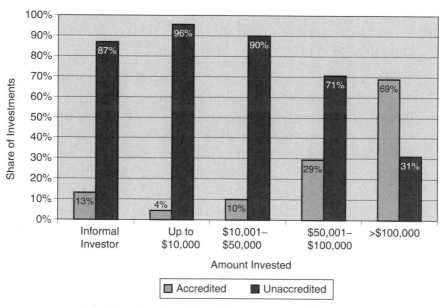

FIGURE 10.1. The Portion of Informal Investments of Different Sizes Made by Accredited and Unaccredited Investors. *Source:* Created from data contained in Reynolds, P. 2004. *Entrepreneurship in the United States Assessment.* Miami: Florida International University.

- Have better deal flow.
- Have better capability to monitor portfolio companies.
- Are better networked with, and respected by, venture capitalists.
- Allow angels to be passive on some deals and active on others.
- Can diversify their investments more effectively.

Thus, the opportunity to invest in a group is an advantage afforded to accredited investors but not unaccredited investors.

Of course, being an accredited investor who is affiliated with an angel group cannot account fully for financially successful angel investing because many angel group members have lost money on their angel investments. So what else makes financially successful angels different from the typical angels?

What group you invest with matters a lot because angel groups are not all equally good at investing in private companies. In fact, many angel groups have not made any money investing in private companies and certainly have not experienced an internal rate of return like that of the leading angel groups. Because of their success, the members the leading groups have very strong relationships and reputations with venture capitalists. They are also highly sought by entrepreneurs who know the value that they provide.

FINANCIALLY SUCCESSFUL ANGELS HAVE EXPERIENCE STARTING COMPANIES, INVESTING IN START-UPS, AND WORKING IN THE INDUSTRIES IN WHICH THEY INVEST

Other than being part of a group with a track record of successful investing, what separates the best angels from the rest? Experience, for one thing. Financially successful angels are almost all experienced as investors in private companies, and they invest in industries that they know. People tend to get better at most things they do the more they do them, and angel investing is no exception. Performance tends to increase with the number of investments that investors have made. In fact, many successful angels—people who have made a lot of money investing in companies that ultimately go public—talk about the errors they made in their initial deals. For instance, several highly successful angels have recounted the same story about their first deal: making an unsecured loan on a handshake. The investments they made later—and that they profited from—weren't unsecured loans, and they weren't handshake deals.[4]

Financially successful angels are almost all experienced in the industries in which they invest.[5] In a survey of high net worth angels affiliated with angel groups, Rob Wiltbank of Willamette University found that the more experience angels have in the industries in which they are investing, the higher is the performance of their investments.[6]

But there's a catch. Experience in the industries in which they invest separates successful angels from typical angels *only* if the investors have experience in industries in which new companies tend to be successful. It's not just industry experience that matters; it's the joint effect of investing in companies in angel-favorable industries like computers and medical devices *and* having experience in those industries that enhances performance.

I suspect that this point is rarely raised by most observers of angel investing because it's hard to turn it into a "how to." If people want to be angel investors and they have a lot of experience in, say, the auto industry, it's hard to tell them how to be successful. They can't remake their careers. But the truth is that investing in the industry in which an auto executive has experience is very unlikely to make that person a successful angel investor. Investing in industries in which investments tend to be successful, but the angel does not know, isn't the answer either because angels need to know the industries in which they invest to be effective. Nevertheless, even if this information isn't very useful for potential angels, it is useful for potential entrepreneurs and policy makers who can target experienced investors that are familiar with the industries in which angel investments tend to be successful.

FINANCIALLY SUCCESSFUL ANGELS KNOW WHICH INDUSTRIES TO INVEST IN

The previous section begs the question: what industries make for financially successful angel investments? The answer: those industries in which the odds are most favorable for the kind of rapid growth that allows companies to achieve high value exits in a short period of time. This means that successful angels put their money into technology companies. Research shows that the technology intensity of an industry is an important predictor of rapid growth, with one study indicating that the proportion of high-tech workers in an industry predicts the proportion of start-ups that make it to the Inc. 500 list of the fastest growing private companies in the United States.[7]

But financially successful angels do more than just pick companies in high-tech industries. After all, a lot of industries, like autos and plastics, are high-tech, but are not very good for angel investing. Successful angels also focus on industries that tend to attract venture capitalists. Why? Because it is easier to get VC follow-on money in industries that venture capitalists like, and venture capital-backed start-ups outperform non-venture capital backed ones when it comes to financial returns to investors.

So what industries do venture capitalists invest in? As Chapter 6 explained, 81 percent of all venture capital dollars are invested in just five industries: computer hardware, computer software (including the Internet), semiconductors and other electronics, communication, and biotechnology, and 73 percent of recipient companies operate in these industries.[8] Because venture capitalists invest in a narrow range of industries, the odds of getting follow-on venture money is dramatically improved by focusing on those industries. Financially successful angels know this and focus their investments in industries that VCs like.

But venture capitalists don't select certain industries just because they like the sound of their names. They like them because those are the industries in which start-ups are most likely to go public. Why? Because an initial public offering is the exit that generates the greatest financial return for investors. (In fact, most of the money made from angel investments has been made from investments in companies that have gone public. For instance, the Band of Angels has lost money on half of the companies in which it has invested, and still had an internal rate of return of 55 percent because of its nine investments that have gone public.) So what are those industries in which start-ups are most likely to go public? They are summarized in Table 10.1.

FINANCIALLY SUCCESSFUL ANGELS ARE HIGHLY SELECTIVE

Financially successful angels select their investments very carefully. Very few companies are founded in high-tech industries, and fewer still are started in the subset of high-tech industries in which most companies that go public are found. So successful angels realize that most of the business opportunities they hear about and the business plans they see aren't in industries in which they can make large finan-

TABLE 10.1. Industries in Which at Least 1 Percent of Start-ups
Founded Each Year Go Public

SIC Code	Industry	IPOs as a Share of Starts
283	Drugs	20.3%
366	Communications Equipment	8.7%
357	Computer and Office Equipment	6.0%
384	Medical Instruments and Supplies	4.7%
367	Electronic Components and Accessories	3.4%
382	Measuring and Controlling Devices	3.3%
369	Miscellaneous Electrical Equipment and Supplies	1.4%
372	Aircraft and Parts	1.3%
208	Beverages	1.0%
484	Cable and Other Pay Television Broadcasting	1.0%
358	Refrigeration and Service Machinery	1.0%

Source: Calculated from data provided by Jonathan Eckhardt and
Thomson Financial, Securities Data Company. (Includes only industries
with an average of at least one IPO per year, and 75 start-ups per year.
IPOs exclude unit offerings, American depository receipts, financial firms,
closed-end mutual funds, real estate investment trusts, spin-offs, reverse
leverage buyouts, foreign firms listing in United States, subsidiary IPOs,
agency offerings, utilities and public offerings of firms with primary shares
outside of the United States.)

cial returns on their investments. Moreover, even within those industries in which IPOs tend to occur, the vast majority of start-ups don't
reach the levels of growth that angels target. As Chapter 8 showed,
even in computer software, only 0.4 percent of start-ups reach $50
million in sales within six years of starting, and only 1.2 percent of
makers of computer peripherals and only 5.5 percent of semiconductor makers reach this level in that amount of time. To get to the point
at which one-in-ten investments makes this growth target, angels have
to find the best start-ups in these industries. So how do the successful
angels do that?

Rather than getting caught up in the optimism of entrepreneurs,
they take a skeptical view of the prospects of start-ups and leave the
dreaming to entrepreneurs. Because most businesses will never achieve

what entrepreneurs say they will, successful angels invest in only those cases where the stars are aligned to give the company a chance to be a very big success. This means ruling out businesses with many strikes against them—weak intellectual property protection, an unclear market, inexperienced entrepreneurs, absence of a real market need, no barriers to competition,[9] lack of scalability, inability to weaken the competitive advantage of incumbents, and so on—and play the odds.

But again, the notion of being selective is only part of the story. You can select only one tenth of 1 percent of the deals you see and still invest only in dogs if you never see good deals. So a big part of what makes selectivity work for successful angels is the generation of very high-quality deal flow. In short, it's not just being selective that makes top angels more successful than typical angels; it's being highly selective among very good opportunities.

FINANCIALLY SUCCESSFUL ANGELS LOOK FOR FINANCIAL DEALS

Financially successful angels also think about angel investing in economic terms and are motivated to generate high returns on their investments. They start with very high return expectations. Given the failure rate of angel investments, successful angels target a thirty times multiple on their invested capital in five years. This alone makes them different from the typical angel investor. According to the data from the Entrepreneurship in the United States Assessment, only 45.4 percent of angel investors expect a rate of return greater than *ten times* their invested capital in *ten* years.

Moreover, financially successful angels invest in businesses that are likely to go public or be acquired in a short period of time. It's basic mathematics to see that the internal rate of return depends a great deal on the time horizon of an investment. Two investments that generate an equal multiple on invested capital will produce very different rates of return if they are earned over different time horizons. For instance, take an investment in a company that generates a return of twice the capital put in. If that multiple is achieved in one year, the internal rate of return on the investment is 100 percent, but it is only 26 percent if the return takes three years to generate.

Finally, successful angels limit the amount of money available for financing private companies. The number of financially rewarding angel investments is constrained by the number of entrepreneurs pursuing business opportunities that stand a chance of becoming high-growth companies. Because the number of good investment opportunities can't be improved by increasing the amount of money available for investment, successful angels avoid chasing deals. By avoiding the temptation to pour money into the process, successful angels avoid competition that drives up valuations and drives down expected returns.

FINANCIALLY SUCCESSFUL ANGELS DON'T OVERVALUE COMPANIES

This brings us to the next important point. Successful angels don't overvalue companies. They don't settle on arbitrary valuations through negotiations with entrepreneurs but instead base their valuations on analysis of the companies.

In fact, financially successful angels tend to undervalue companies because undervaluation increases their financial returns substantially. The initial valuation of a business has a curvilinear effect on return on investment (ROI). That is, a 1 percent decrease in the valuation of a company increases an investor's ROI by more than 1 percent.[10] This means, of course, that successful angels make sure that the valuation of a business is supported by its economics.

One way that successful angels do this is by taking industry into account when valuing companies. Table 10.2 shows the median, or typical, value of a surviving six-year-old company in different industries, as well as the valuation of the typical surviving company in each industry necessary to generate ten times the capital invested with a fifty percent ownership share. The table shows that even at the most precise definition of industry available—the four digit SIC code—dramatic differences exist in the value of companies at the time that angels expect to exit their investments, across even those industries in which angels are said to focus their investments, from a low of $453,000 in computer related services to a high of $11.2 million in semiconductors and related devices. Failing to take this industry variation into account leads investors to overvalue companies because the valuation necessary to earn the desired return on the typical company in many industries lies below the average valuation for all industries.

More important, the typical angel makes the mistake of valuing companies by benchmarking averages across business angels. To be

TABLE 10.2. The Valuation at Start-up Necessary to Earn 10 Times
Invested Capital on Investments in the Median Surviving
Firm in Industries in Which Angels Are Said to Invest

Industry	Value of a Typical Surviving 6-Year-Old Company	Valuation at Investment to Earn 10X on Typical Firm with Half Ownership
Computer Peripheral Equipment	$ 1,545,000	$ 77,250
Computer Programming Services	$ 666,000	$ 33,300
Prepackaged Software	$ 1,158,000	$ 57,900
Computer Integrated Systems Design	$ 738,000	$ 36,900
Data processing and Preparation	$ 600,000	$ 30,000
Information Retrieval Services	$ 2,865,000	$143,250
Computer Related Services, Not Elsewhere Classified	$ 453,000	$ 22,650
Printed Circuit Boards	$ 615,000	$ 30,750
Semiconductors and Related Devices	$11,190,000	$559,500
Electronic Components, Not Elsewhere Classified	$ 3,180,000	$159,000
Electromedical Equipment, X-ray Apparatus and Tubes	$ 855,000	$ 42,750
Pharmaceutical Preparations	$ 9,270,000	$463,500
Surgical Preparations	$ 3,420,000	$171,000
Radio Telephone	$ 468,000	$ 23,400
Other Telephone Communications	$ 525,000	$ 26,250
Radio and Television Broadcasting	$ 2,842,500	$142,125
Communications, Not Elsewhere Classified	$ 450,000	$ 22,500
Radio and Television Apparatus	$ 3,180,000	$159,000
Miscellaneous Publishing	$ 603,000	$ 30,150

Source: Calculated from data contained in Pratt's Stats and a special
tabulation of the Business Information Tracking Series of the U.S. Census.
(These industries are measured at the four-digit SIC code level.)

successful financially, the typical angel needs to value the companies in which he invests at less than the average for angel investors. Because the typical angel is worse than successful angels at picking companies that go public or get acquired at high multiples, his portfolio companies perform worse than those of successful angels. To generate the same rate of return as successful angels, typical angels need to value their companies lower. If, instead, they benchmark the average valuation across all angels, they end up systematically over-valuing their portfolio companies, and end up with poorer performing investments.

FINANCIALLY SUCCESSFUL ANGELS ARE INVOLVED INVESTORS

Because successful angels are skeptical of the claims of entrepreneurs, they investigate companies the same way that venture capitalists do. For instance, they talk to references beyond the list provided by entrepreneurs, ask customers how interested they truly are in the entrepreneurs' products or services, and obtain independent legal opinions about the strength of the companies' intellectual property protection. This greater level of investigation means that successful angels spend more time on due diligence than typical angels. Rob Wiltbank's study of the performance of angel group investors showed that investments on which angels did more than the typical amount of due diligence had an average multiple of 5.9 on the capital invested whereas investments on which angels did less than the typical amount of due diligence had a multiple of only 1.1.[11]

After they make their investments, financially successful angels spend more time with their portfolio companies. Wiltbank's survey of high net worth angel investors who are affiliated with angel groups shows that those angels who meet with their portfolio companies a couple of times per month earn a multiple of 3.7 times their capital invested, on average, whereas those who meet with their portfolio companies only a couple of times per year earn 1.3 times their invested capital, on average.[12] (This may be why financially successful angels make their investments near where they live and work—so they can better assist the start-ups in which they invest.)[13]

But again there is an important caution. Providing assistance alone is not enough. Financially successful angels realize that they must have expertise their portfolio companies need. Otherwise, their greater interaction with the entrepreneurs they finance only amounts to meddling that doesn't improve the companies' prospects.

FINANCIALLY SUCCESSFUL ANGELS ARE DIVERSIFIED INVESTORS IN EARLY STAGE COMPANIES

Financially successful angel investors know that the distribution of returns to their investments is skewed. For instance, Wiltbank's study of investments by high net worth, sophisticated angels associated with angel groups showed that 52 percent of the investments lost money and 7 percent of the investments accounted for three quarters of the total returns.[14] Similarly, Luis Villalobos, a leading angel investor affiliated with Tech Coast Angels, reports that 6 percent of his investment portfolio accounts for 84 percent of his financial returns.[15] Therefore, to make money commensurate with the risk of investing in private companies, investors must be diversified.

Having multiple investments improves the overall performance of an angel investment portfolio. For instance, Wiltbank's study of the performance of investments made by angels in groups showed that the average return across all investments was worse than the average performance for each given angel, which indicates the value of diversification for improving the performance of an investment portfolio.[16]

However, even among samples of highly successful angels—those who belong to angel groups and have an average net worth of over $10 million—the average investor makes too few investments to be diversified, making only about one investment per year (and holding that investment for five years). In contrast, financially successful angels make more investments, holding a portfolio of investments in ten or more start-ups at a time.

Financially successful angels are also less likely than unsuccessful angels to make follow-on investments. In his study of high net worth angels associated with angel groups, Wiltbank found that investments in which angels don't follow-on have a higher return than those in which they do.[17] Why? Investing follow-on capital has an opportunity cost. Whatever money you use to make a follow-on investment comes at the expense of making an investment in a new company. So if you make one-time investments in a larger number of companies and

allow those investments to be diluted down, you will be more diversified than if you make follow-on investments in businesses that need
more money. (Because follow-on investments aren't always made in
businesses that are doing well, you might also benefit from a check
on the tendency to throw good money after bad in making your angel
investments.)

Financially successful angels focus on the seed or start-up round
of financing. One study of high net worth business angels found that
investors in seed stage businesses had fewer investments with an internal rate of return below zero.[18] Again, the reason might have to do with
the best allocation of limited capital. Because the businesses in which
start-ups tend to be very successful demand larger and larger amounts
of capital as they develop, investors can allot a given amount of capital across more investment opportunities if they invest their money at
the earliest stages when capital demands are smallest. As a result, by
investing at the seed and start-up stage, successful angels can be more
diversified with a given amount of capital than they would be if they
invested at later stages.

FINANCIALLY SUCCESSFUL ANGELS
STRUCTURE INVESTMENTS TO MINIMIZE
RISK AND MAXIMIZE RETURNS

Successful angels structure their deals to reduce their risks and maximize their returns. This means that successful angels are much more
likely than typical angels to purchase equity rather than lend money.
Moreover, when successful angels make loans, they usually take the
form of convertible debt, which provides the upside potential of
equity.

Successful angels also establish financial agreements that give them
some control over the companies in which they invest. In fact, one
study of high net worth business angels shows a positive relationship
between the degree to which the investor takes a control-oriented
approach and the rate of return earned on the investment.[19] Taking
control involves the use of contract terms to protect investors against
problems of entrepreneurial moral hazard and poor performance.[20]
Investors also use mechanisms, like management stock ownership,
to align the incentives of the people running the company with their
own.[21] (But successful angels do not seek majority ownership if they

invest in the seed or start-up round of companies that will need multiple rounds of financing; this would dilute the entrepreneurs' ownership too much for them to have incentive to develop the companies and raise additional rounds of money.)

IN CONCLUSION

Only a minority of angels are financially successful investors in private companies. Therefore, if you are an angel or prospective angel and want to make money from your angel investments, are an entrepreneur who wants to work with a successful angel, or a policy maker who wants to encourage angel investment activity among people who know how to do it well, you need to know how financially successful angels invest in private companies.

Financially successful angels tend to be accredited investors who have significant experience investing in private companies, have worked in the industries in which they invest, *and* have experience in industries favorable to angel investing. Unless they are super angels who run their own investment firms, financially successful business angels tend to invest as part of an angel group composed of people who know how to invest successfully in private companies.

Financially successful angels are very selective investors. They have high return expectations and carefully select only the highest potential ventures to finance. Before they invest, they conduct substantial due diligence, and after they invest, they become involved with their portfolio companies, monitoring their investments, and helping the entrepreneurs to make the companies successful (because they have value to add).

Financially successful angels are under no illusions about what makes successful companies successful. They focus on the small number of industries in which venture capitalists invest, and in which IPOs tend to occur, so as to maximize their potential returns from angel investing.

Financially successful angels know that only a small portion of their investments will be successful, even if they focus on the right industries, companies, and entrepreneurs. Therefore, they make multiple investments to diversify their risk across a variety of businesses. They also focus on early stage companies and use their capital to make new investments, rather than following on old ones, because this approach allows them to make more diversified investments with a given amount of capital.

Financially successful angels structure deals with entrepreneurs well. They don't overvalue companies and don't chase opportunities, knowing that competition to invest will drive up valuations and turn good companies into bad deals. They also understand the difference in valuations of young companies across industries and make appropriate valuations, rather than benchmarking from overall averages.

When they make agreements with entrepreneurs, financially successful angels structure their agreements to minimize risk and maximize returns. They take equity rather than lend money. And they use financial instruments that give them some control over the direction of their portfolio companies.

In short, the few financially successful business angels do things differently from the larger group of unsuccessful ones.

ELEVEN

What Makes a Place Good for Angel Investing?

I F YOU'RE AN entrepreneur looking for someone to make an angel investment in your new company, or you're an angel looking to make those investments yourself, or you're a policy maker seeking to use angel investing to drive the growth of your local economy, you need to know if the characteristics of the local environment affect the odds that companies will receive these investments. Some places might be better suited than others for companies to raise external equity and you need to know whether your locale is favorable or unfavorable to this type of finance.

This chapter looks at the similarities and differences in angel investing across different parts of the United States. Specifically, it answers four questions:

- Is angel investing a local business (making differences between places important for this activity)?
- Does the amount of angel financing vary across parts of the United States?
- If so, what kinds of places have more angel investment than others?
- What can governments do to increase the amount of angel activity in an area?

Let's turn now to the first question.

IS ANGEL INVESTING A LOCAL BUSINESS?

Whether angel investing is a local or a national business matters a lot for angels, entrepreneurs, and policy makers. If the angel capital market is a national one, like the public stock market, then differences in the amount of investment capital available in different geographic locations don't matter very much. Entrepreneurs who need angel capital but can't get it where they are can just raise it somewhere else, and angels who have capital but no businesses to fund where they are can just invest their money elsewhere.

Many observers give the impression that the angel capital market is a national one. They say that angels are more interested in financing good companies than in financing local ones and that a lot of angels will therefore invest in good companies wherever they are found. As one observer put it, investing close to home is "not a major consideration" for many angels.[1]

However, the reality is that the angel capital market is a local one; the typical business angel invests almost exclusively in nearby companies.[2] Most studies have found that angels make between 70 and 85 percent of their investments within fifty miles of their homes.[3] For instance, data from the Entrepreneurship in the United States Assessment shows that 72.7 percent of the investments made by angels are in businesses located within fifty miles of the investors.

Even studies of the most sophisticated business angels show a pattern of localized investment. For example, a study of business angels in California who made "Series A" investments in private companies showed that 65 percent of the investors were located within a three-hour drive of the portfolio companies.[4]

Angels focus their investments on nearby companies for several reasons. First, some angels want to be able to monitor their investments by visiting the entrepreneur's place of business ("seeing them sweat" as one angel put it), which is easier to do if the company is nearby.[5] Another explained, "As an investor I want to go out and be able to kick the side of the wall, or kick the desk, and find out where the hell the investment is. I don't want an investment a five-hour plane ride away."[6]

Second, some angel investors want to get involved with their portfolio companies, and this is difficult to do if the company is far away. Distance makes it harder to influence the entrepreneur, and hinders the investor's ability to step in during a crisis.[7] One angel who participated in the Federal Reserve–sponsored focus groups explained that an investor needs to interact with the entrepreneur regularly to have an effect on him and sometimes needs to help fight fires at the company; and neither of those things is easy to do at a distance.[8]

Third, angels often rely on people that they know to identify good investment opportunities.[9] One angel who participated in the Federal Reserve–sponsored focus groups explained that entrepreneurs have better contacts and greater trust with people in their local area, making it easier for them to identify good local investments than to identify favorable investments farther away.[10]

Fourth, angel investors want to build sustainable companies in the community in which they live and work because those companies create local jobs and enhance local economic development.[11]

In short, angel investing is primarily a local business, making it important to figure out if some places have more angel investment activity than others.

DOES THE AMOUNT OF ANGEL ACTIVITY VARY ACROSS PARTS OF THE UNITED STATES?

Although angel investing is less geographically concentrated than venture capital investing,[12] it is far from evenly distributed across parts of the country.[13] To see how unevenly distributed angel investment activity is, we can look at data from the Census Bureau's Survey of Business Owners on new firms founded between 1997 and 2002. By counting the number of businesses founded in those years that received an equity investment from someone who was not a manager, employee, or relative of the founder in each metropolitan statistical area (MSA) with at least 250,000 people (there are 155) and dividing that number by the population, we can measure the per capita rate at which young companies receive external equity investments in each MSA.

As Table 11.1 shows, Boulder-Longmont, Colorado, has the highest per capita rate of angel investing in the country; 275 businesses received an angel investment for every million people in that MSA. At the other end of the spectrum, several areas, such as Brownsville-Harlingen-San Benito, McAllen-Edinburg-Mission, and Corpus Christi, Texas; Saginaw-Bay City-Midland and Lansing-East Lansing, Michigan; Valejo-Napa-Fairfield, California; and Monmouth-Ocean, New Jersey showed *no* angel investing during 1997–2002.

(Before you send me an e-mail indicating that these data must be wrong because you made or received an angel investment in these

TABLE 11.1. Top Ten Metropolitan Statistical Areas with 250,000 or More
People by Per Capita Rate of External Equity Investment

Metropolitan Statistical Area	External Equity Recipient Firms per Million People
Boulder-Longmont, CO	275
Santa Barbara-Santa Maria-Lompoc, CA	177
Reno, NV	170
Raleigh-Durham-Chapel Hill, NC	162
Austin-San Marcos, TX	114
San Jose, CA	107
Tucson, AZ	106
Portland, ME	103
Sarasota-Bradenton, FL	93
Madison, WI	86

Source: Created from data contained in a Special Tabulation of the Survey
of Business Owners of the U.S. Census.

regions during this time period, I want to note that this estimate is
based on responses by entrepreneurs to a survey by the Census Bureau.
If people didn't answer the survey, the investments their companies
received were not recorded. But unless people from some places are
more likely than others to answer surveys about angel investing, these
data are useful for capturing the rate of investment even if they miss a
couple of cases here and there.)

The numbers clearly show that different places in the United
States have very different rates of external equity investment activity.
And these differences exist between places that aren't very far apart
physically. For instance, there is almost four times as much external
investment per capita in the Boulder (Colorado) MSA as in the nearby
Denver metro area. That begs the next question: why?

WHAT KINDS OF PLACES HAVE MORE ANGEL INVESTMENT ACTIVITY THAN OTHERS?

We don't know for sure why rates of external equity investing are so
different across MSAs but we can look at the data for some clues. Two
sources of information—the Federal Reserve focus groups conducted

with angel investors and statistical analysis of the Census data—suggest that six factors affect the amount of this investing that occurs in a locale: the industrial base of the area, its level of wealth, general economic conditions in the area, the stock of universities in the region, the number of entrepreneurs operating in the MSA, and the number of managers found in the locale.[14]

The Relevant Industrial Base

Places that have an industrial base favorable to external equity investing have more external equity investment activity than other places. Investors choose whether to finance the companies that entrepreneurs start; rarely do they offer money to entrepreneurs and ask them to start certain types of companies. Because most entrepreneurs start businesses in the same industries as their previous employers, they tend to start new companies that are related to the industrial base of a region. So if the industries in an area are not the kind that offer good potential returns to external equity investors, that area will have less external investment than areas that have more favorable industries.

Moreover, most investors focus on familiar industries because they find comfort in focusing on things they understand. If a region's economy relies on older, less technology-intensive industries that are believed to be less attractive to external equity investors, then a barrier to investing emerges. The industries that potential investors in the area understand are not particularly conducive to external financing. At the same time, businesses that are conducive to external investing are unfamiliar to the area's pool of potential investors. The result is a lower rate of external equity investing in the area, as compared to others. One participant in the Fed-sponsored focus groups noted this problem, saying: "A huge issue for this town is this split between biotechnology and industrial capital. I've been in meetings where biotechnology entrepreneurs make pitches to angels who made their money in industrial capital. The knowledge gap is overwhelming. How do they critically access what the professor of genetics with this super cool software is saying, and how do they know the impact this will have on an industry that they don't understand? It's real hard to say I want to throw some discretionary capital at this person just because you have it."[15]

Even though most external equity investors don't invest in high-tech companies, the data show a relationship between the proportion of an MSA's business establishments in high-tech industries and its rate of external equity investment activity. Table 11.2 shows the

TABLE 11.2. The Correlations between the Percentage of Establishments in High-Tech Industries and the Per Capita Rate of External Equity Investing for Metropolitan Statistical Areas with 250,000 or More People

Industry	Correlation
R&D in the Physical, Engineering, and Life Sciences	0.45
Software Publishers	0.39
Computer and Peripheral Equipment Manufacturing	0.37
Other Communications Equipment	0.37
Navigational, Measuring, Medical and Control Instruments Manufacturing	0.34
Other Information Services	0.33
Telephone Apparatus Manufacturing	0.32
Pharmaceutical and Medicine Manufacturing	0.32
Computer Systems Design and Related Services	0.31
Semiconductor and Other Electronic Component Manufacturing	0.28
Radio and Television Broadcasting and Wireless Communications Equipment	0.24
All Above Industries Combined	0.38

Source: Created from Data in the Economic Census of the United States and a special tabulation of the Survey of Business Owners of the U.S. Census. Note: These industries are defined by the Bureau of Labor Statistics on the basis of employment and do not correspond to SIC codes.

correlations (all statistically significant) between the per capita rate of external equity investment in all metro areas with 250,000 or more people and the proportion of business establishments found in several high-tech industries. As you can see from the table, the share of businesses in a metro area in these industries is pretty highly correlated with the area's per capita rate of external equity investing, suggesting that places with more high-tech companies have more of this investment activity than other places.

Other measures of a metro area's reliance on technology businesses show similar patterns. For instance, there is a significant positive correlation between the per capita rate of external equity investment and the per capita number of patents created in the MSA ($r = .30$). There are also significant positive correlations with the rate of increase in economic output from high-tech industries over the preceding five years (r=.27), and the degree of concentration of the MSA on high technology (r=.25) (as measured by the Milken Institute, a think tank focused on regional economic development). Moreover, there is a significant positive correlation between the percentage of people living in the MSA whose occupations require the use of computers or mathematics and the per capita number of firms receiving external equity investments (r=.44).

The Wealth of the Area

Many observers don't think that the availability of capital per se is a key element to have successful external equity investing in a region. For instance, many of the participants in the angel investment focus groups argued that there is always plenty of money for good ideas because money is a commodity that travels to locations where there are talented entrepreneurs and good ideas from places where these things are absent.[16]

However, this argument misses a key point about external equity investing. The activity involves the provision of capital to companies that need financing by other people. While people don't have to be wealthy or even to be accredited investors to make external equity investments, they are more *likely* to make these investments if they have more money. Therefore, the more people in an area who have the money to invest in other people's companies, the more external investing there will be. Therefore, places where the *typical* person is wealthier should have more external equity investment activity than places where the *typical* person is poorer.

The Census data show evidence of this pattern. For MSAs of 250,000 or more people, there is a significant positive correlation between the per capita rate of external equity investment activity and per capita income (r=0.32). Moreover, there is a significant negative correlation between the rate of external equity investment activity and the percentage of people in the MSA living in poverty (r=-0.24).

Note, however, that having very wealthy people with a lot of investable assets is not necessarily correlated with having a lot of external equity investment activity in an area. Although some observers have argued that this type of investing is more common in regions where the distribution of capital is highly skewed because the amount of money people are willing to invest in risky asset classes increases with their net worth, the data disagree. The per capita number of people with $1 million or more in investable assets in a metro area is only weakly correlated with the per capita rate of external investing, either for the total set of 292 MSAs on which data are available or the 155 MSAs with a population of 250,000 or more. Moreover, in analyses to predict per capita rate of external equity investing that include both median per capita income *and* the percentage of the population with more than $1 million dollars in investible assets, only the per capita income measure has a significant effect on the rate of external equity investing. That is, the median wealth of a region has *more* of an effect on the rate of external equity investing than the proportion of people with a lot of money to invest.[17] Of course, this pattern is consistent with the observation in Chapter 2 that a whole lot of angels are not accredited investors. The rich may be different from you and me, but it's not because they are solely responsible for angel investing.

General Economic Conditions

As you might expect, there is a relationship between the general economic conditions of a metro area and its external equity investment activity. Places with high unemployment, low levels of wage and salary growth, slow population growth, and weak job growth are generally unattractive places in which to do business. As a result, few people start businesses with enough potential to justify external investment, and there is relatively little external investing.

The data support this argument. For the MSAs with 250,000 or more people, there is a significant positive correlation between the per capita rate of external equity investing and the following measures of general economic conditions:

- The population growth over the preceding seven years ($r = 0.22$).
- The rate of job growth over the previous six years (as measured by the Milken Institute) ($r = .24$).
- The rate of wage and salary growth over the previous five years (as measured by the Milken Institute) ($r = .25$).

And there is a significant negative correlation between the rate of external investing activity and the unemployment rate in the prior year ($r = -.31$). In short, there is a higher rate of this type of investing in places with growing economies than in places with stagnant or declining ones.

Higher Education Infrastructure

A fourth dimension of a place that is positively related to its rate of external equity investment activity is its higher educational infrastructure. Several observers have suggested that universities increase the level of external investing in an area by increasing the pool of talented people. As these observers explain, universities provide a place to educate people to become entrepreneurs and provide a source of smart people who can become employees of the new companies once they graduate.[18]

The empirical evidence supports this point of view. Two measures of the educational infrastructure—the per capita number of Ph.D. graduates from universities in the MSA and the proportion of people with a college education—are positively related to the per capita rate of external equity investing in the MSA. For metro areas of 250,000 people or more, the correlation between the per capita number of Ph.D. graduates from universities and the rate of external equity investing is 0.42 while the correlation between the percentage of the population with a college education and the rate of external equity investment activity is 0.52.

The Presence of Seasoned Entrepreneurs

A fifth element that is thought to be positively related to the amount of external equity investment in a region is the stock of seasoned entrepreneurs. Several observers have argued that a place cannot have a lot of external investment activity unless it has the entrepreneurs to put forward new business ideas because investors are reactive, not proactive. They will fund some portion of businesses that are presented to them, but they aren't going to dream up the business ideas themselves and then find entrepreneurs to pursue them. So the greater the proportion of people in an area who have the willingness and ability to start businesses, the more businesses will be financed by external investors.

Moreover, having more entrepreneurs in an area creates a culture that supports external investing by leading policy makers, the local media, and other institutions to focus their attention on the creation of new companies as an economic development strategy. It also leads people to think that becoming an entrepreneur is a socially desirable vocation, which increases the number of people in the area willing to start companies and attracts to the area people who want to become entrepreneurs. The change in culture also makes it easier for people with available capital to think about investing some portion of their money in private companies. All of this has the end result of increasing the number of external equity investments in an area.[19]

Places with a higher proportion of entrepreneurs among their populations have a higher rate of external equity investment than other places. Statistical analyses that isolate the effect of one factor from the effect of others show that the correlation between the rate of self-employment in MSAs with more than 250,000 people and the per capita rate of external equity investment is 0.36, suggesting a solid positive relationship between the proportion of the population striking out on their own and the per capita rate at which businesses get external equity.

Seasoned Managers

A final element that is positively related to the amount of external equity investment in a region is its stock of seasoned managers. While it might seem paradoxical that places need a lot of seasoned managers to have a lot of this investment, this relationship actually makes a lot of sense. Many investors are looking to put money into companies worthy of their investment. Companies are more worthy of external equity investment if they can attract the management talent necessary to grow. Therefore, places that have a deeper pool of management talent are more likely to have more investment-appropriate companies, and, consequently, a higher rate of external equity investment activity.

The evidence supports this. The correlation between the percentage of the population in managerial occupations and the rate of external equity investment activity across 155 metro areas with populations of 250,000 or more people is 0.46.

WHAT CAN GOVERNMENTS DO TO AFFECT THE AMOUNT OF ANGEL INVESTMENT ACTIVITY IN AN AREA?

Some observers argue that the government should intervene in the angel capital market because "the highly inefficient angel capital market lacks mechanisms for bringing investors and entrepreneurs together, and highly constrictive securities regulations inhibit communication between promising ventures and savvy investors."[20] That is, the justification for government intervention is market failure: If left to its own devices, the angel capital market will fail to finance an adequate number of start-up companies. This argument, of course, raises the question: Is the angel capital market failing?

Is the Angel Capital Marketing Failing?

To date, there is no evidence of failure in the angel capital market. First, the private sector appears to provide sufficient angel capital to companies that need and warrant it.[21] As we saw in Chapter 4, the data do not indicate a shortage of angel capital. The number of angel financed companies is proportional to the number of companies that need angel capital.

Second, there is no evidence that the variation in rates of angel investing across metro areas represents a "failure" of some areas to generate sufficient angel investment activity. Different places may simply have different needs for angel investing based on their industrial or educational infrastructures. These different needs account for the differences across locations in the amount of angel investment that occurs.

Third, there is no evidence that angel investing provides societal benefits that are unrelated to, or inversely related to, the private benefits garnered by angels from investing in start-up companies. So the traditional argument for market failure—that private investors cannot capture the returns on their investments—does not appear to hold for angel investing.

Fourth, government intervention might cause more harm than good. Because the typical angel is not very effective at investing in start-up companies, effective policy toward angel investing necessitates defining the type of investor who should receive government support—something that the government is unlikely to be very good at. Moreover, government policies to encourage angel investing would necessarily involve significant administrative paperwork and requirements, and these could handicap angel investing and keep it from functioning effectively.[22]

In short, there is no evidence of a market failure that justifies government efforts to boost angel investment activity; the market for angel finance appears to be working just fine, making the cost of intervention likely to exceed its benefits.

What Levers Does the Government Have?

Even if you don't buy the argument that the government should stay out of the angel capital market because the market is functioning just fine, there's still the problem of what governments can do to affect the amount of angel investment activity. In general, policy makers have few tools at their disposal to do much of anything. Many of the factors associated with the rate of angel activity in an area—things like the industrial composition of a region, its wealth, its stock of entrepreneurs and managers, and the education of its citizens—are not directly under their control. (If they were, policy makers wouldn't need to worry about angel investing; they could just create the right industries and make their citizens wealthy and well educated.)

Other factors that might increase the amount of angel investing activity in an area are things that are very difficult for governments to implement. For instance, many people avoid investing in new businesses because they do not know how to make these investments or how to evaluate businesses seeking funding.[23] Such a barrier might be overcome by efforts to educate people about how to invest in private companies. But to educate people to invest in these companies effectively, government employees would have to know how to do that successfully.[24] And if they knew that, then why would they be working for the government instead of opening venture capital firms?

What about Tax Policies?

Many people believe that "tax incentives [and] tax relief…motivate angel investors to invest"[25] and that lowering taxes would encourage angel investment activity.[26] The argument, as most policy makers present it, is simple. If taxes were reduced, whether through lower rates on capital gains or credits for making angel investments, people would have a greater incentive to invest in private companies.[27]

The belief in the benefits of reducing taxes as a stimulus to angel investing has led to a widespread use of tax credits to encourage angel investments. (Policy makers prefer tax credits to capital gains tax reduction because the latter cut taxes on only successful investments whereas the former reduce taxes on all investments, making them more effective at motivating investors.[28])

Currently, eighteen U.S. states offer investment tax credits to angel investors, with rates ranging from 10 to 100 percent (see Table 11.3).[29] And the U.S. federal government is proposing a 25 percent tax credit for accredited investors who make early stage investments in new companies.[30] Although these policies have a variety of different features—with some offering higher rates if the investment is in a disadvantaged location; others allowing the credit to be given out over several years or carried forward; still others capping the total

TABLE 11.3. State Angel Tax Credits

State	Tax Credit	Rate (%)
Arizona	Angel Investment Tax Credit	30
Hawaii	High-technology Investment Tax Credit	100
Indiana	Venture Capital Investment Tax Credit	20
Iowa	Qualified Business Investment and Seed Capital Tax Credit	20
Kansas	Angel Investor Tax Credit	50
Louisiana	Angel Investor Tax Credit	50
Maine	Seed Capital Tax Credit	40
New Jersey	High-Technology Investment Tax Credit	10
North Carolina	Qualified Business Investment Tax Credit	25
North Dakota	Seed Capital Investment Tax Credit	45
Ohio	Technology Investment Tax Credit	25
Oklahoma	Small Business Capital Credit	20
Oregon	University Venture Capital Funds	60
Rhode Island	Investment Tax Credit	10
Vermont	Seed Capital Fund	10
Vermont	Angel Venture Investment Capital Gain Deferral Credit	60
Virginia	Qualified Business Investment Credit	50
West Virginia	High-Growth Business Investment Tax Credit	50
Wisconsin	Angel Investor Tax Credit	25

Source: Adapted from Crawford, S. 2006. Angel investment: State strategies to promote entrepreneurship and economic development. Issue Brief. Center for Best Practices, National Governors Association, July 12.

amount of credit or the amount per firm or per year;[31] and some permitting only investments of certain sizes, in certain industries, or of certain types (e.g., passive versus active; stage; etc.)—all of the tax credits have the goal of boosting the financial return to investors in private companies so that investing is more attractive, given the risks involved.[32]

Despite the widespread use of *state* angel tax credits, they are based on a faulty premise. State tax policy doesn't appear to have much effect on the variation in the rate of angel investing across metro areas and creates costly economic distortions. The first problem is that state tax credits for angel investing, or for that matter any state tax policy aimed at angel investors, can't have much of an effect because state taxes aren't a very big portion of most investors' tax bills. Most of the taxes that people pay are federal taxes, and federal taxes are the same for people in Boulder, Colorado, and Brownsville, Texas. Because the bulk of the taxes that angel investors pay on their investments won't change in response to state tax policy, it seems unlikely that a large number of investors will respond strongly to policies that affect only a small portion of their taxes. For instance, why would an investor take money out of state and federal tax-exempt municipal bonds to invest in private companies for which he would get a state tax credit against the 5 or 6 percent of his income that he pays in state taxes but now be subject to federal tax on all his earnings from that investment—which he didn't pay when his money was in municipal bonds?

The second problem with this argument is that the typical angel investor doesn't make very many investments, and those that he makes tend to be small. For typical angel investors to increase their angel investment activity in response to state tax policy, they would have to view the tax benefit from making the change as worthwhile. But a person making $75,000 per year in a state with a 6 percent tax rate pays only $4,500 per year in state taxes. Thus, the *typical* angel investor could wipe out his entire state tax bill by making a single median size angel investment ($10,000) in a state with an angel tax credit of 50 percent. So why would the *typical* angel investor bother to increase his angel investment activity from one investment per year to two in response to this tax policy?

Even the wealthiest, accredited angel investors are unlikely to increase their investment activity in response to this policy. A person making $750,000 per year in a state with a 6 percent income tax rate pays $45,000 per year in state income taxes. According to data collected by Rob Wiltbank, the average angel investor affiliated with an angel group invests $191,000 in each new venture that he finances.[33] With a 50 percent state angel tax credit, this investor can wipe out his entire state income tax bill by making less than half of an average angel investment.

A third problem with this argument is that tax credits might merely shift angel investment activity from one industry to another without increasing the total amount of angel investment undertaken. Many angel tax credits are restricted to investment in certain industries. As a result, the tax credits provide an incentive for angels to invest in some industries and not others. Given the weak incentives that these credits provide for increasing the *amount* of investment that angels make, all they might be doing is spurring angels to shift their investments across industries.

A fourth problem with this argument in favor of state angel tax credits is that the data on the rate of angel investment activity across different metro areas suggests that variations in *state* taxes are unlikely to account for differences in the amount of angel investment activity in different places. All we have to do is look at the states of Texas and California to understand why. While the Austin, Texas, metro area had the fifth highest rate of external equity investment among 155 U.S. metro areas with populations of more than 250,000 people during 1997–2002, the Brownsville-Harlingen-San Benito, McAllen-Edinburg-Mission, and Corpus Christi, Texas, areas were all tied for the lowest rate of external equity investing over the same period. So how can Texas state taxes account for both high and low rates of external investing in different metro areas in Texas? They can't.

And this isn't just an anomaly of Texas. Physically abutting the number six metro area in terms of external equity investing—San Jose, California—is the Valejo-Napa-Fairfield, California, metro area, which is tied for last in the rate of external equity investing. Again state taxes cannot account for the wide variations in rates of external investing across metro areas within California.

Moreover, there is no evidence of a significant relationship between either state capital gains or wage tax rates for the 155 different MSAs with populations of 250,000 or more people. The observed relationship (though not statistically significant) is actually *positive*.

The lack of evidence for the effects of tax policies on the amount of angel investing in an area is important because these policies have significant downsides. For instance, angel tax credits can provide incentives that increase the number of passive, inexperienced angels who provide little value to the companies in which they invest. And increasing the number of business angels in a region might cause competition for deals that would drive up the cost of investments and reduce returns. These policies might even drive venture capitalists out of the market if they unfairly favor business angels at the expense of these investors.

Furthermore, in some instances these policies create incentives for people to take advantage of the tax credits without necessarily affecting their willingness to engage in angel investing. Take, for example, the situation in Kansas City, Missouri, which straddles the states of Missouri and Kansas. Kansas has an angel tax credit but Missouri does not. This has led to the development of a market in which people from

Kansas buy angel tax credits at a discount from people in Missouri who have invested in companies domiciled in Kansas because the Missouri investors cannot make use of the tax credits, while the Kansas investors can.

It is important to point out that the above discussion is about *state* tax credits. It is entirely possible that a *federal* angel tax credit would have a beneficial effect on angel investment activity. Because federal taxes are much greater than state taxes, investors have a much greater incentive to respond to federal tax credits than they do to state tax credits. In addition, federal taxes affect people in all parts of the United States, which means that they influence investors in places with the right industries for successful angel investment as well as places with the wrong industries for that activity. Furthermore, the effect of the tax credit on angel arbitrage opportunities in border locations, like that which occurs between Missouri and Kansas with state angel tax credits, is less of a problem. It helps America a lot more if we can get successful angel investors to shift their investments from Canada or Mexico to the United States than it does if we can get them to shift from Kansas City, Missouri, to Kansas City, Kansas.

Is There Anything That the Government Can Do?

If state tax policies aren't something that we can use to increase the amount of angel investment activity in an area, is there anything that policy makers can do? The answer is yes. Governments can encourage the formation of angel groups. The logic of why is simple. Angel groups make it possible to increase the number of accredited investors that finance start-ups by reducing the amount of money a person needs to invest in high-potential companies. Because of the cost of managing investors, it is difficult for businesses that need a lot of capital to grow to obtain their capital from a large number of small investors.[34] So increasing the average size of angel investments would be beneficial.

But few angels can make large investments alone. Given the risk and illiquidity of investments in start-ups, the typical business angel puts no more than 5 percent of his net worth into this asset class.[35] To be diversified an angel needs have at least ten investments in private companies.[36] Moreover, to provide follow-on money, an angel needs to reserve for future investment an amount equal to twice what he initially invests.[37] If angels need to make ten $10,000 investments (the size of the typical angel investment in the United States) and reserve an additional $20,000 per investment for additional financing, then they need to have \$300,000 available for angel investing. If people limit their angel investments to 5 percent of their net worth, this means that angels need to have \$6 million in net worth to make investments in high-potential companies effectively.[38] It turns out that there are fewer than 366,000 households in the United States worth at least this much money. (There are 366,000 households worth \$5 million or more.)

However, if angels are members of groups, they can make these same investments even if they have significantly lower net worth because the group can pool funds and provide the follow-on money and diversification at smaller amounts per angel. Under current SEC rules, angel group members need to be accredited investors. This means that the opportunity to join an angel group affects the probability that accredited investors with a household net worth between \$1 million and \$5 million will make the kind of high-potential angel investments that the best accredited angel investors tend to make.

Using the data from the IRS on household net worth shown in Table 11.4, we can see that the number of households that have a net worth of at least \$1 million is much larger than those that have a net worth of at least \$5 million. In fact, the creation of angel groups has the potential to increase by a factor of 8.6 the number of accredited angel-investing households that make these kinds of investments, if these households are not currently making angel investments.

Allowing people who would not meet current SEC accreditation requirements to join angel groups—a move that would require federal government action—would further increase the number of angel investors. In fact, given the relatively small number of U.S. households with

TABLE 11.4. Internal Revenue Service Estimates of the Number of Households with \$1 Million or More of Net Worth

Net Worth Category	Number of Households
\$1,000,000 to \$2,499,999	2,569,000
\$2,500,000 to \$4,999,999	574,000
\$5,000,000 to \$9,999,999	243,000
\$10,000,000 to \$19,999,999	77,000
\$20,000,000+	46,000
Total	3,509,000

Source: Adapted from data contained in the IRS Statistics of Income, downloaded from www.irs.gov/taxstats/article/0,,id=120303,00.html.

a net worth between $1 million and $5 million, this change would have a dramatic effect on the number of potential angel group members.

Permitting unaccredited investors to join angel groups would have other benefits as well. It would be likely to improve the quality of their angel investment activity.[39] As part of an angel group, an unaccredited investor could make more diversified investments in higher-potential companies, with greater chances for providing follow-on funding, than he could outside of a group. Thus, current SEC policy doesn't keep unaccredited angels from making the lion's share of angel investments in this country; it just makes it *more difficult* for unaccredited angels to make the *good ones*.

Moreover, the inclusion of unaccredited investors in angel groups would expose those investors to potentially more sophisticated investors who might make better investment decisions and might have access to better investment opportunities. Thus, paradoxically, current SEC policy precludes unaccredited investors, who are argued to have less knowledge of how to invest effectively in start-ups, from co-investing with the very investors who are argued to have more knowledge of how to do so. Because, as Chapter 9 indicates, angel groups can be structured as managed investment funds, it is possible for angel group members to make passive investments. Thus, by permitting unaccredited investors to join angel groups, the SEC would allow their investments to be managed by more knowledgeable and sophisticated investors, much as mutual funds operate.

IN CONCLUSION

This chapter examined the reasons for the variation in the amount of external equity investing that occurs across parts of the United States. The data show that six factors are related to the amount of external equity investing in an area: the industrial base, the wealth of the populace, general economic conditions in the area, and the stock of universities, entrepreneurs, and managers. Because external equity investing is a local business, these differences matter for angels, entrepreneurs, and policy makers.

However, it is not clear that governments should intervene in angel capital markets. There is no evidence of market failure; the differences in the amount of investment activity across locations might simply reflect differences in the economic conditions across parts of the country. Moreover, contrary to popular perception, we have no evidence that state tax policies affect the amount of angel investing that occurs in an area. And we have some evidence that they create distortions in the angel capital market.

If governments want to intervene in the angel capital market, their best policy option is to encourage the formation of angel groups. Because angel group members can make more diversified investments at a lower net worth than individual angels, encouraging the formation of angel groups will increase the number of people who can make angel investments in high-potential businesses in an effective manner.

TWELVE

Conclusions

I F YOU HAVE read this far in the book, you realize that only a small portion of angels make money investing in private companies and that the typical angel is far from the wise investor in the next generation of superstar companies that many observers make him out to be. Unfortunately, you'd never know that from reading the multitude of cheerleading books and articles on angel investing. These sources overstate the amount of angel investing that occurs, the sophistication of that activity, the performance of investors at it, and its impact on the economy. While this cheerleading effort is uplifting—it makes angels feel good, leads entrepreneurs to respect and admire angels, and causes policy makers to view angel investors as a valuable resource for transforming economies into entrepreneurial powerhouses—it isn't very useful.

THE REALITY OF ANGEL INVESTING

A careful look at the data on who angels are, what they do, and the impact they have on the economy leads to results that should surprise people who have bought into the received wisdom. There are fewer angel investors than most people believe. Contrary to popular perception, angel investors compose only 8 percent of all informal investors.

Moreover, very few companies receive an investment from anyone other than the founder, let alone one from an angel. And on an annual basis, the number of companies getting an angel investment is very small. Depending on the source, estimates are that only 50,700 to 57,300 businesses received such investments in a recent year.

The dollar value of the angel capital market is tiny in comparison to other financial markets. At $23 billion per year, the angel capital market is roughly the size of the venture capital market, is only 14 percent of the size of the informal capital market, and is only 3 percent of the size of the mergers and acquisitions market. And it is downright minuscule in comparison to the public equities market.

Angels are far less homogenous than many observers believe. While some angels are accredited investors, others are unaccredited. Some angels are early stage capital providers, but others invest at later stages. Some angels are passive investors, while others are more actively involved. Some angels are quite knowledgeable about investing in start-ups, yet others are quite naïve about this activity. Some angels make large investments; others make small ones. Some angels favor debt; others prefer equity. And while some angels seek high risks and high returns, others seek lower risks and lower returns.

Unlike institutional investors, who invest in start-ups to make money, the motivations of business angels are not so clear-cut. Some angels invest in young companies to remain involved in the "start-up game" without starting companies themselves; others do it to learn something new. Some people get involved in angel investing to find a new job; others do it as a hobby. Some angels invest to make money; others invest to give back to the community in which they live and work. The diversity of reasons that people become angels makes understanding the patterns in what they do more difficult—but also more interesting.

Most people have a preconceived notion of what angel investors look like, and it is wrong. The typical angel isn't wealthy. Nor are all angels the well-educated, older, retired, white, male, former entre-preneurs we hear about in the media. Blacks aren't underrepresented among angel investors once their proportion of informal investors is taken into account; and gender has no effect on the odds of being an angel, relative to being some other type of informal investor.

There's no evidence to support the common assertion that angels are "smarter money" than friends-and-family investors. Angels have no more start-up experience than other kinds of informal investors and tend to be inexperienced investors in start-ups, typically making less than one investment per year. And the attitudes of angels about start-ups and investing in them are similar to those of the rest of the adult population, including other types of informal investors.

Contrary to the arguments frequently made to policy makers, there is no evidence of a shortage of angel capital in this country. A variety of different ways of calculating how much angel capital start-ups need consistently fail to yield estimates of a significant gap between the number of companies that need angel money and the number that get it.

Angels also don't appear to fill the so-called "financing gap" between friends-and-family investors and venture capitalists. In fact, we don't even have proof that such a gap exists. Moreover, few angels even invest in the amounts that would allow them to fill the financing gap. And finally, we have no studies that show the often-reported *causal* relationship between getting an investment from business angels and receiving venture capital.

Angel investments are much more plain vanilla than our stories about them would suggest. The median size of an angel investment is only $10,000, and many angel transactions involve debt. Even among equity investments by sophisticated, high net worth angels—the ones who supposedly are making the more venture capital–like angel investments—40 percent of angel only investment rounds involve nothing more than the straight purchase of common stock. Angels rarely stage their investments; co-investments with, and follow-on investments by, venture capitalists are uncommon; and follow-on investments by angels themselves are rare.

Most angels don't write complex financial contracts governing their investments and rarely have the same clauses in their term sheets as venture capitalists. They don't often get board seats, tend not to have liquidation provisions, infrequently reserve the right to take actions if entrepreneurs fail to meet milestones, and tend not to include anti-dilution provisions (and when they do, these are much less onerous than those used by venture capitalists).

The typical angel's approach to setting his ownership stake tends to be simple. Angels tend not to use the "venture capital method" for valuing early stage businesses and instead tend to rely on simple gut feel. And they tend to take too small a percentage of the companies in which they invest to control their development. In many ways, the typical angel deal might be best characterized by the provision of a small bit of money for a little of a company under generous terms in the hope that the one-time investment will be a winner.

The typical start-up that receives financing from an angel investor looks quite different from the mythical business that many books and articles on angel investing make it out to be. Angels disagree a lot more about the characteristics they look for in start-up companies than most people report. In particular, the statement that angels finance "high-growth" businesses masks a complete lack of consensus on what a high-growth business is.

Angels are often reported to differ from friends-and-family investors because they focus their investments on high-tech, high-growth businesses in large, high-margin markets; however, the data on the patterns of investments made by angels reveal that angels actually invest in a wide range of businesses, including the retail, personal service, and capital-intensive manufacturing businesses that experts say angels won't finance. In reality, angels invest in industries that they know, and different angels know different industries.

The companies that receive external equity investments are also not particularly high performing. A surprisingly large number of the businesses are home based, and a surprisingly small number have an intellectual property-based competitive advantage. Moreover, at the time angels invest in them, the companies are older and more developed than is commonly believed.

The entrepreneurs who receive external equity financing also look different from the picture often presented in the media. They are older and more highly educated than commonly portrayed. They are also more likely to be solo entrepreneurs and are less invested in their start-ups both financially and personally than received wisdom tells us.

Collectively, we have an image of the process through which angels make decisions on which companies to finance that isn't very accurate. The standard description is one of a far more organized and sophisticated process than it actually is. Moreover, the description of typical business angels presents them as more actively involved and more likely to add value beyond money than they actually are.

The performance of angel-backed companies is not as good as received wisdom suggests. Careful estimates constructed from hard data about IPOs and acquisitions suggest that between 0.17 and 0.2 percent of angel investments end in an IPO and between 0.8 and 1.3 percent of angel investments end in an acquisition. The value of angel-backed companies at exit is unlikely to be as high as received wisdom suggests because the average start-up company is worth far less six years after founding than most people believe. Moreover, there are few industries in which the typical start-up is worth the sums of money that many observers of angel investing say angel investments are worth at exit. Finally, angels don't invest in a very large number of high-growth companies because the total number of companies funded from all sources that reach a high level of sales in the time frame that angels are said to target is very small.

The returns on investments made by angel investors are not very high. Even the cream of the crop of angel investors—people with a net worth of $10.9 million, who are members of an angel group, have founded an average of 2.7 companies, have been entrepreneurs for an average of 14.5 years, and who are willing to talk about their experiences investing in start-ups—earn only a 19.2 percent per year rate of return, once the opportunity cost of their time is factored in, less than the rate of return earned by investors in venture capital funds.

Angel groups are an important new development in angel investing. Although they account for a small minority of all angel investors, they are a unique form of angel finance. Their members tend to be accredited investors, which makes their investment processes very different from those of individual angels. In particular, angel groups tend to have standardized approaches to investing, are more selective, and employ more sophisticated terms than individual angels. But only some angels who are eligible to join angel groups choose to do so, raising the important question of why.

Angel groups also tend to vary significantly, differing in age, size, location, legal structure, organizational structure, stage of investment preference, and source of funding. Therefore, understanding the differences among groups is crucial to understanding angel investing in this country.

Only a minority of angels make financially rewarding angel investments. And those who are successful differ from the majority. They tend to be accredited investors with significant experience financing private companies and in the industries favorable to angel investing. They also typically invest as part of an angel group composed of people who know how to finance private companies successfully.

Financially successful angels are very selective investors who focus on the small number of companies in industries that venture capitalists and IPO markets prefer and which have a chance of becoming high-growth businesses. Before they invest, they conduct substantial due diligence; and after they invest, they become involved with their portfolio companies. They also structure deals with entrepreneurs well, using appropriate financial instruments and avoiding overvaluation. Finally, to manage the high risk they face, financially successful angels diversify their angel investments across a variety of businesses.

The level of angel investing activity varies significantly across U.S. metro areas, but differences in state taxes explain little of this variation. Rather, the industrial base of the areas, the residents' wealth, general economic conditions, and the stock of universities, entrepreneurs, and managers account for much of these differences. Moreover, there is little evidence of a market failure in angel capital markets that demands government intervention. Nevertheless, there is one potential role for government policy in the angel capital market: encouraging the formation of angel groups. Increasing the number of groups will increase the number of people who can make angel investments effectively.

I realize that what I have told you isn't very flattering to angel investors and that it is a much more sobering story about angel investing than most. So now that I have poured the cold water of reality on the myths that we tell ourselves about angel investing, it is only fair that I offer some suggestions about what investors, entrepreneurs, and policy makers should do.

WHAT SHOULD WE DO?

Entrepreneurs

Entrepreneurs should do several things. First, they should avoid believing myths about the "specialness" of angels as a category of investors. Rather than getting drawn into the idea that they need angels because angels are "smart money" (and the corresponding view that somehow friends and family are "dumb investors"), they need to think carefully about the true differences between angels and friends and family. While there are some dimensions on which these two groups of investors differ, they aren't as different as the experts have led us to believe. For instance, entrepreneurs shouldn't choose to raise money from angels because they believe that angels have more experience at building companies, because they will get more money from angels, or because angels will lead them to venture capital financing. The typical angel is no different from the typical friends-and-family investor on these dimensions.

Moreover, if angel money is going to cost them more than friends-and-family money, entrepreneurs should ask themselves what they will get from the angels that they can't get from friends and family. In fact, entrepreneurs should ask themselves why they are trying to raise money from outsiders at all. They should evaluate whether paying for capital is a better approach to building their businesses than lowering their capital needs to the amount they have available, starting the businesses, and bootstrapping their growth. Unless it is, they shouldn't be trying to raise money from angels.

Second, entrepreneurs should understand the true alternatives that they have for financing their businesses. Rather than believe such myths as "banks don't finance start-ups, but angels do," entrepreneurs should develop an accurate sense of where to get the money they need. This includes considering sources of debt, like banks and trade creditors. After all, banks and credit card companies offer a good amount of personal credit to entrepreneurs, and as businesses grow and become cash-flow positive, entrepreneurs can often tap lines of credit from financial institutions.

Moreover, entrepreneurs should think about the number of companies that get angel money at all. Given the infrequency with which companies raise angel money, they might be better off concentrating on other sources of financing unless there is some reason to believe that angels are a particularly appropriate source of funds in their case.

Third, entrepreneurs should develop an accurate profile of angel investors. If they believe the myths that have grown up about angel investing and look for angels in the country clubs and restaurants that wealthy retired people frequent, they are going to miss most of them. Raising money for a start-up is hard enough if you know where to look, but searching for one set of people while bypassing another that can provide you with the money you need is making the job much harder than it needs to be.

Fourth, entrepreneurs should understand what angels are looking for in the companies they finance. Here the pattern is ironic. Most of the books and articles about angel investing suggest that business angels have a very narrow profile of the companies in which they are willing to invest—high-growth companies in technology-intensive industries. But the *typical* angel investor *actually* puts his money into lower growth companies that operate in a wider range of industries. So entrepreneurs who want angel money don't have to have the next Google to get it.

Fifth, entrepreneurs should have a realistic sense of when they can get angel money. Unfortunately, this is much later in the lives of their companies than received wisdom would suggest. The standard story describes angels investing at the seed stage, shortly after the company has been founded. But in reality, the *typical* angel invests much later, with almost half of the investments going into established companies. So entrepreneurs need to figure out how to finance their companies without angel money for a lot longer than the experts tell them if they are to last long enough to get the money they want from business angels.

Sixth, entrepreneurs should be aware of what the process of raising money from angels actually looks like rather than just believing the stylized story of careful and sophisticated decision making that is typically presented. Unless they are raising money from the small proportion of angels who are part of an organized group, the process of sourcing deals is likely to be highly focused on the angel's friends and family and will be quite haphazard. And no matter what type of angel the entrepreneur is targeting, the investor's decision-making process will be less sophisticated than most experts suggest and subject to a lot of errors and biases.

Seventh, entrepreneurs should understand what they are going to get out of an investment from a typical business angel. They need to realize that typical investors will spend relatively little time on their ventures and probably don't have the expertise to help them to raise money, build a management team, or create a growth strategy. Therefore, entrepreneurs shouldn't think that they are going to get a lot more than money when they get an investment from a typical angel.

Eighth, entrepreneurs should realize that not all angels are the same. A small minority can provide more than simply dollars. So if they need more than cash, entrepreneurs should focus on those angels. That means targeting well-known angel groups with a track record for success.

Angels

Angels and prospective angels should do several things. First, angels should have realistic expectations about what they will earn from investing in start-ups. The performance of the typical angel investment is nothing like the stories we hear. Few angel-backed companies go public or get acquired, and the value of angel-backed companies at exit is much lower than received wisdom suggests. Therefore, angels need to be prepared for low average returns on their portfolios, particularly after the opportunity cost of their time is accounted for.

Second, angels should ask themselves why they want to make angel investments. If making money is the sole motivator, they should think again. Angel investments are too difficult to make, too illiquid, and insufficiently lucrative for money to be the only reason to make them. Instead of making these investments just for the financial returns, angels should make them because they like helping entrepreneurs or their communities or because they find the process enjoyable.

Third, angels should have realistic expectations of what they will get in return for their investments in start-ups. Most angels can't put a lot of money into start-ups so they are unlikely to be diversified or to back companies that need a large amount of money across multiple financing rounds. They aren't going to get a seat on the board and probably won't get anyone to follow on their investment, especially not a venture capitalist. Rather than having the image of occupying a board seat at the next Google, alongside a partner at Sequoia Capital, angels should have the impression that they will get an illiquid investment in a company whose management may not listen to what they have to say, under terms that make it hard to do anything about it.

Fourth, they should realize that it's not difficult to become a business angel. You don't need to be wealthy, have a great deal of experience investing in new companies, have a lot of time to devote to helping start-ups, or have an elaborate system for sourcing and evaluating deals. All you need to do is find someone who needs money and write a plain vanilla contract to provide the funds that are needed in return for a stake in the company.

Fifth, angels who are also accredited investors should be aware that they also have the option of investing through organized angel groups. Although these groups have some disadvantages that might make them inappropriate for some angel investors, they also offer many advantages, including better deal flow, more diversification, greater ability to tap the expertise of others, and the opportunity to divide up the work of investing in private companies.

Sixth, angels should be aware that to make money from angel investments they need to be very selective investors and focus their attention on the small number of potentially high-growth companies in the handful of industries that VCs and IPO markets prefer. They should invest as part of a group that includes people who know how to make financially rewarding angel investments so they can learn from those investors. Once they have learned how to invest successfully in private companies, angels should conduct careful due diligence and, upon investing, get actively involved with their portfolio companies. Finally, they should structure deals well, use appropriate financial instruments, avoid overvaluation of companies, and diversify their investments across a variety of businesses.

Other Investors in Start-ups

Other investors in start-up companies need to do several things. Friends-and-family investors need to recognize that most angels are quite similar to them. Rather than having strong financial motivations, many angels are seeking to be involved with, and help out, entrepreneurs. As a result, friends-and-family members should treat angels with less awe and be less willing to believe that angels will step in to take the businesses in which they invest down a path toward institutional investment.

Venture capitalists should recognize what drives angel investors and understand that their goals aren't completely aligned with those of venture capitalists. Rather than viewing angels with suspicion, or seeing their actions as somehow "unprofessional," venture capitalists should think of most angels as a different kind of start-up company investor, much as they view banks and other providers of debt capital. Understanding what drives angel investors and how they operate should help venture capitalists figure out what part of the angel community they want to work with, and open up more opportunities for venture capitalists to take the financing baton from angels.

Bankers and other providers of debt should understand that angels might not be providing the equity capital they are looking for to strengthen the balance sheets of private companies. Moreover, lenders should realize that angels invest in a more diverse lot of companies than many people say. They often finance businesses with debt rather than equity and don't always prepare companies for investment by institutional investors.

Policy Makers

Policy makers should do several things. First, they should remember that the angel capital market is small and act accordingly. Because this market is small, policy makers need to think about how few financiers they influence by formulating policy toward business angels, compared to, say, banks or trade creditors, and the overall economic impact of policies to affect the angel capital market compared to other financial markets.

Second, policy makers should be aware of the vast differences within the angel capital market when thinking about how to interface with angel investors or how to influence their activity. Two aspects of the differences among angel investors are particularly important. Only some angel investors are motivated by economic concerns when making their investments in new businesses. Because people who put money into new companies for philanthropic reasons are likely to act very differently from people who invest to make their fortune, it may prove very difficult for policy makers to use angel investors to drive economic development. Any approach that policy makers take—be it offering a financial incentive or appealing to a sense of community—is unlikely to affect more than a minority of business angels.

Moreover, policy makers should remember that the vast majority of business angels are unaccredited investors. As such, they will not be part of angel groups and consequently will be much less visible than the accredited investors who make up those groups. If policy makers are concerned about responding to the needs of the majority of angel investors, they should keep in mind that the organized angel groups that lobby and interact with them represent only a minority of the angel population and may advocate policies that aren't of interest or use to the typical business angel.

Third, policy makers need to carefully assess the reasons they might intervene in the angel capital market. Because there is no evidence of market failure, policy makers need to be very careful to ensure that they are not intervening in response to political pressure from angels who simply want a subsidy.

Policy makers also should carefully consider the premises on which the calls for intervention are based. There is no evidence of a shortage of angel capital that is holding back the growth of entrepreneurial companies. Most companies don't get angel capital because they aren't appropriate for such financing, and increasing the amount of angel capital available will likely lead only to more angel money chasing the same limited number of high-growth companies. This could have the effect of driving up valuations and forcing financially successful angels out of the market.

If policy makers choose to intervene in the angel capital market, they should consider how best to do this. Unfortunately for those in government, many of the factors that affect differences in the amount of angel investing in different parts of the country are things policy makers cannot control directly. Therefore, there is a temptation to employ whatever policies they can, particularly easy-to-implement policies, like state tax credits. Policy makers should resist this temptation because these policies have little effect. Rather, if their goal is to increase the number of angel investors in their community, policy makers should focus on the few things they can affect that have a reasonable chance to work—like increasing the number of people who participate in angel groups.

LAST WORD

In short, business angels play a useful role in the American system of financing private companies, but they aren't the heavenly bodies that many observers make them out to be. While this book has presented a more realistic view of angel investing than most out there, it can't change the behavior of entrepreneurs, angels, and policy makers. That is up to you. With a more accurate understanding of who the angels are, what they do, and the impact of their activities, I hope we all can do a better job of financing private companies.

Notes

Acknowledgments

1. Federal securities laws define the term "accredited investor" as a person whose household net worth exceeds $1 million, or whose income exceeds $200,000 in each of the two previous years if single (or $300,000 if married) and who reasonably expects to maintain the same income level. (See Loritz, J. 2007. *Angel Investment: State Strategies to Promote Entrepreneurship and Economic Growth*. National Governors Association Center for Best Practices, Washington, DC.)

Introduction

1. I use the pronoun "he" to refer to business angels since the majority of them are male.
2. http://financial-dictionary.thefreedictionary.com/Anti-Dilution+Provision.
3. Van Osnabrugge, M., and Robinson, R. 2000. *Angel Investing: Matching Start-up Funds with Start-up Companies—A Guide for Entrepreneurs, Individual Investors, and Venture Capitalists*. San Francisco: Jossey-Bass.
4. This book is based on a wide variety of sources. First, it makes use of several large, representative studies of important populations to understand new business finance, including the Internal Revenue Service's Statistics of Income; the U.S. Census Bureau's Survey of Business Owners; the Federal Reserve Board's Survey of Consumer Finance; the Federal Reserve Board's Survey of Small Business Finances; the Panel Study of Entrepreneurial Dynamics; the Entrepreneurship in the United States Assessment; the Kauffman Firm Survey; and the Global Entrepreneurship Monitor. (The data from the Entrepreneurship in the United States Assessment and the Global Entrepreneurship Monitor are not weighted in the analyses; the data from Federal Reserve Survey of Consumer Finance and the Federal Reserve Survey

of Small Business Finances are.) Second, it incorporates information from several smaller studies conducted by academic researchers. Third, it makes use of my own data collection efforts, including a series of focus groups sponsored by five of the Federal Reserve banks, and personal interviews that I have conducted with business angels, entrepreneurs, and venture capitalists.

5. This return is net of the opportunity cost of the investor's time, which is incurred when an investor makes an angel investment, but not an investment in a venture capital fund. "Opportunity cost" is a term that economists use to measure what people otherwise would have gained from the allocation of their time to an activity. For instance, if a business angel earns $300 per hour as a consultant, and he spends an hour helping an entrepreneur develop a company in which he invested without charging the entrepreneur for his time, the opportunity cost of the angel's time is $300. That is, he could have earned that much money if he had spent the hour with a consulting client instead of with the entrepreneur.

6. There might be a shortage of angel capital in certain industries or in certain locations. However, there are not sufficient data to show this.

Chapter 1

1. Industry Canada. 2001. Angel's Touch!!! Presentation to the Bridging the Investment Gap Conference, June 13–14, Montreal, Canada, p. 4.
2. Ewing Marion Kauffman Foundation. 2002. *Business Angel Investing Groups Growing in North America*, October. Kansas City, MO: Ewing Marion Kauffman Foundation, p. 2.
3. Roberts, M., Stevenson, H., and Morse, K. 2000. Angel investing. *Harvard Business School Note*, 9-800-273, p. 4.
4. Hill, B., and Power, D. 2002. *Attracting Capital from Angels*. New York: John Wiley, p. 252.
5. Shane, S. 2005. Angel Investing. A Report Prepared for the Federal Reserve Banks of Atlanta, Cleveland, Kansas City, Philadelphia, and Richmond. October 1.
6. Hill and Power, *Attracting Capital from Angels*, p. 5.
7. Benjamin, G., and Margulis, J. 2005. *Angel Capital*. New York: John Wiley, p. xxx.
8. Roberts, Stevenson, and Morse, Angel investing.
9. Amatucci, F., and Sohl, J. 2007. Business Angels: Investment Processes, Outcomes, and Current Trends. Working Paper, Center for Venture Research, University of New Hampshire, Durham, NH, p. 2.
10. Shane, Angel Investing.
11. Some experts recommend that angels make investments only in companies whose founders want something more than money. (See Burlingham, B. 1997. My life as an angel. *Inc.*, 19(10). Downloaded from www.inc.com/magazine/19970701/1274.html.)
12. Okabe, B. 2007. How Angel Financing Fits In. Presentation to the Power of Angel Investing Seminar, May 23, Chicago, IL.

13. Shane, Angel Investing.

14. Ibid.

15. Becker-Blease, J., and Sohl, J. 2007. Do women-owned businesses have equal access to angel capital? *Journal of Business Venturing*, 22: 503–21, p. 505.

16. Payne, B. Engaging Angel Investors. Downloaded from www.eventuring. com/eShip/appmanager/eVenturing/eVenturingDesktop?_nfpb=true&_ pageLabel=eShip_linkDetail&_nfls=false&id=Entrepreneurship/Resource/ Resource_546.htm&_fromSearch=false&_nfls=false, p. 7.

17. Shane, Angel Investing.

18. Van Osnabrugge and Robinson, *Angel Investing*.

19. Shane, Angel Investing.

20. While not always knowledgeable about investing in start-ups, naïve business angels are often accredited investors.

21. Shane, Angel Investing.

22. Benjamin, G., and Margulis, J. 2000. *Angel Financing*: How to *Find and Invest in Private Equity*. New York: John Wiley, p. 7.

23. Roberts, Stevenson, and Morse, Angel investing, p. 4.

24. Shane, Angel Investing.

25. Hill and Power, *Attracting Capital from Angels*.

26. Hudson, M. 2006. Angels, Saints and Sinners: Where They Fit in a Community's Entrepreneurial Finance Strategy. Presentation to the CDFA Annual Summit, June 1, Austin, TX, p. 7.

27. Ewing Marion Kauffman Foundation, *Business Angel Investing Groups Growing in North America*, p. 2.

28. Shane, Angel Investing.

29. Ibid.

30. Ibid.

31. Benjamin and Margulis, *Angel Financing*.

32. Shane, Angel Investing.

33. Industry Commission. 1997. Informal Equity Investment. Small Business Research Program Information Paper, April, Melbourne, Australia, p. 7.

34. Sullivan, M. 1991. Entrepreneurs as informal investors: Are there distinguishing characteristics? In N. Churchill, W. Bygrave, J. Covin, D. Sexton, D. Slevin, K. Vesper, and W. Wetzel (eds.), *Frontiers of Entrepreneurship Research*. Babson Park, MA: Babson College.

35. Morrissette, S. 2005. A Profile of Angel Investors: An Invisible Driver of Economic Growth. Working Paper, College of St. Francis, Joliet, IL.

36. Benjamin and Margulis, *Angel Capital*; Mason, C., and Harrison, R. 2002. Barriers to investment in the informal venture capital sector. *Entrepreneurship and Regional Development*, 14: 271–87; Van Osnabrugge and Robinson, *Angel Investing*.

37. Stedler, H., and Peters, H. 2003. Business angels in Germany: An empirical study. *Venture Capital*, 5(3): 269–76.

38. Shane, Angel Investing.

39. Mason, C. 2005. Informal Sources of Venture Finance. Working Paper, University of Strathclyde, Glasgow, United Kingdom.

40. Benjamin and Margulis, *Angel Capital*; Roberts, Stevenson, and Morse, Angel investing.

41. Hill and Power, *Attracting Capital from Angels*, p. 37.

42. Stedler and Peters, Business angels in Germany.

43. Shane, Angel Investing.

44. Ibid.

45. Stedler and Peters, Business angels in Germany.

46. Shane, Angel Investing.

47. Van Osnabrugge and Robinson, *Angel Investing*.

48. Shane, Angel Investing.

49. Hill and Power, *Attracting Capital from Angels*, p. 35.

50. Shane, Angel Investing.

51. Hill and Power, *Attracting Capital from Angels*, p. 34.

52. Shane, Angel Investing.

53. Ibid.

54. Hill and Power, *Attracting Capital from Angels*.

55. Stedler and Peters, Business angels in Germany.

56. Shane, Angel Investing.

57. Ibid.

58. Van Osnabrugge and Robinson, *Angel Investing*.

59. Hill and Power, *Attracting Capital from Angels*.

60. Shane, Angel Investing, p. 8.

61. Van Osnabrugge and Robinson, *Angel Investing*, p. 117.

62. Shane, Angel Investing.

63. Benjamin and Margulis, *Angel Capital*; Roberts, Stevenson, and Morse, Angel investing.

64. Shane, Angel Investing.

65. Angel investments, particularly those of angel groups, are often subsidized by state and local governments, which support these investments as a way to promote economic development. The motivations of angel investors to support economic development may reflect their desire to please their funding sources.

66. Shane, Angel Investing.

67. Personal correspondence with a business angel.

Chapter 2

1. Downloaded from www.census.gov/csd/sbo/index.html.

2. These numbers probably *overstate* the proportion of companies that get external investment because companies with better survival prospects are more likely to get these investments and are also more likely to be alive to answer questions when surveyors call.

3. Reynolds, P. 2007. *New Firm Creation in the U.S.: A PSED I Overview*. Berlin: Springer-Verlag. Reynolds estimates that entrepreneurs provide 40 percent of the capital that they need to start their businesses.

4. Reynolds, *New Firm Creation in the U.S.* These estimates do not include money lent by banks, trade creditors, or other sources, and may be imprecise because some of the money provided by entrepreneurs and informal investors takes the form of debt. The estimate for the amount of informal investment comes from the average amount across the five years reported in Reynolds's study; the venture capital amount is his estimate drawn from other studies.

5. Bygrave, W., Hay, M., Ng, E., and Reynolds, P. 2003. Executive forum: A study of informal investing in 29 nations composing the Global Entrepreneurship Monitor. *Venture Capital* 5(2): 101–16. The U.S. number is at the high end of the distribution of countries on informal investment activity.

6. Mason, C. 2005. Informal Sources of Venture Finance. Working Paper, University of Strathclyde, Glasgow, United Kingdom.

7. Reynolds, P. 2005. *Entrepreneurship in the United States*. Miami: Florida International University.

8. These figures are extrapolated from data contained in the Entrepreneurship in the United States Assessment.

9. Haynes, G., and Ou, C. 2002. A Profile of Owners and Investors of Privately Held Businesses in the United States, 1989–1998. Paper Presented at the Annual Conference of the Academy of Entrepreneurial and Financial Research, April 25–26, City College of New York.

10. Reynolds, *New Firm Creation in the U.S.*

11. The data are too imprecise to provide an exact estimate of the dollar value of the informal equity market, but they indicate that it is substantially smaller than the overall informal capital market.

12. We can use the EUSA data to estimate the number of informal equity investors. Approximately 62 percent of informal investments involved some equity. Given that 7.4 million American adults made informal investments over the three-year period from 2001 to 2003, this suggests that approximately 4.6 million adults made an informal *equity* investment over that time period.

13. Haynes and Ou, A Profile of Owners and Investors of Privately Held Businesses in the United States, 1989–1998.

14. Calculated from data in Haynes and Ou, A Profile of Owners and Investors of Privately Held Businesses in the United States, 1989–1998.

15. Bygrave, Hay, Ng, and Reynolds, Executive forum.

16. Van Osnabrugge, M., and Robinson, R. 2000. *Angel Investing: Matching Start-up Funds with Start-up Companies—A Guide for Entrepreneurs, Individual Investors, and Venture Capitalists*. San Francisco: Jossey-Bass; Wong, A. 2002. Angel Finance: The Other Venture Capital. Working Paper, University of Chicago, Chicago, IL.

17. Benjamin, G., and Margulis, J. 2000. *Angel Financing: How to Find and Invest in Private Equity*. New York: John Wiley, p. xiii. Estimates of the amount of money that angels invest in start-ups every year range from $18 billion to $100 billion. (See Benjamin, G., and Margulis, J. 2001. *The Angel Investor's Handbook*. Princeton, NJ: Bloomberg Press; Van Osnabrugge and Robinson, *Angel Investing*; Cullen, L. 1998. On the side of angels. *Money Magazine*, 27(12): 130–36; Sohl, J. 2003. The U.S. angel and venture capital market: Recent trends and developments. *Journal of Private Equity*, 6(2): 7–18; Sohl, J. 2004. The Angel Investor Market in 2003: The Angel Market Rebounds, but Troublesome Post Seed Funding Gap Deepens. Downloaded from http://unh.edu/cvr/press_release%202004.htm; Hill, B., and Power, D. 2002. *Attracting Capital from Angels*. New York: John Wiley.)

18. The SBA reports that there were 24.4 million U.S. businesses in 2003 of which 99.9 percent had fewer than 500 employees (See www.smallbusiness. com/wiki/Small_business_FAQ#How_many_small_businesses_are_there.3F.)

19. Bygrave, Hay, Ng, and Reynolds, Executive forum.

20. These estimates were calculated from data contained in the Entrepreneurship in the United States Assessment.

21. Wong, Angel Finance.

22. Calculated from data downloaded from www.pwcmoneytree.com/moneytree/ index.jsp and Wong, Angel Finance. Applying the venture capital co-investment rate to the number of companies that Pricewaterhouse Coopers reports receive venture capital each year—4,169—we get an estimate of 19,900 angel investments per year. Dr. Wong finds that each company received an average of 1.5 rounds of investment, suggesting that angel investors made investments in 13,000 companies. If we use the National Science Foundation's calculation of the average number of companies that received an angel investment each year between 1990 and 2004 then the estimate is 7,800 companies. If we use the National Science Foundation's calculation of the average number of companies that received an angel investment each year between 1996 and 2002, then the estimate is 11,500 companies.

23. Wisconsin Department of Revenue, Division of Research and Policy. 2007. *Individual Income Tax Statistics Report for Tax Year 2005*. Madison, WI: Wisconsin Department of Revenue. In Wisconsin, a business is eligible for the angel investment tax credit if it is an early stage company that is less than ten years old, has fewer than 100 employees, has received less than $10 million in private equity, is seeking money for pre-commercialization activities, and is developing a new product or process or is engaged in research and development, manufacturing, agriculture, processing, or assembly.

24. Data from the state of Wisconsin's Revenue Division on the taxpayers who took advantage of the state's angel tax credit in 2005 suggest that a higher share of the dollar value of angel investments comes from accredited investors. Investors with less than $200,000 in income accounted for only

19.4 percent of the *amount* invested in businesses eligible for the angel tax credit in Wisconsin in 2005. However, these data need to be treated with caution because they are data from a single state, based on a tax credit that is limited to certain types of investments, and are estimated solely on the basis of income that reaches the accredited investor level only for a single person. (See Wisconsin Department of Revenue, Division of Research and Policy. 2007. *Individual Income Tax Statistics Report for Tax Year 2005*, Madison, WI.: Wisconsin Department of Revenue.)

25. Payne, B. Engaging Angel Investors. Downloaded from www.eventuring. com/eShip/appmanager/eVenturing/eVenturingDesktop?_nfpb=true&_ pageLabel=eShip_linkDetail&_nfls=false&id=Entrepreneurship/Resource/ Resource_546.htm&_fromSearch=false&_nfls=false, p. 7.

26. Data from the EUSA indicate that 88 percent of angel investors have experience running their own businesses.

27. The Federal Reserve's Survey of Consumer Finances indicates that 27 percent of households that have a net worth that meets the requirements for being an accredited investor also have a business worth more than $1 million. (See Heaton, J., and Lucas, D. 2000. Portfolio choice and asset prices: The importance of entrepreneurial risk. *Journal of Finance*, 55(3): 1163–98.)

28. Benjamin, G., and Margulis, J. 2005. *Angel Capital*. New York: John Wiley, p. 13.

29. Van Osnabrugge and Robinson, *Angel Investing*, p. 5.

30. Ballou, J., Barton, T., DesRoches, D., Potter, F., Robb, A., Shane, S., and Zhao, Z. 2007. *Kauffman Firm Survey: Results from the Baseline and First Follow-Up Surveys*. Kansas City, MO: Kauffman Foundation.

31. Stouder, M., and Kirchoff, B. 2004. Funding the first year of business. In W. Gartner, K. Shaver, N. Carter, and P. Reynolds (eds.), *Handbook of Entrepreneurial Dynamics*. Thousand Oaks, CA: Sage, 352–71.

32. Hill and Power, *Attracting Capital from Angels*, p. 26.

33. Hudson, M. 2006. Why entrepreneurs need angels—and how angels are improving. In R. Litan (ed.), *Kauffman Thoughtbook 2005*. Kansas City, MO: Ewing Marion Kauffman Foundation, 156–60, p. 156.

34. Van Osnabrugge, M. 1999. A comparison of business angel and venture capital investment procedures: An agency theory-based analysis. In P. Reynolds, W. Bygrave, S. Manigart, C. Mason, G. Meyer, H. Sapienza, and K. Shaver (eds.), *Frontiers of Entrepreneurship Research*. Babson Park, MA: Babson College, 30–44, p. 30.

35. Reynolds, P. 2007. *New Firm Creation in the U.S.: A PSED I Overview*. Berlin: Springer-Verlag. Other sources suggest that angels may provide private companies with as much as twice the capital invested by venture capitalists. (See Berger, A., and Udell, G. 1998. The economics of small business finance: The roles of private equity and debt markets in the financial growth cycle. *Journal of Banking and Finance*, 22: 613–73.)

36. This estimate includes data only through 2003. Small Business Administration. 2004. *The Small Business Economy: A Report to the President.* Washington, DC: U.S. Government Printing Office.

37. Reynolds, P. 2005. *Entrepreneurship in the United States.* Miami: Florida International University.

38. Downloaded from www.ipohome.com/marketwatch/ipovolume.asp.

39. Calculated from data downloaded from www.mergerstat.com/newsite/free_report.asp.

40. Berger, A., and Udell, G. 1998. The economics of small business finance: The roles of private equity and debt markets in the financial growth cycle. *Journal of Banking and Finance,* 22: 613–73.

41. Ibid.

Chapter 3

1. Prowse, S. 1998. Angel investors and the market for angel investments. *Journal of Banking and Finance,* 22: 785–92.

2. Benjamin, G., and Margulis, J. 2005. *Angel Capital.* New York: John Wiley, p. 12.

3. You might think that this result comes from separating friends from angel investors, but it doesn't. If we define angel investors as nonfamily investors in companies founded by someone else, we still find that only a minority meet the income or net worth requirements to be accredited investors.

4. www.census.gov/prod/2006pubs/p60-231.pdf.

5. Wisconsin Department of Revenue, Division of Research and Policy. 2007. *Individual Income Tax Statistics Report for Tax Year 2005.* Madison, WI: Wisconsin Department of Revenue.

6. The proportion of angel equity investors who are employed full or part time is similar.

7. The proportion of angel equity investors who are retired or not in the labor force is similar.

8. Morrissette, S. 2005. A Profile of Angel Investors: An Invisible Driver of Economic Growth. Working Paper, College of St. Francis, Joliet, IL; Wetzel, W., and Freear, J. 1996. Promoting informal venture capital in the United States: Reflections on the history of the Venture Capital Network. In Harrison, R., and Mason, C. (eds.), *Informal Venture Capital: Evaluating the Impact of Business Introduction Services.* New York: Prentice Hall, 61–74; Gaston, R. 1989. *Finding Private Venture Capital for Your Firm: A Complete Guide.* New York: John Wiley; Sohl, J. 2005. Angel Investment Market Grows 10 Percent in 2006. Center for Venture Research. Downloaded from www.unh.edu/Centers_CVR/2006pressrelease.cfm.

9. However, gender *does* affect the tendency to be an informal investor. An analysis of the Federal Reserve's Survey of Consumer Finances by George Haynes of Montana State University and Charles Ou of the Office of Advocacy of the U.S. Small Business Administration showed that being male has a significant positive effect in regressions to predict being an informal

equity investor, controlling for a variety of other demographic factors. (See Haynes, G., and Ou, C. 2002. A Profile of Owners and Investors of Privately Held Businesses in the United States, 1989–1998. Paper Presented at the Annual Conference of the Academy of Entrepreneurial and Financial Research, April 25–26, City College of New York.)

10. Sohl, Angel Investment Market Grows 10 Percent in 2006.

11. Reynolds, P. Forthcoming. *New Firm Creation in the U.S.: A PSED I Overview*. Berlin: Springer-Verlag.

12. Reynolds, P. 2005. *Entrepreneurship in the United States*. Miami: Florida International University. The patterns for Hispanics are not the same across all studies. In an analysis of the Federal Reserve's Survey of Consumer Finances, George Haynes of Montana State University and Charles Ou of the Office of Advocacy of the U.S. Small Business Administration found that being Hispanic had a significant negative effect on the likelihood of being an informal investor. (See Haynes and Ou, A Profile of Owners and Investors of Privately Held Businesses in the United States, 1989–1998.)

13. However, the sample size is very small, making this estimate imprecise.

14. Van Osnabrugge, M., and Robinson, R. 2000. *Angel Investing: Matching Start-up Funds with Start-up Companies—A Guide for Entrepreneurs, Individual Investors, and Venture Capitalists*. San Francisco: Jossey-Bass; Hill, B., and Power, D. 2002. *Attracting Capital from Angels*. New York: John Wiley; Morrissette, A Profile of Angel Investors; Wetzel, W., and Freear, J. 1996. Promoting informal venture capital in the United States; reflections on the history of the Venture Capital Network. In Harrison and Mason, *Informal Venture Capital*, 61–74; Gaston, *Finding Private Venture Capital for Your Firm*; Aram, J. 1989. Attitudes and behaviors of informal investors toward early-stage investments, technology-based ventures, and co-investors. *Journal of Business Venturing*, 4(5): 333–47.

15. Van Osnabrugge and Robinson, *Angel Investing*; Hill and Power, *Attracting Capital from Angels*; Morrissette, A Profile of Angel Investors; Wetzel, W., and Freear, J. 1996. Promoting informal venture capital in the United States; reflections on the history of the Venture Capital Network. In Harrison and Mason, *Informal Venture Capital*, 61–74; Gaston, *Finding Private Venture Capital for Your Firm*; Aram, Attitudes and behaviors of informal investors.

16. Aizcorbe, A., Kennickell, A., and Moore, K. 2003. Recent changes in U.S. family finances: Evidence from the 1998 and 2001 Survey of Consumer Finances. *Federal Reserve Bulletin*, 89: 1–32.

17. Many authors have argued that most angels are highly educated, but they have based their evidence on highly selected data. (See, for example, Van Osnabrugge and Robinson, *Angel Investing*; Hill and Power, *Attracting Capital from Angels*; Morrissette, A Profile of Angel Investors; Gaston, *Finding Private Venture Capital for Your Firm*; Aram, Attitudes and behaviors of informal investors.)

18. Van Osnabrugge and Robinson, *Angel Investing*, p. 106.

19. Benjamin and Margulis, *Angel Capital*, p. 119.

20. The regressions included race, age, gender, net worth, labor force status, and whether the individual was an owner-manager of a business.

21. Similar patterns were observed for angels who make equity investments.

22. Benjamin and Margulis, *Angel Capital*, p. 119.

23. Hill and Power, *Attracting Capital from Angels*, p. 11.

24. According to regressions run on data from the Entrepreneurship in the United States Assessment.

25. Wiltbank, R. 2007. Angel Investor Research. Downloaded from www.willamette.edu/~wiltbank/AngelInvestorResearch2.ppt.

26. Hill and Power, *Attracting Capital from Angels*, p. 3.

27. Riding, A. 2005. Estimating Informal Investment in Canada. Paper Prepared for Small Business Policy Branch Industry Canada, March, Ottawa, Canada.

28. Farrell, A. 1998. Informal venture capital investment in Atlantic Canada: A representative view of "angels." A Report Submitted to Atlantic Canada Opportunities Agency, February, Ottawa, Canada.

29. Hamilton, B. 2004. Angel Investing in the 1990's. Working Paper, Washington University, St. Louis, MO.

30. Ibid.

31. Benjamin and Margulis, *Angel Capital*; Prowse, Angel investors and the market for angel investments; Morrissette, A Profile of Angel Investors.

32. The same is true for angel equity investments.

33. Van Osnabrugge, M. 1998. Do serial and non-serial investors behave differently? An empirical and theoretical analysis. *Entrepreneurship Theory and Practice*, Summer: 23–42.

34. The regressions included race, age, gender, net worth, labor force status, education, and whether the individual was an owner-manager of a business.

35. Benjamin, G., and Margulis, J. 2000. *Angel Financing: How to Find and Invest in Private Equity*. New York: John Wiley.

36. The regressions included race, age, gender, net worth, labor force status, education, and whether the individual was an owner-manager of a business.

37. Angels are more likely than the rest of the adult population to say that there will be good start-up opportunities in their geographical area in the coming months and that those starting a business are accorded a lot of respect and status, but are no more likely than other types of informal investors to think this.

Chapter 4

1. Freear, J., and Sohl, J. 2001. The characteristics and value-added contributions of private investors to entrepreneurial software ventures. *Journal of Entrepreneurial Finance*, 6(1): 84–103; Benjamin, G., and Margulis, J. 2001. *The Angel Investor's Handbook*. Princeton, NJ: Bloomberg Press.

2. This story describes situation in the United States. In other countries, the situation is different.

3. Farrell, A. 2000. A Literature Review and Industry Analysis of Informal Investment in Canada: A Research Agenda on Angels. Research Paper Prepared for the Small Business Policy Branch as Part of the Small and Medium-Sized Enterprise (SME) Financing Data Initiative, Government of Canada, Ottawa.

4. Sohl, J. 2003. The U.S. angel and venture capital market: Recent trends and developments. *Journal of Private Equity*, Spring: 7–16; Coveney, P., and Moore, K. 1998. *Business Angels*. New York: John Wiley; Prowse, S. 1998. Angel investors and the market for angel investments. *Journal of Banking and Finance*, 22: 785–92.

5. Industry Commission. 1997. Informal Equity Investment. Small Business Research Program Information Paper, April, Melbourne, Australia.

6. Coveney and Moore, *Business Angels*.

7. Benjamin and Margulis, *The Angel Investor's Handbook*, p. 4.

8. May, J., and Simmons, C. 2001. *Every Business Needs an Angel*. New York: Crown Books, pp. 33–34.

9. Geshwiler, J., May, J., and Hudson, M. 2006. State of Angel Groups: A Report on ACA and ACEF. April 27, New York, NY.

10. Industry Canada. 2001. Angel's Touch!!! Presentation to the Bridging the Investment Gap Conference, June 13–14, Montreal, Canada.

11. Van Auken, H., and Carter, R. 1989. Capital acquisition in small firms. *Journal of Small Business Management*, 27: 1–9.

12. Berger, A., and Udell, G. 1998. The economics of small business finance: The roles of private equity and debt markets in the financial growth cycle. *Journal of Banking and Finance*, 22: 613–73.

13. Reynolds, P., and White, S. 1997. *The Entrepreneurial Process: Economic Growth, Men, Women, and Minorities.* Westport, CT: Greenwood. Very young companies can obtain debt financing even if they lack the cash flow to service their debt because their founders turn to credit cards and personal loans, or personally guarantee the debt of their new companies, to obtain the financing they need.

14. Benjamin and Margulis, *The Angel Investor's Handbook*, p. xx.

15. Benjamin and Margulis, *The Angel Investor's Handbook*.

16. Mason, C., and Harrison, R. 2000. The size of the informal venture capital market in the United Kingdom. *Small Business Economics*, 15: 137–48.

17. Ou, C., and Haynes, G. 2003. Uses of Equity Capital by Small Firms— Findings for the Surveys of Small Business Finances (for 1993 and 1998). Paper presented at the 14th Annual Conference on Entrepreneurial Finance and Business Ventures, April 3–May 2, DePaul University, Chicago, IL.

18. www.hvcc.com/definit1.html.

19. Mason, C., and Harrison, R. 1996. Why "business angels" say no: A case study of opportunities rejected by an informal investor syndicate. *International Small Business Journal*, 14(2): 35–51.

20. Haynes, G. 2001. Wealth and Income: How Did Small Businesses Fare from 1989 to 1998? Report for the U.S. Small Business Administration, Contract number SBAHQ-00-M-0502, Washington, DC.

21. Reynolds, P., and White, S. 1997. *The Entrepreneurial Process: Economic Growth, Men, Women, and Minorities*. Westport, CT: Greenwood.

22. The patterns are similar for employer firms.

23. Benjamin, G., and Margulis, J. 2000. *Angel Financing: How to Find and Invest in Private Equity*. New York: John Wiley.

24. Limited liability companies are included among the acceptable legal forms because they came into widespread use only after the Federal Reserve data were collected and anecdotal evidence suggests that limited liability companies receive angel investments.

25. May, J., and Simmons, C. 2001. *Every Business Needs an Angel*. New York: Crown Books.

26. Only a small portion of the new businesses surveyed indicated that they had met the conditions for being classified as "employer firms."

27. Many observers say that angels expect a ten times return on their invested capital.

28. Benjamin and Margulis, *Angel Financing*, p. 77.

29. Fenn, G., and Liang, N. 1998. New resources and new ideas: Private equity for small businesses. *Journal of Banking and Finance*, 22: 1077–84.

30. Riding, A., and Belanger, B. 2006. Informally financed SMEs. *Small Business Financing Profiles*. Government of Canada, September, Ottawa, Canada.

31. Calculated from data provided in the special tabulation.

32. These are the most current data available. The Survey of Business Owners is conducted every five years; to get five-year growth rates, you have to look at companies that were founded at a time when the previous Survey of Business Owners can report their sales. Because the 2007 survey data have not yet been released, I had to look at the 2002 survey data, which meant examining companies founded in 1996 over the 1997 to 2002 period.

33. Villalobos, L., and Payne, B. 2007. Valuation of Seed/Start-up Ventures. Presentation to the Power of Angel Investing Seminar, May 23–25, Chicago, IL.

34. Atkinson, R., and Court, R. 1998. *The New Economy Index: Understanding America's Economic Transformation*. November, Progressive Policy Institute, Washington, DC.

35. The average business that sought funding projected first-year sales of $654,000 and fifth-year sales of $60 million.

36. Okabe, B. 2007. Valuation of Early Stage Companies. Presentation to the Power of Angel Investing Seminar, May 24, Chicago, IL.

37. Personal correspondence with Todd Federman, director of the Northcoast Angel Network.

Chapter 5

1. Morrissette, S. 2005. A Profile of Angel Investors: An Invisible Driver of Economic Growth. Working Paper, College of St. Francis, Joliet, IL; Van Osnabrugge and Robinson, *Angel Investing: Matching Start-up Funds with Start-up Companies—A Guide for Entrepreneurs, Individual Investors, and Venture Capitalists*. San Francisco: Jossey-Bass; Hill, B., and Power, D. 2002. *Attracting Capital from Angels*. New York: John Wiley; Gaston, R. 1989. *Finding Private Venture Capital for Your Firm: A Complete Guide*. New York: John Wiley; Aram, J. 1989. Attitudes and behaviors of informal investors toward early-stage investments, technology-based ventures, and co-investors. *Journal of Business Venturing*, 4(5): 333–47; Freear, J., Sohl, J., and Wetzel, W. 1994. Angels and non-angels: Are there differences? *Journal of Business Venturing*, 9(2): 109–23; Benjamin, G., and Margulis, J. 2005. *Angel Capital*. New York: John Wiley; Prowse, S. 1998. Angel investors and the market for angel investments. *Journal of Banking and Finance*, 22: 785–92; Van Osnabrugge, M. 2000. A comparison of business angel and venture capitalist investment procedures: An agency theory-based analysis. *Venture Capital*, 2(2): 91–109; Sohl, J. and Sommer, B. 2007. Angel Investing: Changing Strategies During Volatile Times. Working Paper, Center for Venture Research, University of New Hampshire, Durham, NH.; Wong, A. 2002. Angel Finance: The Other Venture Capital. Working Paper, University of Chicago, Chicago, IL; Coveney, P., and Moore, K. 1998. *Business Angels*. New York: John Wiley.

2. Van Osnabrugge and Robinson, *Angel Investing*; Wong, Angel Finance; Rob Wiltbank's survey of 121 accredited angel investors also found that they had $136,318 in outstanding investment. (See Wiltbank, R. 2007. Angel Investor Research. Downloaded from www.willamette.edu/~wiltbank/AngelInvestorResearc2.ppt.)

3. Goldfarb, B., Hoberg, G., Kirsch, D., and Triantis, A. 2007. Are Angels Preferred Venture Investors? Working Paper, University of Maryland, College Park, MD.

4. www.fundingpost.com/glossary/series-a-preferred-stock.asp.

5. The regressions included race, age, gender, net worth, labor force status, education, and whether the individual was an owner-manager of a business.

6. Wong, Angel Finance.

7. Ibid.

8. Kelly, P., and Hay, M. 2001. Helping Hand or Watchful Eye? An Agency Theory Perspective on Private Investor Involvement in Entrepreneurial Ventures. Downloaded from www.babson.edu/entrep/fer/Babson2001/XXI/XXIB/XXIB/xxi-b.htm.

9. Wong, Angel Finance.

10. Ibid.

11. Prowse, Angel investors and the market for angel investments.

12. Downloaded from www.angel-investor-guide.com/startup_funding.aspx.

13. Even studies of nonrepresentative samples of known business angels show a surprising amount of debt financing. One study of thirty-four angel investments in the United Kingdom found that 40 percent involved only equity and 20 percent involved only debt. (See Mason, C., and Harrison, R. 1996. Informal venture capital: A study of the investment process, the post-investment experience and investment performance. *Entrepreneurship and Regional Development*, 8: 105–25.)

14. www.rbeck.com/ryan_beck3/invest_glosry_CnCo.htm.

15. Wainwright, F., and Groeninger, A. 2005. Note on Angel Investing. Tuck School of Business Administration at Dartmouth Center for Private Equity and Entrepreneurship, Case Number 5-0001; Benjamin, G., and Margulis, J. 2001. *The Angel Investor's Handbook*. Princeton, NJ: Bloomberg Press; Linde, L., and Prasad, A. 2000. *Venture Support Systems Project: Angel Investors*. Cambridge, MA: MIT Entrepreneurship Center.

16. www.investorwords.com/986/common_stock.html.

17. Amis, D., and Stevenson, H. 2001. *Winning Angels*. London: Pearson Education, p. 183.

18. Ibid.

19. Amis and Stevenson, *Winning Angels*, p. 210.

20. www.globefund.com/v5/content/glossary/.

21. Benjamin, G., and Margulis, J. 2001. *The Angel Investor's Handbook*. Princeton, NJ: Bloomberg Press.

22. Wong, Angel Finance.

23. Ibid.

24. Roberts, M., Stevenson, H., and Morse, K. 2000. Angel investing. *Harvard Business School Note*, 9-800-273.

25. Hill and Power, *Attracting Capital from Angels*. However, convertible debt is not without disadvantages. Investors can have their return premium washed away by later round investors who do not accept it.

26. Wong, Angel Finance.

27. Benjamin, G., and Margulis, J. 2001. *The Angel Investor's Handbook*. Princeton, NJ: Bloomberg Press.

28. Wong, Angel Finance.

29. Mason, C., and Harrison, R. 1996. Informal venture capital: A study of the investment process, the post-investment experience and investment performance. *Entrepreneurship and Regional Development*, 8: 105–25.

30. Van Osnabrugge and Robinson, *Angel Investing*.

31. Wong, Angel Finance.

32. Van Osnabrugge, M. 2000. A comparison of business angel and venture capitalist investment procedures: An agency theory-based analysis. *Venture Capital*, 2(2): 91–109.

33. Goldfarb, B., Hoberg, G., Kirsch D., and Triantis, A. 2007. Are Angels Preferred Venture Investors? Working Paper, University of Maryland, College Park, MD.

34. Amatucci, F., and Sohl, J. 2007. Business Angels: Investment Processes, Outcomes, and Current Trends. Working Paper, Center for Venture Research, University of New Hampshire, Durham, NH.

35. Kelly, P., and Hay, M. 2003. Business angel contracts: The influence of context. *Venture Capital*, 5(4): 287–312.

36. Amatucci, and Sohl, Business Angels.

37. Kelly, P., and Hay, M. 2000. The Private Investor-entrepreneur Contractual Relationship: Understanding the Influence of Context. Downloaded from www.babson.edu/entrep/fer/XII/XIIB/html/xii-b.htm.

38. Amatucci and Sohl, Business Angels.

39. Benjamin, G., and Margulis, J. 2001. *The Angel Investor's Handbook*. Princeton, NJ: Bloomberg Press.

40. Ibid., p. 36.

41. Amis, D., and Stevenson, H. 2001. *Winning Angels*. London: Pearson Education.

42. Linde, L., and Prasad, A. 2000. *Venture Support Systems Project: Angel Investors*. Cambridge, MA: MIT Entrepreneurship Center.

43. Amis, D., and Stevenson, H. 2001. *Winning Angels*. London: Pearson Education; Linde, L., and Prasad, A. 2000. *Venture Support Systems Project: Angel Investors*. Cambridge, MA: MIT Entrepreneurship Center.

44. Benjamin, G., and Margulis, J. 2001. *The Angel Investor's Handbook*. Princeton, NJ: Bloomberg Press.

45. Amis and Stevenson, *Winning Angels*.

46. Roberts, Stevenson, and Morse, Angel investing.

47. Ibid.

48. www.crownenoble.com/Glossary_I.html.

49. Benjamin, G., and Margulis, J. 2000. *Angel Financing: How to Find and Invest in Private Equity*. New York: John Wiley.

50. Amis and Stevenson, *Winning Angels*.

51. Ibid.

52. Prowse, Angel investors and the market for angel investments; Van Osnabrugge and Robinson, *Angel Investing*; Gaston, *Finding Private Venture Capital for Your Firm*; Freear, J., Sohl, J., and Wetzel, W. 1992. The investment attitudes, behavior and characteristics of high net worth individuals. In N. Churchill, S. Birley, W. Bygrave, D. Muzyka, C. Wahlbin, and W. Wetzel (eds.), *Frontiers of Entrepreneurship Research*. Babson Park, MA: Babson College, 274–387.

53. Benjamin and Margulis, *Angel Capital*.

54. Wong, Angel Finance.

55. Ibid.

56. Benjamin, G., and Margulis, J. 2001. *The Angel Investor's Handbook*. Princeton, NJ: Bloomberg Press.

57. Wong, Angel Finance.

58. Benjamin and Margulis, *Angel Capital*.

59. http://vcexperts.com/vce/library/encyclopedia/glossary_view.asp?glossary_ id=274.

60. Burlingham, B. 1997. My life as an angel. *Inc.*, 19(10): July. Downloaded from www.inc.com/magazine/19970701/1274.html.

61. Wong, Angel Finance.

62. www.ma-research.com/glossary.php?letter=w.

63. Mason, C., and Harrison, R. 1996. Informal venture capital: A study of the investment process, the post-investment experience and investment performance. *Entrepreneurship and Regional Development*, 8: 105–25.

64. Goldfarb, B., Hoberg, G., Kirsch D., and Triantis, A. 2007. Are Angels Preferred Venture Investors? *Working Paper*, University of Maryland, College Park, MD.

65. Amis, and Stevenson, *Winning Angels*.

66. Van Osnabrugge and Robinson, *Angel Investing*.

67. Goldfarb, B., Hoberg, G., Kirsch D., and Triantis, A. 2007. Are Angels Preferred Venture Investors? *Working Paper*, University of Maryland, College Park, MD.

68. Benjamin, G., and Margulis, J. 2001. *The Angel Investor's Handbook*. Princeton, NJ: Bloomberg Press.

69. Wong, Angel Finance.

70. Ibid.

71. Van Osnabrugge and Robinson, *Angel Investing*.

72. Wong, Angel Finance.

73. Hill and Power, *Attracting Capital from Angels*; Van Osnabrugge and Robinson, *Angel Investing*.

74. Mason, C., and Harrison, R. 1996. Informal venture capital: A study of the investment process, the post-investment experience and investment performance. *Entrepreneurship and Regional Development*, 8: 105–25.

75. Wiltbank, R., and Boeker, W. 2007. Returns to Angel Investors in Groups. Working Paper, Ewing Marion Kauffman Foundation, Kansas City, MO.

76. Mason, C., and Harrison, R. 1996. Informal venture capital: A study of the investment process, the post-investment experience and investment performance. *Entrepreneurship and Regional Development*, 8: 105–25.

77. Hill and Power, *Attracting Capital from Angels*.

78. Wainwright, F., and Groeninger, A. 2005. *Note on Angel Investing*. Tuck School of Business Administration at Dartmouth Center for Private Equity and Entrepreneurship, Case Number 5-0001.

79. Shane, S. 2005. Angel Investing. A Report Prepared for the Federal Reserve Banks of Atlanta, Cleveland, Kansas City, Philadelphia, and Richmond. October 1.

80. Riding, A., and Short, D. 1987. Some investor and entrepreneur perspectives on the informal market for risk capital. *Journal of Small Business and Entrepreneurship*, 4: 19–30.

81. Harrison, R., and Mason, C. 2000. Venture capital market complementarities: The links between business angels and venture capital funds in the United Kingdom. *Venture Capital*, 2(3): 223–42.

82. Mason, C., and Harrison, R. 2002. Is it worth it? The rates of return from informal venture capital investments. *Journal of Business Venturing*, 17: 211–36.

83. Wong, Angel Finance.

84. Hudson, M. 2007. ACA Briefing and Angel Group Stats. Presentation to the Angel Capital Association, May 24, Chicago, IL.

85. The data were downloaded from www.nsf.gov/statistics/seind06/c6/c6s6.htm.

86. Wong, Angel Finance.

87. Ibid.; Kelly and Hay, Helping Hand or Watchful Eye?

88. Wong, Angel Finance.

89. Van Osnabrugge, M. 1998. Do serial and non-serial investors behave differently? An empirical and theoretical analysis. *Entrepreneurship Theory and Practice*, Summer: 23–42.

90. Wong, Angel Finance.

91. Amatucci and Sohl, Business Angels.

92. Linde, L., and Prasad, A. 2000. *Venture Support Systems Project: Angel Investor*. Cambridge, MA: MIT Entrepreneurship Center.

93. Van Osnabrugge, M., and Robinson, R. 2000. *Angel Investing: Matching Start-up Funds with Start-up Companies —A Guide for Entrepreneurs, Individual Investors, and Venture Capitalists*. San Francisco: Jossey-Bass, p. 155.

94. Wiltbank, R., and Boeker, R. 2007. Angel Performance Project. Power Point Presentation, Angel Capital Association Annual Meeting, May 23, Chicago, IL.

95. The data were downloaded from www.nsf.gov/statistics/seind06/c6/c6s6.htm.

96. These estimates also fail to note that only a small proportion of angel investments have characteristics that make them appropriate for follow-on investment. (See Wong, Angel Finance.)

97. Amatucci and Sohl, Business Angels.

98. Harrison, R., and Mason, C. 2000. Venture capital market complementarities: The links between business angels and venture capital funds in the United Kingdom. *Venture Capital*, 2(3): 223–42.

99. Wong, Angel Finance.

100. Riding, A., Dal Cin, P., Duxbury, L. Haines, G., and Safrata, R. 1993. *Informal Investors in Canada: The Identification of Salient Characteristics*. Ottawa: Carleton University.

101. Mason, C., and Harrison, R. 2002. Barriers to investment in the informal venture capital sector. *Entrepreneurship and Regional Development*, 14: 271–87.

102. Amis, D., and Stevenson, H. 2001. *Winning Angels*. London: Pearson Education.

103. Amis, D., and Stevenson, H. 2001.

104. Shane, *Angel Investing.*

105. Benjamin and Margulis, *Angel Capital*; Prowse, Angel investors and the market for angel investments.

106. Benjamin and Margulis, *Angel Capital*; Benjamin and Margulis, *Angel Investor's Handbook*; Benjamin and Margulis, *Angel Financing*. Several of the eight points are made in each of these books.

107. Hill and Power, *Attracting Capital from Angels.*

108. Wainwright, F., and Groeninger, A. 2005. *Note on Angel Investing.* Tuck School of Business Administration at Dartmouth Center for Private Equity and Entrepreneurship, Case Number 5-0001.

109. Van Osnabrugge and Robinson, *Angel Investing*, p. 173.

110. Amis and Stevenson, *Winning Angels.*

111. Wainwright, F., and Groeninger, A. 2005. *Note on Angel Investing.* Tuck School of Business Administration at Dartmouth Center for Private Equity and Entrepreneurship, Case Number 5-0001; Benjamin and Margulis, *Angel Financing*; Becker-Blease, J., and Sohl, J. 2007. Do women-owned businesses have equal access to angel capital? *Journal of Business Venturing*, 22: 503–21.

112. Mason, C., and Harrison, R. 2002. Barriers to investment in the informal venture capital sector. *Entrepreneurship and Regional Development*, 14: 271–87.

113. Mason, C., and Harrison, R. 1996. Informal venture capital: A study of the investment process, the post-investment experience and investment performance. *Entrepreneurship and Regional Development*, 8: 105–25.

114. Shane, *Angel Investing.*

115. Benjamin and Margulis, *Angel Financing*, p. 111.

116. Van Osnabrugge and Robinson, *Angel Investing.*

117. Wainwright and Groeninger, *Note on Angel Investing.*

118. Prowse, Angel investors and the market for angel investments.

119. Riding and Short, Some investor and entrepreneur perspectives on the informal market for risk capital.

120. Wainwright and Groeninger, *Note on Angel Investing*; Benjamin and Margulis, *Angel Financing*; Wong, Angel Finance; Sohl and Sommer, Angel Investing; Van Osnabrugge, M. 2000. A comparison of business angel and venture capitalist investment procedures: An agency theory-based analysis. *Venture Capital*, 2 (2): 91–109; Coveney and Moore, *Business Angels.*

121. Becker-Blease and Sohl, Do women-owned businesses have equal access to angel capital?

122. Goldfarb, B., Hoberg, G., Kirsch D., and Triantis, A. 2007. Are Angels Preferred Venture Investors? Working Paper, University of Maryland, College Park, MD.

123. Wong, Angel Finance.

124. Shane, *Angel Investing.*

125. Roberts, Stevenson, and Morse, Angel investing.

126. Wong, Angel Finance.

127. Becker-Blease and Sohl, Do women-owned businesses have equal access to angel capital?; Wong, Angel Finance.

128. Wong, Angel Finance.

129. Ibid.

130. Ibid.

131. Ibid.

Chapter 6

1. www.angelinvestorsforum.com/.

2. This is for real. See the Web site www.raisingangelfinancing.com/.

3. Mason, C., and Harrison, R. 1996. Why "business angels" say no: A case study of opportunities rejected by an informal investor syndicate. *International Small Business Journal*, 14(2): 35–51.

4. Many sources report that angels are looking for a good management team and use aphorisms like "It is better to bet on the jockey than on the horse" or "An A team will do better with a B idea than a B team will do with an A idea." These statements are interesting because they seem to be at odds with the terms that at least some angels are now putting in their term sheets. Some angels give themselves participating preferred stock, which decreases the incentive for talented entrepreneurs to seek financing from angels. So if angels are so interested in getting the best entrepreneurs, why do they structure deals to generate the highest possible financial returns at the expense of attracting the best entrepreneurs?

5. Prowse, S. 1998. Angel investors and the market for angel investments. *Journal of Banking and Finance*, 22: 785–92; Van Osnabrugge, M., and Robinson, R. 2000. *Angel Investing: Matching Start-up Funds with Start-up Companies—A Guide for Entrepreneurs, Individual Investors, and Venture Capitalists*. San Francisco: Jossey-Bass.

6. Benjamin, G., and Margulis, J. 2005. *Angel Capital*. New York: John Wiley.

7. Ibid.

8. Sohl, J. 1999. The early-stage equity market in the USA. *Venture Capital*, 1(2): 101–20.

9. www.angelcaptitaleducation.org/dir_resources/for entrepreneurs.

10. Hanbury-Brown, S. 2007. What Makes a Deal an Angel Deal? Presentation to the Angel Capital Association, May 24, Chicago, IL.

11. Personal correspondence with Lynn-Ann Gries.

12. Downloaded from www.techcoastangels.com/Public/Content. aspx?ID=EA6BF3BE-964F-11D4-AD7900A0C95C1653&Redir=False.

13. Payne, B. Engaging Angel Investors. Downloaded from www.eventuring. com/eShip/appmanager/eVenturing/eVenturingDesktop?_nfpb=true&_pageLabel=eShip_linkDetail&_nfls=false&id=Entrepreneurship/Resource/Resource_546.htm&_fromSearch=false&_nfls=false.

14. Van Osnabrugge and Robinson, *Angel Investing*, p. 149.

15. Benjamin, G., and Margulis, J. 2001. *The Angel Investor's Handbook*. Princeton, NJ: Bloomberg Press, p. 63.

16. Van Osnabrugge and Robinson, *Angel Investing*; Wong, A. 2002. Angel Finance: The Other Venture Capital. Working Paper, University of Chicago, Chicago, IL; Stedler, H., and Peters, H. 2003. Business angels in Germany: An empirical study. *Venture Capital*, 5(3): 269–76; Sohl, J. 2005. The Angel Investor Market in 2005. Center for Venture Research, downloaded from www.unh.edu/news/docs/CVR_2005.pdf. While these surveys give the impression of support for the argument that angels focus on high-tech industries, this is an illusion. All the surveys make the same mistake of surveying people who are disproportionately likely to invest in high-technology markets and then proclaim that angels are particularly likely to invest in these markets. This, of course, is a fallacy akin to surveying teenage users of iPods about what kind of music they like and then drawing the conclusion that no one listens to classical music anymore. If you don't ask the listeners of classical music about their music preferences, you won't find any listeners of classical music, just as you won't find any angels investing in start-ups in low-tech industries if you don't ask the investors in low-tech industries about their investments.

17. Wiltbank, R. 2006. Angel Investor Research. Downloaded from www.willamette.edu/~wiltbank/AngelInvestorResearch2.ppt.

18. Businesses are generally scalable if one of three conditions holds: there are economies of scale in production or distribution (fixed costs can be spread over additional volume); costs go down with the volume produced (increasing returns businesses); or revenues are recurring (incremental sales have an annuity-like quality once initial sales are made to customers). (See Amis, D., and Stevenson, H. 2001. *Winning Angels*. London: Pearson Education.)

19. Payne, B. Engaging Angel Investors.

20. Van Osnabrugge and Robinson, *Angel Investing*; Hill, B., and Power, D. 2002. *Attracting Capital from Angels*. New York: John Wiley; Brettel, M. 2003. Business angels in Germany: A research note. *Venture Capital*, 5(3): 251–68; Stedler and Peters, Business angels in Germany; Linde, L., and Prasad, A. 2000. *Venture Support Systems Project: Angel Investors*. Cambridge, MA: MIT Entrepreneurship Center; Mason, C., and Harrison, R. 1996. Informal venture capital: A study of the investment process, the post-investment experience and investment performance. *Entrepreneurship and Regional Development*, 8: 105–25; Benjamin, G., and Margulis, J. 2000. *Angel Financing: How to Find and Invest in Private Equity*. New York: John Wiley.

21. Amis and Stevenson, *Winning Angels*; Hill and Power, *Attracting Capital from Angels*; Brettel, Business angels in Germany; Payne, Engaging Angel Investors; Roberts, M., Stevenson, H., and Morse, K. 2000. Angel investing. *Harvard Business School Note*, 9-800-273; Benjamin and Margulis, *Angel Capital*.

22. Shane, S. 2005. Angel Investing. A Report Prepared for the Federal Reserve Banks of Atlanta, Cleveland, Kansas City, Philadelphia, and Richmond. October 1.
23. Amis and Stevenson, *Winning Angels*.
24. Payne, Engaging Angel Investors; Stedler and Peters, Business angels in Germany.
25. Benjamin and Margulis, *Angel Financing*.
26. Benjamin and Margulis, *Angel Capital*.
27. Hill and Power, *Attracting Capital from Angels*.
28. Van Osnabrugge and Robinson, *Angel Investing*, p. 129.
29. Benjamin and Margulis, *Angel Investor's Handbook*, p. 15.
30. Feeney, Haines, and Riding, Private investors' investment criteria; Linde and Prasad, V*enture Support Systems Project*.
31. Hill and Power, *Attracting Capital from Angels*.
32. Wiltbank, R. 2007. Angel Investor Research. Downloaded from www.willamette.edu/~wiltbank/AngelInvestorResearch2.ppt.
33. Van Osnabrugge, M. 2000. A comparison of business angel and venture capitalist investment procedures: An agency theory-based analysis. *Venture Capital*, 2(2): 91–109.
34. Calculated from data downloaded from www.nsf.gov/statistics/seind06/c6/c6s6.htm.
35. Amis and Stevenson, *Winning Angels*; Wainwright, F., and Groeninger, A. 2005. *Note on Angel Investing*. Tuck School of Business Administration at Dartmouth Center for Private Equity and Entrepreneurship, Case Number 5-0001.
36. Sohl, J. 2005. Angel Investment Market Grows 10 Percent in 2006. Center for Venture Research. Downloaded from www.unh.edu/Centers_CVR/2006pressrelease.cfm; Aernoudt, R. 1999. Business angels: Should they fly on their own wings? *Venture Capital*, 1(2): 187–95; Coveney, P., and Moore, K. 1998. *Business Angels*. New York: John Wiley; Feeney, Haines, and Riding, Private investors' investment criteria; Stedler and Peters, Business angels in Germany; Wiltbank, R. 2006. Angel Investor Research. Downloaded from www.willamette.edu/~wiltbank/AngelInvestorResearch2.ppt; Wiltbank, R. 2006. At the Individual Level: Outlining Angel Investing in the United States. Downloaded from www.willamette.edu/~wiltbank/AtTheIndividualLevel7.pdf; Hudson, M. 2007. ACA Briefing and Angel Group Stats. Presentation to the Angel Capital Association, May 24, Chicago, IL; Benjamin and Margulis, *Angel Capital*.
37. Aram, J. 1989. Attitudes and behaviors of informal investors toward early-stage investments, technology-based ventures, and co-investors. *Journal of Business Venturing*, 4(5): 333–47; Sohl, J. 2004. The Angel Investor Market in 2003: The Angel Market Rebounds, but a Troublesome Post Seed Funding Gap Deepens. Downloaded from http://unh.edu/cvr/press_release%202004.htm; Wiltbank, At the Individual Level; Wong, Angel Finance.

38. Wong, Angel Finance.

39. Ibid.

40. Downloaded from www.nsf.gov/statistics/seind06/c6/c6s6.htm#c6s6l4.

41. Surveys of ad hoc samples of people known to be accredited business angels show that between 46 percent and 83 percent of angel investments occur at the seed or start-up stage (see Sohl, J. 2005. Angel Investment Market Grows 10 Percent in 2006. Center for Venture Research. Downloaded from www.unh.edu/Centers_CVR/2006pressrelease.cfm; Aernoudt, Business angels: Should they fly on their own wings?; Coveney and Moore, *Business Angels*, and Riding, Private investors' investment criteria; Stedler and Peters, Business angels in Germany; Wiltbank, R. 2006. Angel Investor Research. Downloaded from www.willamette.edu/~wiltbank/AngelInvestorResearch2. ppt; Wiltbank, At the Individual Level; Hudson, M. 2007. ACA Briefing and Angel Group Stats. Presentation to the Angel Capital Association, May 24, Chicago, IL), but these statistics just demonstrate the problems that occur when researchers examine samples that are not representative of the overall population of angel investors.

42. Riding, A., and Belanger, B. 2006. Informally Financed SMEs. *Small Business Financing Profiles*, Government of Canada, September, Ottawa.

43. Calculated from a special tabulation of the Survey of Business Owners.

44. Benjamin and Margulis, *Angel Investor's Handbook*; Payne, B. Engaging Angel Investors. Downloaded from www.eventuring.com/eShip/appmanager/ eVenturing/eVenturingDesktop?_nfpb=true&_pageLabel=eShip_ linkDetail&_nfls=false&id=Entrepreneurship/Resource/Resource_546. htm&_fromSearch=false&_nfls=false.

45. Benjamin, and Margulis, *Angel Investor's Handbook*; Benjamin and Margulis, *Angel Capital*; Hill and Power, *Attracting Capital from Angels*.

46. This pattern may be the result of differences in the types of businesses that female entrepreneurs tend to start. One study that looked at the outside equity financing of 235 businesses led by women found that the receipt of outside equity financing was more common if the businesses was in manufacturing or information technology. Receipt of this financing was also more likely if the entrepreneur had a graduate education or if the founder had invested considerable money in the business. (See Carter, N., Brush, C., Greene, P., Gatewood, E., and Hart, M. 2003. Women entrepreneurs who break through to equity financing: The influence of human, social and financial capital. *Venture Capital*, 5(1): 1–28.)

47. These data were calculated from a special tabulation of the Survey of Business Owners.

48. Calculated from data downloaded from www.census.gov/prod/eco2/ sbo200cscbt.pdf.

49. The Federal Reserve Survey of Small Business Finances shows similar patterns.

50. Calculated from data downloaded from www.census.gov/prod/eco2/ sbo200cscbt.pdf.

51. Calculated from data downloaded from www.census.gov/csd/sbo/ cbosummaryoffindings.htm.

52. Benjamin and Margulis, *Angel Financing*.

53. Feeney, Haines, and Riding, Private investors' investment criteria; Mason and Harrison, Informal venture capital; Brettel, Business angels in Germany; Hill and Power, *Attracting Capital from Angels*; Mason, C., and Stark, C. 2004. What do investors look for in a business plan? *International Small Business Journal*, 22(3): 227–48; Roberts, Stevenson, and Morse, Angel investing; Riding, A., and Short, D. 1987. Some investor and entrepreneur perspectives on the informal market for risk capital. *Journal of Small Business and Entrepreneurship*, 4: 19–30; Benjamin and Margulis, *Angel Capital*; Benjamin and Margulis, *Angel Financing*; Riding, A., Dal Cin, P., Duxbury, L. Haines, G., and Safrata, R. 1993. *Informal Investors in Canada: The Identification of Salient Characteristics*. Ottawa: Carleton University; Linde and Prasad, *Venture Support Systems Project*.

54. Greenberg, W. 2006. Angel Investing. Presentation to Senator Emzi's Inventors Conference. April 20, Washington, DC.

55. Benjamin, Margulis, *Angel Financing*, p. 127.

56. Benjamin and Margulis, *Angel Investor's Handbook*, p. 141.

57. Hill and Power, *Attracting Capital from Angels*; May, J., and Simmons, C. 2001. *Every Business Needs an Angel*. New York: Crown Books.

58. Of course, angel-backed new ventures founded by teams of three or more people might be more successful than angel-backed companies founded by a single individual. However, we don't have the data to figure out whether teams matter for the performance of angel-backed firms. They probably help since the performance of new businesses founded by teams, in general, is better than those founded by single individuals, and there is little reason to think that angel-backed companies would differ from the norm in this regard. (See Cooper, A., Dunkelberg, W., and Woo, C. 1988. Survival and failure: A longitudinal study. In Kirchhoff, B., Long, W., McMullan, W, Vesper, K., and Wetzel, W. (eds.), *Frontiers of Entrepreneurship Research*. Babson Park, MA: Babson College, 225–37; Reynolds, P., and White, S. 1997. *The Entrepreneurial Process: Economic Growth, Men, Women, and Minorities*, Westport, CT: Greenwood; Schutgens, V., and Wever, E. 2000. Determinants of new firm success. *Papers in Regional Science*, 79: 135–59.)

59. Feeney, Haines, and Riding, Private investors' investment criteria; Amis and Stevenson, *Winning Angels*.

60. Benjamin and Margulis, *Angel Capital*; Benjamin and Margulis, *Angel Financing*; May and Simmons, *Every Business Needs an Angel*; Van Osnabrugge and Robinson, *Angel Investing*; Roberts, Stevenson, and Morse, Angel investing.

61. Riding, A., and Belanger, B. 2006. Informally financed SMEs. *Small Business Financing Profiles*. Government of Canada, September, Ottawa, Canada.

62. Van Osnabrugge and Robinson, *Angel Investing*; Benjamin and Margulis, *Angel Capital*; Roberts, Stevenson, and Morse, Angel investing; Benjamin and Margulis, *Angel Financing*.

63. Stedler and Peters, Business angels in Germany.

64. Roberts, Stevenson, and Morse, Angel investing.

65. Benjamin and Margulis, *Angel Financing*; Benjamin and Margulis, *Angel Capital*.

66. May and Simmons, *Every Business Needs an Angel*; Roberts, Stevenson, and Morse, Angel investing.

67. Amis and Stevenson, *Winning Angels*.

68. Preston, S. 2006. A Match Made in Heaven: Collaborating Successfully with Your Angel Investors. Presentation to the Northwest Entrepreneur Network, February 10, Bellevue, WA.

69. Hill and Power, *Attracting Capital from Angels*.

70. Benjamin and Margulis, *Angel Capital*; Feeney, Haines, and Riding, Private investors' investment criteria; Benjamin and Margulis, *Angel Financing*; Riding, Dal Cin, Duxbury, Haines, and Safrata, *Informal Investors in Canada*; May and Simmons, *Every Business Needs an Angel*; Roberts, Stevenson, and Morse, Angel investing; Amis and Stevenson, *Winning Angels*.

71. Riding, Dal Cin, Duxbury, Haines, and Safrata, *Informal Investors in Canada*; Feeney, Haines, and Riding, Private investors' investment criteria.

72. Feeney, Haines, and Riding, Private investors' investment criteria; Amis and Stevenson, *Winning Angels*.

73. Preston, S. 2006. A Match Made in Heaven: Collaborating Successfully with Your Angel Investors. Presentation to the Northwest Entrepreneur Network, February 10, Bellevue, WA; Roberts, Stevenson, and Morse, Angel investing; Payne, B. Engaging Angel Investors. Downloaded from www.eventuring. com/eShip/appmanager/eVenturing/eVenturingDesktop?_nfpb=true&_pageLabel=eShip_linkDetail&_nfls=false&id=Entrepreneurship/Resource/Resource_546.htm&_fromSearch=false&_nfls=false; Hill and Power, *Attracting Capital from Angels*.

Chapter 7

1. Stedler, H., and Peters, H. 2003. Business angels in Germany: An empirical study. *Venture Capital*, 5(3): 269–76.

2. Amis, D., and Stevenson, H. 2001. *Winning Angels*. London: Pearson Education.

3. Van Osnabrugge, M., and Robinson, R. 2000. *Angel Investing: Matching Start-up Funds with Start-up Companies—A Guide for Entrepreneurs, Individual Investors, and Venture Capitalists*. San Francisco: Jossey-Bass.

4. Prowse, S. 1998. Angel investors and the market for angel investments. *Journal of Banking and Finance*, 22: 785–92.

5. Van Osnabrugge and Robinson, *Angel Investing*.

6. Benjamin, G., and Margulis, J. 2000. *Angel Financing: How to Find and Invest in Private Equity*. New York: John Wiley.

7. Prowse, S. 1998. Angel investors and the market for angel investments. *Journal of Banking and Finance*, 22: 785–92.

8. Hill, B., and Power, D. 2002. *Attracting Capital from Angels*. New York: John Wiley.

9. Freear, J., Sohl, J., and Wetzel, W, 1994. The private investor market for venture capital. *The Financier*, 1(2): 7–15; Van Osnabrugge and Robinson, *Angel Investing*; Freear, J., Sohl, J., and Wetzel, W. 1992. The investment attitudes, behavior and characteristics of high net worth individuals. In N. Churchill, S. Birley, W. Bygrave, D. Muzyka, C. Wahlbin, and W. Wetzel (eds.), *Frontiers of Entrepreneurship Research*. Babson Park, MA: Babson College, 274–387.

10. Benjamin, G., and Margulis, J. 2005. *Angel Capital*. New York: John Wiley.

11. Riding, A., Dal Cin, P., Duxbury, L. Haines, G., and Safrata, R. 1993. *Informal Investors in Canada: The Identification of Salient Characteristics*. Ottawa: Carleton University; Hill and Power, *Attracting Capital from Angels*; Feeney, L., Haines, G., and Riding, A. 1999. Private investors' investment criteria: Insights from qualitative data. *Venture Capital*, 1(2): 121–45.

12. Amis and Stevenson, *Winning Angels*.

13. Shane, S. 2005. Angel Investing. A Report Prepared for the Federal Reserve Banks of Atlanta, Cleveland, Kansas City, Philadelphia, and Richmond. October 1.

14. Van Osnabrugge and Robinson, *Angel Investing*.

15. Shane, Angel Investing.

16. Freear, J., Sohl, J., and Wetzel, W. 1995. Angels: Personal investors in the venture capital market. *Entrepreneurship and Regional Development*, 7: 85–94.

17. Wiltbank, R. 2006. At the Individual Level: Outlining Angel Investing in the United States. Downloaded from www.willamette.edu/~wiltbank/AtTheIndividualLevel7.pdf.

18. Shane, Angel Investing.

19. Van Osnabrugge and Robinson, *Angel Investing*, p. 116.

20. Amis and Stevenson, *Winning Angels*; Wainwright, F., and Groeninger, A. 2005. *Note on Angel Investing*. Tuck School of Business Administration at Dartmouth Center for Private Equity and Entrepreneurship, Case Number 5–0001; Benjamin and Margulis, *Angel Capital*; Angel Capital Association. 2007. An Introduction to Angel Investing. Downloaded from www.angelcapitalassociation.org/.

21. Van Osnabrugge, M. 2000. A comparison of business angel and venture capitalist investment procedures: An agency theory-based analysis. *Venture Capital*, 2(2): 91–109.

22. Angel Capital Association. 2007. An Introduction to Angel Investing. Downloaded from www.angelcapitalassociation.org/.

23. Amis and Stevenson, *Winning Angels*.

24. Van Osnabrugge and Robinson, *Angel Investing*.

25. May, J., and Simmons, C. 2001. *Every Business Needs an Angel*. New York: Crown Books.

26. Van Osnabrugge and Robinson, *Angel Investing*.

27. Amis and Stevenson, *Winning Angels*.

28. May and Simmons, *Every Business Needs an Angel*.

29. Amis and Stevenson, *Winning Angels*.

30. Van Osnabrugge and Robinson, *Angel Investing*.

31. Amis and Stevenson, *Winning Angels*.

32. Benjamin, G., and Margulis, J. 2001. *The Angel Investor's Handbook*. Princeton, NJ: Bloomberg Press.

33. Van Osnabrugge and Robinson, *Angel Investing*.

34. Amis and Stevenson, *Winning Angels*.

35. Benjamin and Margulis, *The Angel Investor's Handbook*.

36. May and Simmons, *Every Business Needs an Angel*.

37. Amis and Stevenson, *Winning Angels*.

38. Benjamin and Margulis, *Angel Financing*.

39. Van Osnabrugge and Robinson, *Angel Investing*, p. 162.

40. Ibid.

41. Farrell, A., and Howorth, C. 2002. Representativeness and Overconfidence in Novice and Habitual Business Angels. Downloaded from www.babson.edu/entrep/fer/BABSON2002/TOC/TOC.htm.

42. Shane, Angel Investing.

43. Benjamin and Margulis, *Angel Financing*; Hill, and Power, *Attracting Capital from Angels*; May and Simmons, *Every Business Needs an Angel*.

44. Van Osnabrugge and Robinson, *Angel Investing*; Feeney, Haines, and Riding, Private investors' investment criteria.

45. Stedler and Peters, Business angels in Germany.

46. Amatucci, F., and Sohl, J. 2007. Business Angels: Investment Processes, Outcomes, and Current Trends. Working Paper, Center for Venture Research, University of New Hampshire, Durham, NH.

47. Van Osnabrugge and Robinson, *Angel Investing*.

48. Benjamin and Margulis, *The Angel Investor's Handbook*; Benjamin and Margulis, *Angel Capital*.

49. Van Osnabrugge and Robinson, *Angel Investing*.

50. Riding, Dal Cin, Duxbury, Haines, and Safrata, *Informal Investors in Canada*; Feeney, Haines, and Riding, Private investors' investment criteria.

51. Madill, J., Haines, G., and Riding, A. 2005. The role of angels in technology SMEs: A link to venture capital. *Venture Capital*, 7(2): 107–29.

52. Brettel, M. 2003. Business angels in Germany: A research note. *Venture Capital*, 5(3): 251–68. Several studies have shown that investors tend to reject businesses whose plans are based on unrealistic assumptions. (See Feeney, Haines, and Riding, Private investors' investment criteria; Mason, C., and Harrison, R. 2002. Barriers to investment in the informal venture capital sector. *Entrepreneurship and Regional Development*, 14: 271–87.)

53. Benjamin and Margulis, *Angel Capital*; Coveney, P., and Moore, K. 1998. *Business Angels*. New York: John Wiley.

54. Mason, C., and Harrison, R. 2002. Barriers to investment in the informal venture capital sector. *Entrepreneurship and Regional Development*, 14: 271–87.

55. Riding, Dal Cin, Duxbury, Haines, and Safrata, *Informal Investors in Canada*.
56. Feeney, Haines, and Riding, Private investors' investment criteria; Mason, C., and Harrison, R. 2002. Barriers to investment in the informal venture capital sector. *Entrepreneurship and Regional Development*, 14: 271–87.
57. Hill and Power, *Attracting Capital from Angels*.
58. Van Osnabrugge and Robinson, *Angel Investing*.
59. Coveney and Moore, *Business Angels*.
60. Benjamin and Margulis, *Angel Financing*.
61. Mason, C., and Harrison, R. 1996. Informal venture capital: A study of the investment process, the post-investment experience and investment performance. *Entrepreneurship and Regional Development*, 8: 105–25.
62. Van Osnabrugge and Robinson, *Angel Investing*.
63. Shane, Angel Investing.
64. Hill and Power, *Attracting Capital from Angels*, p. 55.
65. Benjamin and Margulis, *The Angel Investor's Handbook*, p. 124.
66. Okabe, B. 2007. Due Diligence for Angel Investors. Presentation to the Power of Angel Investing Seminar, May 24, Chicago, IL.
67. Amis and Stevenson, *Winning Angels*.
68. Okabe, Due Diligence for Angel Investors.
69. Roberts, M., Stevenson, H., and Morse, K. 2000. Angel investing. *Harvard Business School Note*, 9-800-273; Van Osnabrugge and Robinson, *Angel Investing*; May and Simmons, *Every Business Needs an Angel*; Benjamin and Margulis, *The Angel Investor's Handbook*.
70. Wiltbank, R., and Boeker, W. 2007. Angel Performance Project. Presentation to the Kauffman Foundation Entrepreneurship and Innovation Data Conference, November 2, Kansas City, MO.
71. Wiltbank, R. 2006. At the Individual Level: Outlining Angel Investing in the United States. Downloaded from www.willamette.edu/~wiltbank/AtTheIndividualLevel7.pdf.
72. Hill and Power, *Attracting Capital from Angels*.
73. Van Osnabrugge, A comparison of business angel and venture capitalist investment procedures.
74. Ibid.
75. Van Osnabrugge and Robinson, *Angel Investing*.
76. Van Osnabrugge, A comparison of business angel and venture capitalist investment procedures.
77. Fenn, G., and Liang, N. 1998. New resources and new ideas: Private equity for small businesses. *Journal of Banking and Finance*, 22: 1077–84.
78. Freear, J., Sohl, J., and Wetzel, W. 1992. The investment attitudes, behavior and characteristics of high net worth individuals. In N. Churchill, S. Birley, W. Bygrave, D. Muzyka, C. Wahlbin, and W. Wetzel (eds.), *Frontiers of Entrepreneurship Research*. Babson Park, MA: Babson College, 274–387; Freear, J., Sohl, J., and Wetzel, W. 1995. Angels: Personal investors in the

venture capital market. *Entrepreneurship and Regional Development*, 7: 85–94; Van Osnabrugge and Robinson, *Angel Investing*.

79. Van Osnabrugge and Robinson, *Angel Investing*, p. 188.

80. May and Simmons, *Every Business Needs an Angel*, p. 100.

81. Benjamin and Margulis, *Angel Financing*, p. 178.

82. Amis and Stevenson, *Winning Angels*.

83. Wiltbank, R. 2006. At the Individual Level: Outlining Angel Investing in the United States. Downloaded from www.willamette.edu/~wiltbank/ AtTheIndividualLevel7.pdf.

84. Ibid.

85. Ibid.

86. Shane, Angel Investing.

87. May and Simmons, *Every Business Needs an Angel*, p. 147.

88. Roberts, Stevenson, and Morse, Angel investing; Riding, Dal Cin, Duxbury, Haines, and Safrata, *Informal Investors in Canada*; Amis and Stevenson, *Winning Angels*; Benjamin and Margulis, *The Angel Investor's Handbook*; Benjamin and Margulis, *Angel Capital*; Madill, J., Haines, G., and Riding, A. 2005. The role of angels in technology SMEs: A link to venture capital. *Venture Capital*, 7(2): 107–29.

89. Benjamin and Margulis, *The Angel Investor's Handbook*, p. 2.

90. Wiltbank, R. 2006. At the Individual Level: Outlining Angel Investing in the United States. Downloaded from www.willamette.edu/~wiltbank/ AtTheIndividualLevel7.pdf.

91. Duxbury, L., Haines, G., and Riding, A. 1996. A personality profile of Canadian informal investors. *Journal of Small Business Management*, 34(2): 44–55.

92. Wiltbank, At the Individual Level.

93. Madill, J., Haines, G., and Riding, A. 2005. The role of angels in technology SMEs: A link to venture capital. *Venture Capital*, 7(2): 107–29.

94. Ardichvilli, A., Cardozo, R., Tune, C., and Reinach, J. 2000. The role of angel investors in the assembly of non-financial resources of new ventures. Downloaded from www.babson.edu/entrep/fer/TOC/ TOC%20Text.html.

95. Wong, A. 2002. Angel Finance: The Other Venture Capital. Working Paper, University of Chicago, Chicago, IL.

96. Calculated from data in Wiltbank, R., and Boeker, W. 2007. Angel Performance Project. Presentation to the Kauffman Foundation Conference on Entrepreneurship and Innovation Data, November 2, Kansas City, MO. (Draft version)

97. Van Osnabrugge and Robinson, *Angel Investing*.

98. One study even found that 48 percent of angels believe that their expertise and experience was the main nonfinancial benefit that they provide. (See Coveney and Moore, *Business Angels*.)

Chapter 8

1. Hill, B., and Power, D. 2002. *Attracting Capital from Angels*. New York: John Wiley.
2. Riding, A., Dal Cin, P., Duxbury, L. Haines, G., and Safrata, R. 1993. *Informal Investors in Canada: The Identification of Salient Characteristics*. Ottawa: Carleton University; Feeney, L., Haines, G., and Riding, A. 1999. Private investors' investment criteria: Insights from qualitative data. *Venture Capital*, 1(2): 121–45; Benjamin, G., and Margulis, J. 2005. *Angel Capital*. New York: John Wiley; Wainwright, F., and Groeninger, A. 2005. *Note on Angel Investing*. Tuck School of Business Administration at Dartmouth Center for Private Equity and Entrepreneurship, Case Number 5-0001.
3. Mason, C., and Harrison, R. 1999. The rates of return from informal venture capital investments: Some UK evidence. Paper Presented at the Babson Conference-Kauffman Foundation Entrepreneurship Research Conference, University of South Carolina, Columbia, SC, May 12–15. Even the Band of Angels, a group that might be the best angel group in the United States doesn't do this well. The Band of Angels reports that it has invested in 194 companies and has had 9 IPOs (see www.bandangels.com/news/index.php).
4. Calculated from data downloaded from http://bear.cba.ufl.edu/ritter/New%20Folder/IPOs2006Factoids.pdf.
5. Shane, S. 2005. Angel Investing. A Report Prepared for the Federal Reserve Banks of Atlanta, Cleveland, Kansas City, Philadelphia, and Richmond. October 1.
6. Mason, C., and Harrison, R. 1999. The Rates of Return from Informal Venture Capital Investments: Some UK evidence. Paper Presented at the Babson Conference-Kauffman Foundation Entrepreneurship Research Conference, University of South Carolina, Columbia, SC, May 12–15.
7. Downloaded from www.bandangels.com/news/index.php.
8. Office of Advocacy. 1998. Mergers and Acquisitions in the United States, 1990–1994. Downloaded from www.sba.gov/ADVO/stats/m_a.html.
9. See www.census.gov/prod/2003pubs/02statab/business.pdf.
10. www.nvca.org/pdf/Q407ExitPollReleaseFINAL.pdf.
11. Ibid.
12. www.nsf.gov/statistics/seind06/c6/c6s6.htm.
13. Ibid.
14. Hill and Power, *Attracting Capital from Angels*.
15. Okabe, B. 2007. Valuation of Early Stage Companies. Presentation to the Power of Angel Investing Seminar, May 24, Chicago, IL.
16. One author argued that companies that go public on NASDAQ are typically priced at 4.2 times revenue. (See Hammond, J. 2007. Planning for Exits: How Our Returns Could Have Been Even Better. Presentation to the Angel Capital Association, May 24, Chicago, IL.)

17. Zuckerman, G. 2006. How the pros tell if a stock is a bargain. *Wall Street Journal*, December 3. Downloaded from http://online.wsj.com/article_print/ SB116510103905339242.html.

18. Zheng, S. 2007. Are IPOs really overpriced? *Journal of Empirical Finance*, 14: 287–309.

19. Pukthuanthong-Le, K., and Varaiya, N. Forthcoming. IPO pricing, block sales, and long term performance. *Financial Review*.

20. Ibid.

21. Haar, N., Starr, J., and MacMillan, I. 1988. Informal risk capital investors: Investment patterns on the East Coast of the USA. *Journal of Business Venturing*, 3: 11–29.

22. This comparison of the Band of Angels' data to the overall angel investing performance indicates that we need to treat studies of the performance of angel investments with *extreme* caution. Angels may be less likely to report their poorer investments, which would inflate the magnitude of their returns. Moreover, the angels who have been surveyed are far from representative of the overall population of angel investors. The data naturally overweight more established angels since less established angels may not yet have had many exits. If performance is positively related to experience, then the results will be overstated. Respondents are also likely to over represent the most successful angels since they are easiest to identify and probably the most willing to talk to surveyors.

23. Another problem is that informal equity investments confound friends-and-family investments with angel investments.

24. Prior to Wiltbank's effort, there were other studies of the performance of angel investments. One study looked at 1,200 angel investors' liquidated investments and found that over an average of eight years, 39 percent lost money, 19 percent broke even, 30 percent generated more than a 50 percent internal rate of return, and 12 percent generated more than a 100 percent internal rate of return. (See Benjamin, G., and Margulis, J. 2001. *The Angel Investor's Handbook*. Princeton, NJ: Bloomberg Press.) Another study of 128 exited investments made by 51 business angels in the United Kingdom found that 34 percent lost all the investment, 13 percent returned only as much as the capital invested, 23 percent had a return of more than 50 percent and only 10 percent generated more than a 100 percent return. (See Mason, C., and Harrison, R. 1999. The Rates of Return from Informal Venture Capital Investments: Some UK Evidence. Paper Presented at the Babson College-Kauffman Foundation Entrepreneurship Research Conference, University of South Carolina, May 12–15, Columbia, SC.) However, these studies are less well designed than Wiltbank's study, which makes the results that they provide less likely to be accurate.

25. Only 13 percent of the angels surveyed in Wiltbank's study answered the questionnaire.

26. The converse is not true. If the data show high performance, those results could easily be driven by a few, highly successful angels and not represent the performance of the typical angel investor.

27. Wiltbank, R., and Boeker, W. 2007. Angel Performance Project. Presentation to the Kauffman Foundation Conference on Entrepreneurship and Innovation Data, November 2, Kansas City, MO.

28. Wiltbank, R., and Boeker, W. 2007. Returns to Angel Investors in Groups. Working Paper, Ewing Marion Kauffman Foundation, Kansas City, MO.

29. Ibid.

30. Wiltbank, R. 2006. At the Individual Level: Outlining Angel Investing in the United States. Downloaded from www.willamette.edu/~wiltbank/AtTheIndividualLevel7.pdf.

31. Because all of the angel investors in Wiltbank's sample are accredited investors, we can estimate the cost to them of spending 426 hours on a venture. The minimum income level to meet SEC accreditation requirements is $200,000 per year for a single person, which we can use as a conservative estimate of minimum annual income of someone in the sample. IRS data shows that the average adjusted gross income of people who earn more than $200,000 per year was $608,545 in 2005. (Calculated from data downloaded from www.irs.gov/taxstats/indtaxstats/article/0,,id=96981,00.html.) Assuming that people who earn $608,545 per year work an average of forty hours per week and take two weeks of vacation per year, we can estimate the opportunity cost of an accredited angel's time conservatively at $304.27 per hour. (Readers should note that this is a very conservative estimate. The typical angel is married. Therefore, most of the angels in the sample would have to exceed $300,000 per year in income to meet SEC accreditation requirements. Moreover, the respondents have an average net worth of $10.9 million. People with an average net worth that high probably have incomes considerably higher than $200,000 per year.)

32. Wiltbank, R. 2006. Angel Investor Research. Downloaded from www.willamette.edu/~wiltbank/AngelInvestorResearch2.ppt.

33. For the period ending in September 2004. See www.prnewswire.com/cgi-bin/stories.pl?ACCT=109&STORY=/www/story/01-19-2005/0002862967&EDATE.

Chapter 9

1. Angel groups should not be confused with "super angels," very high net worth individuals who make large magnitude investments in start-up companies, through organizations that employ professional staff to evaluate deals and monitor investments. (See Shane, S. 2005. Angel Investing. A Report Prepared for the Federal Reserve Banks of Atlanta, Cleveland, Kansas City, Philadelphia, and Richmond. October 1.) The relationships between different the dimensions of angel groups that are reported in this chapter are based on regressions that include a variety of different variables. For instance, the regression to predict the age of the angel group included the size of the group; the external investment rate in the area; the patent rate in the area; whether the group was located in an angel tax credit state; whether the group

was located in California; whether the group was a limited liability company, non-profit mutual benefit corporation, or S or C corporation; whether the group likes to invest at start-up stage, the early stage, the expansion stage, or the late stage; whether the group is manager-led; whether the group allows sidecar funds; whether the group must invest in the state; and whether the investment region is within four hours drive of the group.

2. Sobieski, I. 2006. Sustainability Issues in Angel Investing. Presentation to the Angel Capital Association, April 26, New York, NY.

3. For instance, the median age of angels who are members of the groups that make up the Angel Capital Association is significantly older than the median age of individual angels. (See Hudson, M. 2007. ACA Briefing and Angel Group Stats. Presentation to the Angel Capital Association, May 24, Chicago, IL.)

4. Hudson, ACA Briefing and Angel Group Stats; Becker-Blease, J., and Sohl, J. 2007. Do women-owned businesses have equal access to angel capital? *Journal of Business Venturing*, 22: 503–21; Benjamin, G., and Margulis, J. 2005. *Angel Capital*. New York: Wiley Finance.

5. Hudson, ACA Briefing and Angel Group Stats.

6. Ibid.

7. U.S. Small Business Administration. 2002. *Small Business Investment Company Program*, Washington, DC: U.S. Government Printing Office.

8. Amis, D., and Stevenson, H. 2001. *Winning Angels*. London: Pearson Education, p. 39.

9. Angel Capital Association. 2007. Angel Group Confidence Report. March 27, Angel Capital Association, Kansas City, MO.

10. Center for Venture Research. 2005. The Angel Investor Market in 2005: The Angel Market Exhibits Modest Growth. Downloaded from www.unh.edu/Centers_CVR/2006pressrelease.cfm.

11. Hudson, ACA Briefing and Angel Group Stats.

12. Ewing Marion Kauffman Foundation. 2002. *Business Angel Investing Groups Growing in North America*. Downloaded from www.emkf.org.

13. Ibid.

14. May, J. 2002. Structured angel groups in the USA: The Dinner Club experience. *Venture Capital*, 4(4): 337–42.

15. Hudson, ACA Briefing and Angel Group Stats.

16. Ibid.

17. Preston, S. 2007. Angel Investment Groups, Networks and Funds: A Guidebook to Developing the Right Angel Organization for Your Community. Downloaded from www.kauffman.org/items.cfm?itemID=590.

18. May, J., and Simmons, C. 2001. *Every Business Needs an Angel*. New York: Crown Books.

19. Angel Capital Association, Angel Group Confidence Report.

20. Ewing Marion Kauffman Foundation, *Business Angel Investing Groups Growing*.

21. Shane, Angel Investing.

22. Ibid.

23. Ibid.

24. Ibid.

25. Van Osnabrugge, M., and Robinson, R. 2000. *Angel Investing: Matching Start-up Funds with Start-up Companies—A Guide for Entrepreneurs, Individual Investors, and Venture Capitalists*. San Francisco: Jossey-Bass.

26. Wainwright, F., and Groeninger, A. 2005. *Note on Angel Investing*. Tuck School of Business Administration at Dartmouth Center for Private Equity and Entrepreneurship, Case Number 5-0001.

27. Sobieski, Sustainability Issues in Angel Investing.

28. Shane, Angel Investing.

29. Ewing Marion Kauffman Foundation. 2003. Angel Investing Group Best Practices. Downloaded from www.emkf.org.

30. Ewing Marion Kauffman Foundation, *Business Angel Investing Groups Growing*.

31. Shane, Angel Investing.

32. Payne, W., and Macarty, M. 2002. The anatomy of an angel investing network: Tech Coast Angels. *Venture Capital*, 4(4): 331–36.

33. Angel Capital Association, Angel Group Confidence Report.

34. Shane, Angel Investing.

35. Ibid.

36. Sobieski, Sustainability Issues in Angel Investing.

37. Verrill, D. 2006. Angel Group Leader Compensation Roundtable. Presentation to the Angel Capital Educational Foundation, April 27, New York, NY.

38. Angel Capital Association, Angel Group Confidence Report.

39. Sobieski, Sustainability Issues in Angel Investing.

40. Van Osnabrugge and Robinson, *Angel Investing*.

41. Shane, Angel Investing.

42. Ewing Marion Kauffman Foundation, *Business Angel Investing Groups Growing*.

43. Verrill, D. 2006. Angel Group Leader Compensation Roundtable. Presentation to the Angel Capital Educational Foundation, April 27, New York, NY.

44. Preston, Angel Investment Groups, Networks and Funds.

45. Shane, Angel Investing.

46. Some angel groups even include a co-investment requirement in their by-laws (see Shane, Angel Investing).

47. Angel Capital Association, Angel Group Confidence Report.

48. Hudson, M. 2007. ACA Briefing and Angel Group Stats. Presentation to the Angel Capital Association, May 24, Chicago, IL.

49. Shane, Angel Investing.

50. Ibid.

51. Riding, A., Dal Cin, P., Duxbury, L., Haines, G., and Safrata, R. 1993. *Informal Investors in Canada: The Identification of Salient Characteristics*. Ottawa: Carleton University.

52. Shane, Angel Investing.
53. Riding, Dal Cin, Duxbury, Haines, and Safrata, *Informal Investors in Canada*.
54. Shane, Angel Investing.
55. Ibid., p. 12.
56. Preston, Angel Investment Groups, Networks and Funds.
57. Shane, Angel Investing.
58. May, Structured angel groups in the USA.
59. May and Simmons, *Every Business Needs an Angel*.
60. Linde and Prasad, *Venture Support Systems Project*; Riding, Dal Cin, Duxbury, Haines, and Safrata, *Informal Investors in Canada*.
61. Shane, Angel Investing, p. 11.
62. May, Structured angel groups in the USA.
63. Shane, Angel Investing.
64. Ibid.
65. May, Structured angel groups in the USA.
66. This comment was made by an angel at the Power of Angel Investing meeting in Chicago on May 23, 2007.
67. Van Osnabrugge and Robinson, *Angel Investing*.
68. Shane, Angel Investing.
69. Wainwright and Groeninger, *Note on Angel Investing*.
70. Shane, Angel Investing.
71. Ibid., p. 13.
72. Hill, B., and Power, D. 2002. *Attracting Capital from Angels*. New York: John Wiley.
73. Shane, Angel Investing.
74. Riding, Dal Cin, Duxbury, Haines, and Safrata, *Informal Investors in Canada*.
75. Linde and Prasad, *Venture Support Systems Project*; Riding, Dal Cin, Duxbury, Haines, and Safrata, *Informal Investors in Canada*; Jensen, M. 2002. Angel investors: opportunity amidst chaos. *Venture Capital*, 4(4): 295–304.
76. Shane, Angel Investing, p. 21.
77. Shane, Angel Investing.
78. Ibid.
79. Ibid.
80. Anonymous. 2005. Giving ideas wings. *Economist*, September 16, 38(8495).
81. Van Osnabrugge and Robinson, *Angel Investing*.
82. Shane, Angel Investing.
83. Burlingham, B. 1997. My life as an angel. *Inc.*, 19(10): July. Downloaded from www.inc.com/magazine/19970701/1274.html.
84. Anonymous. 2005. Giving ideas wings. *Economist*, September 16, 38(8495).
85. May and Simmons, *Every Business Needs an Angel*.
86. Shane, Angel Investing.
87. Ibid.
88. Sobieski, Sustainability Issues in Angel Investing.
89. Ewing Marion Kauffman Foundation, *Business Angel Investing Groups Growing*.

90. Hill and Power, *Attracting Capital from Angels*, p. 194.

91. Ewing Marion Kauffman Foundation, Angel Investing Group Best Practices.

92. Shane, Angel Investing.

93. Angel Capital Association, Angel Group Confidence Report; Mason, C., and Harrison, R. 1996. Why "business angels" say no: A case study of opportunities rejected by an informal investor syndicate. *International Small Business Journal*, 14(2): 35–35; Feeney, L., Haines, G., and Riding, A. 1999. Private investors' investment criteria: Insights from qualitative data. *Venture Capital*, 1(2): 121–45; Riding, Dal Cin, Duxbury, Haines, and Safrata, *Informal Investors in Canada*.

94. Shane, Angel Investing; Ewing Marion Kauffman Foundation, *Business Angel Investing Groups Growing*.

95. Amatucci, F., and Sohl, J. 2007. Business Angels: Investment Processes, Outcomes, and Current Trends. Working Paper, Center for Venture Research, University of New Hampshire, Durham, NH.

96. Ibid.

97. Van Osnabrugge and Robinson, *Angel Investing*.

98. Shane, Angel Investing.

99. Ibid.

100. Ibid.

101. Ibid.; Ewing Marion Kauffman Foundation, *Business Angel Investing Groups Growing*.

102. Shane, Angel Investing.

103. Ewing Marion Kauffman Foundation, Angel Investing Group Best Practices.

104. Shane, Angel Investing.

105. Ibid.

106. Angel Capital Association. 2007. An Introduction to Angel Investing. Downloaded from www.angelcapitalassociation.org/; Mason, C., and Harrison, R. 1996. Why "business angels" say no: A case study of opportunities rejected by an informal investor syndicate. *International Small Business Journal*, 14(2): 35–51.

107. Shane, Angel Investing.

108. Angel Capital Association, An Introduction to Angel Investing; Freear, J., Sohl, J., and Wetzel, W. 1992. The investment attitudes, behavior and characteristics of high net worth individuals. In N. Churchill, S. Birley, W. Bygrave, D. Muzyka, C. Wahlbin, and W. Wetzel (eds.), *Frontiers of Entrepreneurship Research*. Babson Park, MA: Babson College, 274–387; Angel Capital Association, Angel Group Confidence Report.

109. Shane, Angel Investing.

110. Ibid.

111. Ibid.

112. Ibid.

113. Ibid.

114. Ibid.

Chapter 10

1. Wiltbank, R., and Boeker, W. 2007. Returns to Angel Investors in Groups. Working Paper, Ewing Marion Kauffman Foundation, Kansas City.
2. Wiltbank, R. 2007. Angel Investor Research. Downloaded from www.willamette.edu/~wiltbank/AngelInvestorResearch2.ppt.
3. Hession, J. 2003. Financing High-Tech and Emerging Growth Companies, Presentation. Downloaded from www.medtechignite.com/resources/FinancingHighTechCompanies.ppt.
4. Van Osnabrugge, M. 1998. Do serial and non-serial investors behave differently? An empirical and theoretical analysis. *Entrepreneurship Theory and Practice*, Summer: 23–42.
5. Ibid.
6. Wiltbank and Boeker, Returns to Angel Investors in Groups.
7. Eckhardt, J., and Shane, S. Creative Destruction or Creative Accumulation? Working Paper, University of Wisconsin, Madison, WI.
8. Calculated from data downloaded from www.nsf.gov/statistics/seind06/c6/c6s6.htm.
9. Van Osnabrugge, M. 1998. Do serial and non-serial investors behave differently? An empirical and theoretical analysis. *Entrepreneurship Theory and Practice*, Summer: 23–42.
10. Amis, D., and Stevenson, H. 2001. *Winning Angels*. London: Pearson Education.
11. Wiltbank and Boeker, Returns to Angel Investors in Groups.
12. Ibid.
13. Wong, A. 2002. Angel Finance: The Other Venture Capital. Working Paper, University of Chicago, Chicago, IL.
14. Wiltbank and Boeker, Returns to Angel Investors in Groups.
15. Villalobos, L., and Payne, B. 2007. Valuation of Seed/Start-up Ventures. Presentation to the Power of Angel Investing Seminar, May 24, Chicago, IL.
16. Wiltbank and Boeker, Returns to Angel Investors in Groups.
17. Ibid.
18. Wiltbank, R. 2005. Investment practices and outcomes of informal venture investors. *Venture Capital*, 7(4): 343–57.
19. Wiltbank, R., Read, S., Dew, N., and Sarasvathy, S. 2006. Prediction and Control under Uncertainty: The Outcomes of New Venture Investors. Working Paper, Willamette University, Salem, OR.
20. Prowse, S. 1998. Angel investors and the market for angel investments. *Journal of Banking and Finance*, 22: 785–92.
21. Ibid.

Chapter 11

1. Benjamin, G., and Margulis, J. 2000. *Angel Financing: How to Find and Invest in Private Equity*. New York: John Wiley, p. 84.
2. Coveney, P., and Moore, K. 1998. *Business Angels*. New York: John Wiley.

3. Morrissette, S. 2005. A Profile of Angel Investors: An Invisible Driver of Economic Growth. Working Paper, College of St. Francis, Joliet, IL; Aram, J. 1989. Attitudes and behaviors of informal investors toward early-stage investments, technology-based ventures, and coinvestors. *Journal of Business Venturing*, 4(5): 333–47; Riding, A., and Short, D. 1987. On the estimation of the investment potential of informal investors: A capture-recapture approach. *Journal of Small Business and Entrepreneurship*, 5(4): 26–40.

4. Goldfarb, B., Hoberg, G., Kirsch D., and Triantis, A. 2007. Are Angels Preferred Venture Investors? Working Paper, University of Maryland, College Park, MD.

5. Shane, S. 2005. Angel Investing. A Report Prepared for the Federal Reserve Banks of Atlanta, Cleveland, Kansas City, Philadelphia, and Richmond. October 1, p. 31.

6. Benjamin and Margulis, *Angel Financing*, p. 115.

7. May, J., and Simmons, C. 2001. *Every Business Needs an Angel*. New York: Crown Books.

8. Shane, Angel Investing.

9. Hill, B., and Power, D. 2002. *Attracting Capital from Angels*. New York: John Wiley.

10. Shane, Angel Investing.

11. Ibid. Angels tend to make investments out of their area only if they are super-angels with a lot of money, a lot of connections around the country, and a lot of investment experience; or if someone else that they know and trust from outside the local area is co-investing with them.

12. Van Osnabrugge, M. 2000. A comparison of business angel and venture capitalist investment procedures: An agency theory-based analysis. *Venture Capital*, 2(2): 91–109.

13. Wong, A. 2002. Angel Finance: The Other Venture Capital. Working Paper, University of Chicago, Chicago, IL.

14. Another possible explanation is past performance at angel investing. To have successful angel investing, a region needs to have some initial successes on which future investing builds because the willingness of people to make additional investments depends on their performance with previous investments. Thus, places that have had successful angel investing in the past are more likely to have people who want to make future investments. In addition, successful investing provides a pool of capital from which future angel investments can be made. Furthermore, successful angel investing changes the culture of a region and makes it more socially acceptable for people to engage in start-up activity, which increases the likelihood that angels will have companies to fund.

15. Shane, Angel Investing, p. 25.

16. Shane, Angel Investing.

17. If it is the average wealth of an area and not the proportion of very wealthy people that affects the rate of angel investment activity in an area, then lowering the state estate tax rate would not be likely to affect the amount of angel investment activity in a state.

18. Shane, Angel Investing.

19. Ibid.

20. Benjamin, G., and Margulis, J. 2001. *The Angel Investor's Handbook.* Princeton, NJ: Bloomberg Press, p. xxi.

21. Industry Commission. 1997. Informal Equity Investment. Small Business Research Program Information Paper, April, Melbourne, Australia.

22. Shane, Angel Investing.

23. Bank of England. 2001. *Financing of Technology-Based Small Firms.* February, London, United Kingdom.

24. San Jose, A., Roure, J., and Aeroudt, R. 2005. Business angel academies: Unleashing the potential for business angel investing. *Venture Capital,* 7(2): 149–65.

25. Van Osnabrugge, M., and Robinson, R. 2000. *Angel Investing: Matching Start-up Funds with Start-up Companies—A Guide for Entrepreneurs, Individual Investors, and Venture Capitalists.* San Francisco: Jossey Bass, p. 72.

26. Harrison, R., and Mason, C. 2000. Influences on the supply of informal venture capital in the UK: An exploratory study of investor attitudes. *International Small Business Journal,* 18(4): 11–28.

27. Shane, Angel Investing; European Commission. 2002. Benchmarking Business Angels. November 4, Brussels, Belgium.

28. Harrison, R., and Mason, C. 2000. Influences on the supply of informal venture capital in the UK: An exploratory study of investor attitudes. *International Small Business Journal,* 18(4): 11–28.

29. Crawford, S. 2006. Angel Investment: State Strategies to Promote Entrepreneurship and Economic Development. Issue Brief, Center for Best Practices, National Governors Association, July 12, Washington, DC.

30. DeBaise, C. 2007. On angels' wings. *Wall Street Journal,* March 19: R6, R9.

31. Sandler, S. 2004. *Venture Capital and Tax Incentives: A Comparative Study of Canada and the United States.* Toronto: Canadian Tax Foundation.

32. European Commission. 2002. Benchmarking Business Angels. November 4, Brussels, Belgium.

33. Wiltbank, R. 2006. At the Individual Level: Outlining Angel Investing in the United States. Downloaded from www.willamette.edu/~wiltbank/AtTheIndividualLevel7.pdf.

34. May and Simmons, *Every Business Needs an Angel.*

35. Angel Capital Association. 2007. An Introduction to Angel Investing. Downloaded from www.angelcapitalassociation.org/.

36. Ibid.

37. Shane, Angel Investing; European Commission. 2002.

38. Benjamin and Margulis, *Angel Financing.*

39. Current laws do not preclude unaccredited investors from putting money into start-up companies; they only keep start-up companies from raising money from more than thirty-five unaccredited investors at a time. Even then, companies can do this as long as they provide a proper, legally documented disclosure to investors.

Index